Gordie Howe's Son

Gordie Howe's Son

A Hall of Fame Life in the Shadow of Mr. Hockey

Mark Howe
with Jay Greenberg

HarperCollinsPublishersLtd

Gordie Howe's Son

Published by HarperCollins Publishers Ltd

Originally published in Canada in a hardcover edition
by HarperCollins Publishers Ltd: 2013
This trade paperback edition: 2014

Interior photos courtesy of the author except where specified otherwise.

HarperCollins Publishers Ltd
2 Bloor Street East, 20th Floor
Toronto, Ontario, Canada
M4W 1A8

www.harpercollins.ca

Library and Archives Canada Cataloguing in Publication
information is available upon request.

ISBN 978-1-44342-350-2

Printed in the United States of America
RRD 9 8 7 6 5 4 3 2

To Travis, Azia and Nolan. Hearing what wonderful and caring persons you are will always be my proudest honor and greatest award.

—MH

To Mona and her passion.

—JG

CONTENTS

FOREWORD BY

Wayne Gretzky

As a kid, I had Gordie Howe's autographed picture on my wall, wore an authentic Red Wings Number 9 jersey on my back, and even had my hair cut exactly like his, down to the little bald spot. So when I had a chance to meet my idol at age 10, it could have gone one of two ways: either an unreal feeling or a feeling of disappointment.

For me, it proved to be one of the greatest days I ever had as a child. Gordie was bigger, better and nicer than I had even imagined. Before that Kiwanis Club banquet in my hometown of Brantford, Ontario, he told me, "Kid, keep practicing that backhand," something I never forgot. And when they called on me to speak and I was so scared I started to cry, he bailed me out.

Gordie whispered to me, "Say, 'I'm sorry, I'm lost without a pair of skates,' and walk off." But once I got up there, I couldn't even remember that. So he came to the microphone and said, "When someone has done what this kid has done, he doesn't have to say anything."

He proved as gracious to me that night as I thought he was graceful on the ice. While everybody, including me, was in awe of how tough he was, that wasn't what this skinny kid was trying to emulate.

I had been watching how incredibly good he was as a passer, stickhandler and shooter. And now I was able to see what a tremendous person he was and what a role model he could be for me.

I got to spend more time with him when he came to visit his youngest son, Murray, my teammate in Junior B hockey in Toronto. Over the years, Gordie and I became good friends.

My dream to play a game with him came true at age 17, when I was selected to the World Hockey Association All-Star team for a three-game series against Moscow Dynamo. When they gave me a jersey that was way too big, Gordie took me into the trainer's room and actually sewed it himself so that it would fit better.

Jacques Demers, the coach, told me I was going to center Gordie and his son Mark. Playing with Gordie was one of the few things in my career that made me nervous. But again, he knew just the right thing to say.

"Boy, I'm really nervous about this game," I said to Gordie on the bench. He half-yawned and said, "I am too," and it cracked me up and calmed me down. The three of us combined for 10 points in the first two games of the series, which we swept. Playing with him remains one of the greatest thrills in my hockey career. And how many people can say they centered two Howes?

I first saw Mark play for the Detroit Junior Red Wings when he was 15 and clearly the best player on the ice, even against 18- and 19-year-olds. He won an Olympic medal at age 16, the youngest hockey player ever to do that.

There are people who say Mark's natural talent might have been greater than his dad's. I know he was the only player I ever saw be an All-Star defenseman in the WHA one year, and then the next year be one of the league's top scorers as a forward.

Mark had a lot of points in the NHL, too, and there is little question he would have scored more had he thought the Flyers needed that from him. In the two Stanley Cup finals Edmonton played against Philadelphia—including the one in 1987 when the Flyers took us to game seven—Mark was the ultimate team player, as smart as he was quick and skilled.

The Howes are a tremendous family and I was truly blessed to have had the opportunity to play with and against them. As I became lucky enough to zero in on some of Gordie's records, he and his wife, Colleen, were always there and fully supportive.

To this day, I tell my family and friends that Gordie Howe is the greatest player who ever lived. And I've been fortunate to be friends with the nicest superstar you could ever know!

Enjoy the reading. I'm sure you will love learning about Gordie, Mark and the entire Howe family.

—Wayne Gretzky

PROLOGUE

Gordie Howe's Number 9 continued to hang in the rafters of Detroit's Olympia Stadium even as my dad resumed his career in a rival league and returned to the NHL in the uniform of another team, the Hartford Whalers.

So when I played the final three of my 22 seasons with the Red Wings, and the Number 2 I had worn with Philadelphia already was taken in Detroit by my good friend and former Flyers defense partner Brad McCrimmon, I put on Number 4. That was the Detroit number of Hall of Famer Bill Gadsby, whose family was best of friends with ours. I had always worn Number 9 with the Detroit Junior Red Wings, who had the same uniform as the Red Wings, but Dad, of course, took Number 9 when we played together in Houston. When I came to the Red Wings, I never even considered asking for it.

That thought had crossed the mind of but one person, the only one who could deem it appropriate. But the idea came to him too late.

"I don't know if you remember this, Dad, or not," I said during the last thank-you of my Hall of Fame induction speech on November 14, 2011. "Just after I retired—and the key word is *after* I retired—16 years ago, you mentioned that you wished I had worn your Number 9 for the Red Wings for one game. Your timing was pretty bad.

"You have never asked me for anything in your life. So I would like to honor your request at this time on a much bigger stage."

I reached into a bag and pulled out a Number 9 Red Wing jersey, which I put on over my tuxedo jacket. I not only became the fourth son of a Hockey Hall of Famer to be inducted, but also every son thanking a father for support, sacrifices and, most of all, the pride he felt in his child.

We are called Hockey's number-one family. But before a filled Allen Lambert Galleria at the Hockey Hall of Fame in Toronto and a national television audience in two countries, I hoped my gesture could strike a chord with any viewer's family. At least I know I moved my dad as he swallowed the lump in his throat and walked to the stage to shake my hand.

"I'm not going to thank you for being my linemate for six years," I said in my speech. "I am not going to thank you for elbowing the guy who may have taken a dirty shot at me.

"I am not going to thank you for being the greatest hockey player ever. I want to thank you for being the husband, the father and person that you are. You are the role model by which I tried to live my life. I am so proud to call you my dad.

"Dad, I love you."

CHAPTER 1

Gifts from Mom and Dad

I first realized I had a famous father when he would take me places and everybody wanted his autograph. But I just thought that was normal. For as long as I remember, Gordie Howe has been my dad more than Mr. Hockey.

Interviewers have asked, "What's it like being Gordie Howe's son?" I've always assumed it was no different than being anybody's son who grew up in a loving, supportive family.

Of course, I felt differently the night he scored his 545th goal to pass Maurice Richard for the all-time lead in the NHL. I was eight years old and the cheering at Detroit's Olympia that night—November 10, 1963—seemed to last forever. I remember thinking, "Wow, I'm the only person in here who can say, 'That's my dad!'"

A wealth of pride, however, was the only wealth into which I was born. In the '50s and '60s, not even being the planet's best hockey player translated into big dollars. When I came into the world on May 28, 1955—15 months after my brother Marty—Gordie Howe, the star of the Stanley Cup champion Red Wings, earned a salary of $10,000. That's worth $86,000 today, when the minimum NHL salary is $525,000.

Making the middle class was a huge step up for Dad, though. As the sixth of nine kids—another two were stillborn—of Katherine and Ab Howe, my father was raised in Saskatoon, Saskatchewan, in a house with no running water, necessitating that he shower at school. Thank God he liked oatmeal, which he sometimes had to eat three times a day. But the house in which his family lived so embarrassed him that until he made enough money to buy his parents a new place in Saskatoon, my father would not invite teammates to come visit over the summer.

Dad grew up delivering groceries in 30-below-zero weather and hunting the gophers that drove the Prairie farmers crazy, which would bring in a dollar a tail. I'm told that because of his struggles in school, he was a really shy and under-confident guy away from the rink. But that was only part of the reason he eyed my mother, Colleen, for weeks at his hangout, the Lucky Strike Bowling Lanes near the Olympia, before finally approaching her. Dad didn't feel he had enough money for a proper date.

According to Mom, Dad was worried about making the mortgage payments when our growing family—Marty was five, I was four, sister Cathy an infant, and baby Murray on the way a year later—moved from the little ranch house on Stawell Avenue in northwest Detroit to the bigger, split-level home at 28780 Sunset Boulevard in Lathrup Village.

It seems amazing that the first time my grandparents ever saw their son play an NHL game was on Gordie Howe Night at the Olympia—in his 13th season. But you have to realize that there wasn't money to pay for their transportation to Detroit. Until we had the means to buy a second car, my mother would bundle Marty and me for trips to the train station as late as 4 a.m. in order to pick up Dad from road trips.

When he wasn't traveling, my father did what had been expected of him since he was a kid: helping cook and clean. Even after he could afford to do so, Dad wouldn't pay people to do work on the house that he could perform himself. So Marty and I were given chores to earn our $5-a-week allowances. Even before I was old enough to be put in charge of cutting the lawn and removing snow, my once-a-week responsibility was to take everything out of our garage, clean it, and then put everything back.

I had a pretty good understanding of an honest day's work for a day's pay, a concept that was helped along in fifth grade when I was reminded there was a cost for bad decisions. One day after school, some friends and I had stopped at a little neighborhood drug store and didn't have any money on us, so we stole candy and cakes. I took some Twinkies.

About an hour and half later, my hockey game in the driveway was in full swing when a police car pulled up. I had eaten my evidence, but one of the other kids had gotten caught when he got home. He told on all of us, so they were rounding up the other suspects. I tried to deny it, but in front of all my friends the police dragged me, totally embarrassed, into the house.

I took a belt whipping that day, but not from Dad. I remember him physically reprimanding me only once. I don't recall what I did, but it must have been pretty bad because he slapped me in the ass with such force it felt like he broke my back. On this day, it was Mom who hit me so hard with the belt that blood was seeping from my lashes.

I refused to give in and cry. Actually, Mom did an hour later, when she came to me shedding tears because she had hit me. But I certainly learned that day not to steal.

In our house, there were reprimands when we deserved them, but never any threats. Always, there was an awareness of our responsibilities, intensified by being Gordie Howe's kids.

Dad had struggled in school because he suffered from mild and undiagnosed dyslexia. When Detroit signed him at age 16 out of a training camp in Windsor, Ontario—for a first-year pay of $2,300 and the promise of a Red Wings jacket—and sent him to their farm team in Galt, Ontario, he dutifully showed up for the first day of high school. But, suddenly realizing he knew no one, my father gave his books away, walked to a metal plant, and took a job instead.

In his year at that factory, Dad actually worked his way into a low-level supervisory position. But he always regretted dropping out of school and felt that somebody from the hockey club should have stopped him. I think that's why he took up crossword puzzles—a big-time passion of his—to improve his vocabulary. We did them together, and still do to this day.

So it wasn't just Mom who valued education in the Howe household. Homework had to be done before I could get to my game, either at a rink or in my driveway. I would always race home from school to get it out of the way. Fortunately, school came pretty easily to me, because it was a means to an end. The greatest thing my father passed on to me besides a sense of responsibility was a love of the game like his own.

"Is your father at work?" asked someone on the phone that I answered at age five.

"My dad doesn't work, he plays hockey," my mother remembers me saying. For me, too, the game was no chore.

Dad also gifted me his ability to skate. Mom and Dad always said that while the other kids' ankles would bow in, mine would bow out for some reason—probably genetic. I'm told I learned at age two by leaning on a folding chair that I would push around the ice, giving me something to help pull myself up when I fell.

By age four, I was playing on my first team: Teamsters 299, sponsored by the union. I remember a little about the outdoor rink—Butzel Arena—just up the street from our house in Lathrup Village. There were a couple of little bleachers and one tiny room where we could put our skates on. But you had to shovel the ice after it snowed.

Believe it or not, when I was really young, the Olympia was the only indoor rink in Detroit. My parents got together with some people and obtained the use of a closed factory in which they put up boards so that when it snowed you could still play, even if it was on natural ice in an unheated building. The train tracks that ran into the building were inactive, but as a five-year-old, I still worried about a train coming.

Mom and Dad created a rink in our front yard, too, setting their alarm clocks to come out at all hours of the night to move the hose they had attached to a ladder so they could flood the next section. After a couple of years without much sleep, my parents tried something easier by letting me skate on the ice on the cover atop our Lathrup Village backyard pool. But because I cut the winter pool cover with my skates and they worried about me falling through, that lasted only one year.

Later, they put up wooden planks and plastic, which eliminated the need to move the hose. The lights I hung around the arena for play after dark were also used for our Christmas decorations, and one year we won an originality award from the town of Lathrup Village.

Finally, a neighbor who owned a construction company came to our aid when he plowed a 200-by-85-foot rink—piled-up dirt served as the boards—in a vacant lot across the street. The town would open up a fire hydrant to flood the surface. That beat our little home rink in the front yard for reasons that included the location of the latter in front of a picture window, which I had broken one night when the puck bounced off the goal post. Dad was away and it was cold. Mom was not a happy camper.

By my count, I broke 12 windows in the house over the years. When I was playing in the driveway, I usually had a net, but, always going for the corners, I would sometimes miss, so it was *bang, bang, bang* against the aluminum garage door. After hours of that one day, Mom finally came out and said, "Put the door up." So I did, and I think the very first ball I shot went through the garage, breaking the glass door leading into the kitchen and continuing down the hallway into the living room. In one straight shot, the ball ended up under the sofa at the far end of the house, leaving glass all over the kitchen.

Mom then asked me to put the door back down. She never told me to stop shooting, though. And we received encouragement from our parents about all of our passions, not just hockey.

When my sister, Cathy, hit her preteen years and began to object to being dragged to her brothers' games, she ran track and became an excellent water skier. I don't think any of us thought Murray, the best student in the family, was going anywhere in hockey; we believed he played because he thought it was expected of a Howe. Murray, now a doctor, insists he didn't feel that pressure and that he really loved the game. I know he did, but there was little question he admired my dad so much that he wanted to follow in his footsteps.

Whatever pressure we felt came only from within. When Dad would attend our games, he would just watch, never yell or second-guess the coaching or do any of the things other parents would do. There wasn't a lot of unsolicited advice from him or from my mom. Basically, you learned how to do everything on your own, and when you had questions, they always were there with the answers. And I believe the sense of family that guided almost everything we did came not only from the big one in which Dad grew up, but from the one my mother never really had.

Her parents, Margaret Sidney and Howard Mulvaney—a trombonist who played with Benny Goodman, among other big bands—married and divorced young. Basically, Mom was raised by her great-aunt Elsie and great-uncle Hughie, who became the only people we knew well on that side of the family. The odd time at Christmas, we would go to Mom's mother's place in Detroit, but the relationship was not great. Mom said her stepfather from her mother's second marriage, Budd Joffa, was very good to her, but after Margaret's second divorce, my mom lost track of him.

Howard, her biological father, was good at woodworking. So Mom, trying to spend more time with him and also help him out a bit financially, hired him once to do some restoration work for us and make some furniture. She also gave him a truck for the work he had done, but he totaled it while driving drunk a few weeks later. His drinking problem was so evident that Mom didn't want him around her children, which put a huge strain on their relationship. He more or less drank himself out of our lives.

Mom always tried to patch things up with her parents, make them at least okay, but deep down, they weren't. It's my belief she did so much work with children's charities because she drew a short straw when it came to her own parents.

Of course, she also couldn't do enough for her husband and

children, which Dad never took for granted. One time while we were eating dinner, he and Mom were in a squabble about something. After a while, he said, "I need to cool off for a minute," so he got in the car and I hopped in with him. He had just started it up when I said, "I can't believe what Mom's saying. She is so mean."

He snapped at me, "Don't ever talk about your mother that way." I said, "I'm on your side!" And he repeated, "Don't ever talk about your mother that way."

They had a lot of patience for each other. Because she didn't like how people with the hockey club took advantage of his time for appearances and things, she wished he would stand up more for himself. But I don't think he ever thought she was nagging him about it; actually, he probably agreed with her. Still, because Dad wasn't one to bark back, Mom would wind up with the bad rap because the Gordie Howe everyone loved couldn't do enough for people.

Because Dad was on the road or at practice or needing his nap on game days, Mom took charge of our hockey educations. She had some disagreements with the way minor programs were run by what was then the Amateur Hockey Association of the United States, so she formed some independent teams for us. Mom selected coaches not just to teach her own boys, but everybody's on the club. After she had done her due diligence, I think she let the coaches, none of whom were screamers, do their thing. Jim Chapman, whom I had up to age 10, and who unfortunately later died in a car accident, was a very patient teaching coach.

Of course, the most essential hockey lesson Marty and I had to learn was how to cope with being the sons of the greatest player on earth. Even from a ridiculously early age, I would hear fans yelling, "You're not as good as your father," to which Marty sometimes would yell back, "Who is?" Pretty good answer. But as our teams, in search of better competition, would go to Canada to play games, there would be a lot more—and tougher—trash talk.

When our club became the first from the United States to enter the annual pee wee tournament in Quebec City, there were around

14,000 people at Le Colisée. All eyes were upon Gordie Howe's eight- and nine-year-old sons, me on left wing, Marty on defense. Pretty intimidating. If, as we grew older, Marty ever fought any jealousy about me, the little brother becoming the better player in people's eyes, I don't think we ever discussed it. We spent most of our time talking about dealing with being Gordie Howe's kids. And the best advice on that came from our mom.

"You have to learn to let it go in one ear and out the other," she said. "It is what it is, learn to accept it. Maybe there's a negative side with all the attention you get. But let me make a list of all the positive things, like being able to go down to the Olympia and skate for six to eight hours. You can say, 'I'm Gordie Howe's son,' and go anyplace in that building you want."

Every Red Wing would get two tickets per game. Later in Dad's career, when Mom was too busy with running his business stuff to go to every game, I would go out onto Grand River Avenue, sell the tickets at the face value of $7.50 each, then walk past a friendly ticket taker and go sit in the press box.

That wasn't the only example of my entrepreneurship. One Christmas, I surprised my parents with a request for a $450 top-of-the-line snowblower—I had done my research—with which to expand operations throughout the neighborhood. They loaned me the money. I had 25 contracts for three to five dollars per driveway and paid them back completely by Christmas the following year.

Fortunately, I never had to pay for a seat at our kitchen table with Bobby Baun, Bill Gadsby or other Red Wings after games, another perk of being Gordie's kid. Mom would let me stay up—I even got the meal ready for them and drew the beers from the tap we had in the basement—and I would ask Frank Mahovlich about his aim on the goal he had scored that night, or question Bobby Baun about whether the shot he blocked had hurt him. Mostly, though, I just listened. My mother later said that at age nine, I already was preparing myself to be a professional.

A couple of times a year, when Dad was supposed to be dropping

Marty and me off at elementary school on the way to practice, I would plead to go to the rink with him, and every once in a while, he would say okay. Mom was fine with that because I was a conscientious student and she knew time with Dad was precious to us. When he was home during the day after practice, we would be at school. During the playoffs, the team would be in Toledo for up to four or five weeks because Jack Adams, the general manager, wanted the players away from "distractions" like wives and kids. So when the Red Wings would be coming home late from a trip, I would ask Mom if I could wake up to see Dad for a little bit. She would say okay and I would get to spend 10 minutes with him before he would put me back to bed and get to sleep himself.

As long as my homework was done, I could go to the Red Wings games, even on school nights, which gave me the chance to see Dad some more. If the Wings were winning, I would leave my seat with about five minutes to go in the game and stand along the barricade—the players had to go through the Olympia concourse to get to the locker room—waiting for Dad to grab me and take me into the locker room.

Norm Ullman, Number 7 for Detroit, would always sit on one side of the bench. Dad, Number 9, was in the middle and Alex Delvecchio (Number 10) on the other side. I would sit with them while the coach would rant and rave. Dad remembered that once, when I was really young, I asked, "Who's that little fat guy?" meaning Jack Adams, and the next game, the policy was: no more kids in the locker room. I don't know how long that rule lasted, but while Sid Abel, and then Gadsby, coached, it certainly no longer was enforced.

All the players were great to me. I can't remember one who wasn't, although I was embarrassed pretty badly by Toronto's Eddie Shack one time when I was serving as water boy/stick boy/tape boy in the visiting locker room.

There used to be a 45-rpm record called "Gordie Howe is the Greatest of Them All" that would be played in Detroit at playoff time. Eddie was on the training table in the middle of the visitors' locker room, getting taped, and just as he saw I was going to ask him for his autograph, he started singing that song. I got so embarrassed I had to hide in the stick room.

Everybody made fun of Eddie, who was unable to write because of his dyslexia. So he got a stamp made with his alleged signature. When the crowds would form around him outside the locker room, he would pull out his pad and stamp away. I thought that was just the neatest thing.

Over to the left in the Red Wings' locker room was the stick rack. As I got older, I would grab a stick that Nick Libett or Dean Prentice would saw down to my size, and then the trainer, Lefty Wilson, would come out of the back, screaming at me (in mock anger) for stealing sticks. Everybody in the locker room would chuckle.

I wanted those sticks to play ball hockey on the stairs to the back balcony, where a railing and a wall created a sort-of goal. Even dressed up in my suit and tie—that's what you wore to the games in those days—I would go off to the balcony, hopefully with another player's kid—sometimes Jerry Sawchuk or Kenny Delvecchio—who could be the goaltender.

After Dad showered, he would sign every autograph, which I loved because that meant another 20 or 30 minutes to play on the stairs. But that also was him again teaching me by example, showing how he took care of the public and what a humble man he was. Dad graciously accepted the many things offered his way, but didn't behave as though he had grown to expect them.

I saw him lose patience in public only three or four times. When, instead of asking nicely, somebody would demand an autograph with a "Sign here!" Dad would usually sign the word "Here." That's his sense of humor. Once, at an Italian restaurant near the Olympia, Dad had food halfway to his mouth when some guy shoved a piece of paper right against the fork and said, "Sign this!" Dad had a few things to say that were not nice, but fitting for what the guy had done.

Another time, Marty and I were playing in a junior game in Chatham, Ontario, against a team with which we had a pretty good rivalry. Throughout the game, people were all over Marty and me with "Your old man sucks," and all over Dad with "You're over the hill—you ought to retire, you bum."

Afterward, people asked, "Hey Gordie, can I have your autograph?" But after two and a half hours of verbal abuse, they had no chance of getting it. He didn't say anything other than, "I'm not signing tonight."

Then there was the time just my father and I were in the car when some kid cut him off on Southfield Road, near home. Dad drove around in front of the guy, but the kid got back in front again and slammed on his brakes for spite.

When the cars came up to a light, Dad put ours in park and started out. The guy looked back and took off through the light. When Dad got back into the car, all he said was, "Don't tell your mother."

I read about one other time where some guy spit on a Red Wing right in front of Dad as the team got on the bus after a game. Apparently, Dad left the creep crumpled against the back wheel of the vehicle. The guy sued and the team had to make a settlement.

It took something really abusive to provoke Dad. His thoughtfulness could be incredible. When he was finished cleaning his own windshield at the gas station, my father would do somebody else's. Every once in a while, he would shovel the neighbors' driveways, rake their leaves or mow their lawns without being asked.

One time when there was a snowstorm and my team couldn't get back from a game in southern Ontario, he was out with the snowblower in the wee hours, taking care of my obligations in the neighborhood. And as he has gotten older, my father continues to do even more of those kind things for people.

Always, there has been this incredible grace to him. Every once in a while, when he had to go to Toronto, I would ride with him. Dad was a notoriously fast driver; we were headed up the 401 doing something like 95–100 miles per hour when he got pulled over near Chatham.

Dad kept autographed pictures in the glove box of the car. In getting out his registration, he would intentionally put the pictures on the floor within the cop's line of vision.

When this patrolman said, "Oh Gordie, it's you," Dad gave him the line, "Yeah, how you doing? Got any kids?"

The cop said, "Yeah, I got three." And Dad said, "Would you like an autograph for them?"

The patrolman said, "No thanks, Gordie, we already got three sets of those." Seems the same guy had been stopping Dad for years. I remember the cop saying, "Look, Gordie, we're concerned for your life. If you get a flat tire going this fast, anything can happen. We just want you to slow down." Sure, he was letting Dad go because he was Gordie Howe, but not entirely. Dad just has a way with people.

One day, he playfully scooped up some ice shavings and threw them over the glass on some quadriplegic kids who were watching practice. One of them was laughing as the snow ran down his face, but when the next Red Wing did it, too, that kid was pissed off. He loved it only when Gordie Howe did it.

That's Dad's natural gift, a mystique or whatever you want to call it, the best part of what he is. His interaction with people is phenomenal and is what keeps him ticking today.

In 1965, when I was 10, Dad signed a $10,000 yearly deal with Eaton's department store to travel coast to coast in Canada, visiting every store in the chain during July. Usually, when he got about halfway across the country, like to Winnipeg, I would fly out and travel with him for the final two weeks.

What I remember most about those trips were these picture cards he would pass out every day. Each night at 8 or 9 p.m., when we got back to the hotel, Dad would pre-sign 2,000 to 2,500 cards so he could spend more time the next day writing in things like "To John, best wishes" and thus have a little more time for each person.

If it was a town with only one Eaton's, you would spend a couple of hours at the store, and then they would take us golfing or fishing. Marty, who wasn't a golfer but liked the fishing part of it, went a couple of times. Mostly, it was Dad and me. And every second with him was a treasure.

CHAPTER 2

Growing Up Fast

The kind and cool dad I grew up with was not the same Gordie Howe opponents saw—or felt, especially when he was upset. Riding downtown to the game, he would say, "Keep an eye on so-and-so tonight," and inevitably, that guy would wind up in a corner with blood spewing from his face. I saw Dad do some pretty cruel things that I knew were premeditated.

The one scene I can still picture vividly involved the Blackhawks' Keith Magnuson, who obviously must have done something to really piss Dad off. There was a right-circle face-off in Chicago's zone, with Magnuson lined up behind Stan Mikita. The puck went to Magnuson, who, head down, started to take off behind the net. Dad went at him with a vicious elbow right in the middle of Magnuson's face. He might already have been out cold as he was falling, but Dad still grabbed Magnuson by the back of the head, brought it down and almost put his knee through Keith's face.

Magnuson was done for the night, while Dad went to the penalty box for something like two minutes for elbowing and two minutes for roughing. That was all. Back then, there was only one television camera and one referee who couldn't see everything, so players took justice into their own hands, something rare in the current game. Today, I think Dad would have a hard time playing because, with the way penalties are called, he probably would be suspended all the time. And I don't think he ever was.

While my father was far and away hockey's all-time leading goal and point scorer when he retired, his toughness probably became more legendary than his skills. So certainly, as kids, we were expected to stick up not only for ourselves but for members of the family as well. Apparently, once when I was really small, I came running into the house, yelling, "Somebody is picking on Marty." Dad, half-kiddingly, said something like "Why don't you stand up for your brother? Get a stick and hit the kid over the head." So I picked up a stick—they were never in short supply around the house—and started out the door. Dad had to chase me down or else I would have cracked the guy.

Then there was the time in junior high that I walked into the house after school and Marty was sitting at the kitchen table. It surprised me to see him there because he always took the bus home and I always beat him by 15 to 20 minutes by running. That way, I could get right to my homework, and then my hockey game. But before I could ask how it was that he already was there, Marty put his finger in front of his mouth, telling me to be quiet.

Next thing I knew, Mom came down the stairs, ranting and raving. Marty had gotten into a fight at school and had been suspended for three days. His locker partner, a guy who sat in back of him in homeroom and with whom he didn't get along, had started to mouth off about Dad and the Red Wings, who were pretty bad by those years. When my brother turned around and told the kid to shut up, the guy challenged Marty, who popped the guy in the nose.

When Dad came home from practice, Mom started lecturing him for being a bad example before she stormed off again upstairs. Dad had no idea what she was talking about. "What happened?" he asked. After Marty told the whole story, Gordie took a quick look around for Mom to make sure she wasn't listening, patted him on the shoulder and said, "Good job."

Dad gave me advice about handling myself just once. He said, "If somebody is coming to hit you, just try to go right through them. Don't be backing down."

I guess he got that attitude through strong-minded parents who had survived the Great Depression. He looked at the puck as his personal possession, so there would be retribution toward any player who took it away from him, even cleanly. It wasn't important to him that I match his mean streak. He just didn't want me to be pushed around.

I was growing into a big kid, 180 or 185 pounds by age 14, which allowed me to play three to five years ahead of my age group. But, of course, I wasn't going to win any physical wars against guys 17 to 19 years old. My way of getting them back was to put the puck in the net and win the game. My mindset was that the opponent might win the battle, but I would win the war. I might leave with a sore body, but I would be smiling.

I inherited mental toughness from both my parents. But my willingness to play with pain came from Dad. One time, not feeling well at dinner, he went upstairs, and then we heard this big thud on the floor. We ran and found my father had fallen down six stairs of our split-level house and was lying on the floor all crumpled up. At the hospital, he was diagnosed with kidney stones—which, according to anybody who has suffered from them, are the most painful things they ever have felt. Dad was admitted overnight to have surgery in the morning, but he passed the stones at around 8 a.m. The Red Wings were playing at 3 o'clock that afternoon and, just released from the hospital, Dad had something like two goals and two assists and was the game's first star. I came to believe that his nerve endings stopped short of the top floor. And perhaps he passed a little of that on to me, too.

One bitterly cold day, I talked Marty and his friends into skating with me on the ice at the Rackham Golf Course near the Detroit Zoo. After about an hour, everybody but me went inside. By the time Dad came to pick us up, I couldn't feel my hands or toes. When I got home and put my hands under cold water, it felt like they were burning.

That was one of the more agonizing days of my young life that I remember. There was another that, fortunately, I don't. I was the only kid in the sixth grade who could run up, grab the chin-up bar in the playground of Lathrup Elementary School, and flip the whole way around. Or, at least I was until the day I missed and fell on my head.

Mom and Dad, who were flying home from Toronto that day, were escorted into a private room at the Windsor airport and told that I had been taken to the hospital, unconscious, as a result of a fall at school. Imagine their long ride to the hospital, particularly with my mother furious that I had been taken to a facility different from the one designated on the emergency card at the school. She had me transferred later in the day, by which time I had regained enough of my senses—apparently, at the school I had been lying on the ground, smiling and waving—to insist I was fine. But they wouldn't let me out of bed for four or five days. I was giving one nurse a hard time because I wanted to go to the toilet, so she said, "Fine, Hot Dog, get out of bed." After one step, she had to catch me. I said, "Okay, I'll use the bedpan." I think I spent seven days in the hospital, and they wouldn't let me play hockey for at least six weeks.

I had 22 seasons in the pros, including six in the wild, goon-laden World Hockey Association and 10 years in Philadelphia with the franchise that had won two Stanley Cups as the Broad Street Bullies. Still, the worst concussion I ever suffered was in sixth grade when I fell off the monkey bars.

That wasn't the only problem I had with my head as a kid, though. When I was in third grade, they stuck me in a hospital for 10 days to try to find out why I was getting migraines. It would start with this buildup of pressure, then my vision would blur and I would feel sick to my stomach. It never was brought on by physical activity, but by getting overly excited, like on Halloween—I only got to go trick-or-treating once in my life—or if there was stress about something like a big test at school. When I felt a migraine coming on, I would go to the principal's office and Mom would come pick me up. This happened about 40 or 50 times a year.

A substitute teacher once didn't believe me—thought I was just trying to get out of class. I said, "I'm telling you, I am going to get sick," so she said, "Stay here and we'll see how you do." Fifteen minutes later, I threw up all over the room. I said, "Told ya." She said, "Get out of here."

Nobody else in the family suffered from these, and they never have found a reason for mine. I can remember them sometimes getting so bad I would bang my head against the headboard trying to relieve the pressure. But by age 14 I learned how to deal with them. As early as possible when I felt one coming on, I'd catch a nap. I would wake up an hour later and be fine.

My first stitches were not self-induced, however. At age 10, I took a puck in the top lip during a game at Sault Ste. Marie, Ontario. The shot of Novocain was really the only bad part, but while the doctor was stitching and tightening, Mom was making cringing faces. I finally asked the doctor to stop. He asked, "Why, is it sore?" I said, "No, but can you get her out of here? She's killing me."

Marty once got cut over the eye in a game at Gordie Howe Hockeyland, a rink across town in St. Clair Shores, Michigan, that my parents built with four other investors during the 1960s. On the way home, we stopped at Beaumont Hospital, where he received 10 stitches. The following Sunday, we again were playing in St. Clair Shores and planned to stop at Beaumont after the game to get the stitches removed. As luck would have it, this time *I* got cut over the eye.

At the hospital, the doctor said, "You need 10 stitches." I said, "My brother had 10; you've gotta give me 11." So he actually put in 11 while the nurses were looking at me like, "What is wrong with this child?" To me, almost everything was a competition, even extending to sibling rivalry.

Because I was six years older than Murray, my relationship with him was different than with Marty. Murray was a sweet kid and was always supportive of me, even if Marty and I gave him the odd "swirly"—hanging him upside down in the toilet and flushing. Marty was the instigator. I usually was the follower. Murray had to keep the door to the bathroom locked, knowing we would try to harass him.

We wouldn't just eat the Cocoa Krispies that Murray loved more than anything in the world, we'd put the empty box back so he'd be doubly disappointed when he went to pour them into his bowl and nothing came out. When my parents took pity and bought a case for him, Murray hid the boxes from us all over the house, and then forgot where he put some of them. They were found years later.

Another time, my brothers and I were fishing on a very choppy Lake Michigan and a seasick Murray was throwing up. But because Marty and I were having our best day ever and were allowed three fish per person, we refused to take him in until we also caught Murray's three. It only took an extra half-hour, although I'm sure it seemed longer to him.

That's what siblings do—torture each other. One night, when I must have been around 10 and we were with a babysitter, Marty was bothering me about something—I don't remember what. On a table between our beds, there was an aquarium that really was more his than mine, so I said, "If you don't stop, I'm going to wreck the aquarium!"

He said, "You wouldn't dare." I replied, "You daring me?" I went to give it the ol' fake punch, but went a quarter-inch too far and the glass shattered, water pouring all over the place. We discovered one of the fish about two years later. And Mom never found out exactly what had happened.

Only years after the fact did I tell her about the time I climbed out the back window of our moving station wagon, used the luggage rack to pull myself onto the roof of the car, and then lowered my head over the windshield, freaking out my brother. He had been driving for only three months. We were on this gravel road near the cottage Mom and Dad had bought at Bear Lake near Grayling, Michigan, and when another car came around a curve, Marty panicked, hit the brake, and I went flying farther than Carl Lewis's best-ever long jump.

Thank God I got one foot down, and then my next one, but then I skidded, filling my hands and knees with gravel. Next day, I started getting some red lines from infection and had to show Mom.

"We were going to roast marshmallows on the beach and I fell down the steps," I lied.

"I'm not believing that," she said. "But we have to get you to the hospital."

It wasn't until I was well into adulthood—and had a couple of drinks at a function one night—that I volunteered to her how stupid I had been. She just shook her head.

Marty and I were on the same teams growing up, but not always on the same page. It was hard to get him to play in my driveway games. Because I got used sticks, nets and Terry Sawchuk's old goaltending equipment from the Olympia, those games were first-class, attracting all the neighborhood kids, but usually not my brother.

He was a better athlete than I, a faster and stronger runner who set many school track and field records. He also was the better football player. One time, he had a conflict between football practice and a hockey playoff game and the football coach said, "If you miss practice, you're off the team." The hockey game was against a team that had given us our only loss of the season, so he decided to play, and the football coach kept his word. That brought Marty back to hockey as his main sport. Today, he says that was the best decision he could have made.

My own football career ended in seventh grade, with Dad watching. The coaches were working on defense, so they had us younger guys filling in with some of the eighth graders on offense. I was the quarterback, at least for that practice, so the coach—his name was Dave Sebring—told me to call the play.

In the huddle, some of the eighth graders said, "Let's call the bomb." I said, "What?" In our whole playbook there was not one play that utilized two wide receivers, so I called it like you would in the schoolyard: "Two guys go long."

I threw to one of them for a touchdown and the coach asked me, "What play did you call?"

I said, "The bomb." He waited a couple seconds and asked, "What play did you call?" I said, "The bomb!" He started yelling at me, "What bleeping play did you call?" Again, I said, "The bomb!" So he got out the playbook and said, "Where is that in here?"

I said, "It's not." He said, "Run laps!" So as they were practicing, I ran around the field like a fool for an hour, even though I knew I was going to quit.

Gordie, who watched all this, walked up to the coach afterward and said, "I think Mark may have played in his last football game." I turned in my equipment because football wasn't nearly as much fun as hockey—although that day, it certainly was for Dad. He loved that story.

What I really loved, next to hockey, was golf. Dad was a plus-handicap, and the day I shot par for the first time, at age 17, was also the first time I beat him. We were at Michaywe Pines near Gaylord, Michigan—the course had just opened—and we were tied going into the last hole. I birdied it while he bogeyed, and I won by two. That was VG-Day for me, boy, beating Gordie—not that I was competitive or anything.

Marty never wanted to play golf. So in the year that he had his driver's license and I didn't yet, I would have to bribe him to drive me to the course by promising him six hours of fishing for one round of golf. No matter how, I had to find a way.

When I got my driver's license the next year, I borrowed the Town Car Dad received for doing promotional work for Lincoln-Mercury and went to Twin Birch, a nine-hole course near the cottage. I met a man for the first time and went around with him twice. It was a really short course—some of the holes were 300 to 320 yards—and I think I played the front nine at four under par and the second nine at two under.

The guy kept telling me what a good golfer I was, how far I could hit the ball. He said I should take some lessons and that he could get me a golf scholarship. All I kept telling him was, "No, I'm going to be a hockey player." I think that drove the man crazy, because here's a kid he thought could be a pro golfer and all I talked about was hockey.

When we finished, he watched this 16-year-old get into this big Town Car with "HOWE 9" on its plates. About a month later, this guy wrote Mom and Dad, telling the story of how frustrated he had been until he saw the license plate and figured out who I was.

Because we would play upward of 100 hockey games a year and practice two or three days a week, there was time for golf only in the summers. By age 15, I was leading a Tier II league in scoring while playing against kids 18 and 19, so I knew I was pretty good on the ice and didn't want to risk a serious injury that might jeopardize a possible hockey career.

Nevertheless, I was a big kid and one of the strongest in our high school, so coaches didn't give up on getting me to come out for other sports. They tried to entice me by saying it would be easier to get an A or a B in their classes, but I used to tell them I would get an A or a B anyway.

The wrestling coach found a different way: keeping me after class and making me late for my next one. After a week of this, I finally made a deal with him. I said, "I'll wrestle, but I won't practice—just do the meets." And even though I knew nothing about wrestling, he let me do it.

At my first meet, after they taught me the basic rules on the bus, I was beating this kid 14–1. Next thing I knew, he'd turned around and pinned me. I was on the mat, saying "Bleep this" and "Mother that."

The team won the meet regardless. When we got on the bus, the coach said, "Great job, guys. But for those of you who don't know, there's no swearing in wrestling." And that's what I remember most about my wrestling experience.

I was also a good catcher in Little League. Got my baseball ability from Dad, too—in his first years with the Red Wings, before he got married, he used to play in a summer league in Saskatoon with pros. Dad showed me an article once that said he was hitting something like .560. The Red Wings ended summer baseball for him because they didn't want him to get injured. But sometimes Tigers star Al Kaline, with whom Dad was in the auto parts business for a time, would invite him down for batting practice and he would hit home runs at Briggs (later Tiger) Stadium.

One day, I was getting ready for a game by throwing with Dad and he said, "Ever caught a knuckleball? I'll throw you a couple." First one popped me in the nose. I had blood spewing, my eyes were teary, and, of course, stupid me wanted him to throw another one. He said, "Nah, nah," but I insisted. "I'll catch this one," I said. Bingo, it hit me right in the forehead. Dad said, "All right, you're done with knuckleballs."

As long as I wasn't done with hockey. When I took shop in junior high, my wood project was a tray with all the NHL team logos on it. For a metal project, I made a goal frame out of steel and used old, discarded netting from the Olympia to complete my work. I also would do the odd end table, but the hockey stuff was more useful to me.

If the Red Wings were on the road on a Saturday and Sunday and I could find somebody to drive me downtown, I would skate and shoot pucks by myself for six to eight hours. A great guy in concessions named Jessie would prepare the two of us a lunch of hot dogs, popcorn and soda. I would return the favor by sometimes bringing donuts for breakfast.

Probably because I was so focused on hockey, I had only a passing curiosity about the things that can get adolescents in trouble, like alcohol. Mom never was a drinker, and I can count on one hand the number of times I ever saw Dad have more than two beers in one night. Whenever we would host a team party, I would go to Dad first and ask if I could have a beer. He'd say, "You have to ask your mother." So I would tell her, "Dad said it was okay to have a beer."

Mom would say, "If he said so, you can have one." So I would get one, then go back to Dad and tell him, "Mom said to make sure it was okay with you." And he would say, "Go ahead." So I would work my way into two beers, not just one.

One day in my early teens, after walking home from school, I had my homework out, the TV on and decided to pour myself a cold one. Mom came downstairs and said, "What's that?"

I said, "My homework."

She scowled, "No, *that,*" pointing to the beer. That was the end of having a beer with my homework. But as I got older, inevitably there was more exposure to adult things.

The Christmas Eve when I was 13, Danny Olesevich, the Red Wings' assistant trainer, got sick. Dad called me from practice and asked, "Do you want to come with us to be the trainer for the game tomorrow in Pittsburgh?"

Hey, no-brainer. I flew with the team. Guys were deciding where to go for dinner on their $20-a-day NHL meal money, and a few of them even went to McDonald's. Dad took me with about four or five other Red Wings to a place where we could get a bite and they could get a couple of beers. Suddenly, a dancer came out on this stage in a short skirt, wearing white go-go boots. Dad said to me, "Whoa, we can't have you in here." But the guys said, "No leave him, he's fine," and we finished the meal and left.

I guess I was saved from much naïveté by spending so much time around people older than myself. But the one place where I always was a kid was at Bear Lake, where my family bought a cottage, mostly with their Eaton's money.

There were four or five beachfront units, all owned by good friends who would have a sailing regatta at least once every weekend. The clear, spring-fed lake was stocked with rainbow trout and I would water-ski all day every day or go into the backwoods on a dirt bike.

It was 96 steps from the back door of the cottage to the lake. When you made that trip 10 times a day, you knew exactly how many. Usually, we would go up there on a Friday and leave either Sunday or Monday, but when Marty and I got older, Mom and Dad would trust us to be there midweek by ourselves. In fact, Marty was there alone with my grandparents when my grandmother suffered the fall that ended her life.

Mom and Dad had run to Toronto for some one-day event. I was in Detroit, taking driver's ed. I guess my grandmother heard a noise at around two or three in the morning, got up to see what it was and fell down the steps of the cottage, hitting her head. Blood was gushing all over the place.

Grandpa woke up Marty, who held Grandma Kate's head with a towel. They called me at home at about 3 a.m. to tell me what had happened and that Grandma's chances of surviving were slim. I was the only one with contact information for my parents—no cell phones in those days—so I called the hotel in Toronto, praying Dad wouldn't answer the phone because I couldn't bear the thought of telling him.

Sure enough, he picked up, so I asked for Mom. It was hard enough telling her, and harder still for her to tell Dad, I'm sure. When she did, he broke down.

Mom called back and said Uncle Vern, Dad's oldest brother, who was head of the maintenance crew at the Olympia at the time, was going to pick me up and take me to Bear Lake while my parents returned from Toronto. About an hour later, I got a call from Dad informing me my grandmother had passed away.

Because of the distance, we hadn't seen Dad's big family much while growing up. But I remember Grandma Kate as a sweet, yet tough woman who beat me at arm wrestling when I was 13, who did jigsaw puzzles with me, and who made good pies. The bears at Waskesiu Lake at Prince Albert National Park in Saskatchewan thought so, too, clawing through a cottage kitchen screen one time to eat them.

Together, we flew to Saskatoon for the funeral, Dad and Vern up in first class, feeding Grandpa Ab drinks. After a while, they told the flight attendants to start serving them water because there was no way they could keep up with their father.

Dad told me that Grandpa had been a track star in his youth. He played the fiddle, too, when he was younger, but what I remember most about him were his massive hands. Big as Dad's are, Grandpa's were even bigger.

When he headed the paving crew that put in the sidewalks of Saskatoon, he would make side money by wagering 30 cents that his incredibly strong son could lift six concrete bags—each of which weighed about 65 or 75 pounds—at once.

"Don't let me down," Grandpa would tell Dad. Talk about pressure. At age 16, Dad had a double hernia operation. No surprise there.

After Grandma's death, Ab remained in the home that Mom and Dad bought them in Saskatoon. When he was dying of cancer at 92 and all his children had gathered, Dad's sisters went to Grandpa's for breakfast one morning and found him with his eyes closed, apparently not breathing. They came out of the room crying. Everybody ran in, only to see Grandpa open his eyes and say, "Ha, ha. Fooled you!" Not dead yet, although at that moment everybody wanted to kill him. He passed away the next day.

That's where Dad got his sense of humor, in addition to his work ethic. As a father, Ab had so many mouths to feed on so little money that he hadn't gone to Gordie's games. But when I hit my teens and it was becoming increasingly clear there was a chance for me to play pro, Dad made certain I could avail myself of unique opportunities.

I was only 14 when the Red Wings gave me a uniform at training camp in Port Huron, Michigan, and I got to play with all the guys for four days. Talk about quickly learning great lessons. I'll never forget my first scrimmage, lined up at left wing against Dean Prentice, who scored three goals in a 3–0 win. All he told me was, "Kid, you have to learn how to backcheck."

Every once in a while, Dad would get me on the ice for regular-season practices. One time, I missed the net with a shot and shattered the glass, delaying practice for about a half hour. A few days later, I missed the net again and shattered another piece. So they told Dad, "That's it until the kid learns to hit the net." I got in a few more practices, though not many. But the Red Wings were good to me and I treasured every opportunity to learn.

On the way to Dad's games, I would be quiet so he could focus. But every once in a while, he would volunteer, "Don't just watch the game, watch how people are playing it."

For a lot of years, Nick Libett was one of the league's best left wings, your prototypical up-and-down winger who would score 20 goals a season and keep his man from getting opportunities. I spent a lot of time watching where Nick went in different situations and how he reacted. And of course, when Chicago would come to town, I would keep my eyes on Bobby Hull, who was the best left wing in the game and maybe of all time. I also remember watching Toronto's Ronnie Ellis, a strong checker and skater. Ronnie the Robot, they called him, up and down that wing, never coming inside the dots, because that's what hockey was back then.

But there were never long tutorials from Dad. And he didn't bring the game home after a loss—good thing, because I did that too often.

When we were pretty young, somebody took a picture of Dad dropping the puck for a face-off between Marty and me. Later, an artist did a rendering of that photo as a gift to us. One time, when Dad was showing a writer that painting, he said something like, "Do you see it?' He was referring to the fact that Marty was smiling—like he was supposed to be doing—for the picture, while my head was down, thinking about nothing besides winning the face-off.

Certainly, no coach ever had to tell me to take the game more seriously. After being rejected at age 12 by the Dearborn Fabricators, Marty's midget-level team (where players were generally 14 to 16 years old), I cried my eyes out—not only because this would be the first year I didn't play with my older brother, but because I really wanted to make that team.

Carl Lindstrom, the coach, explained that I would get to play 40 minutes a game with my bantam team, Myr Metal, but would only have been a third-liner on Marty's team. So I played bantam one more year and we won the national championship in Minnesota. The next week, I was back home, as was Dad—whose Red Wings had missed the playoffs—when Marty's midget team was going to the national tournament in Erie, Pennsylvania. We were all driving there in a motor home my godfather, Ed Taube, had borrowed. The equipment was being stored in the shower, somehow the water got turned on, and we had to air-dry the stuff out the windows.

Then, when we were about 20 miles from Erie, smoke started coming out of the engine. We were running really late, so Mom and

I stayed with the van while Marty, Dad and Ed hitchhiked. There was Gordie Howe, standing alongside the road just outside Erie, holding hockey sticks, with his thumb out. Mom said it would have been like seeing Arnold Palmer hitchhiking with his golf bag. They got picked up by a guy in a Mustang fastback and made it to the game on time, although Marty's team lost. I teased Lindstrom, "See, if you would have had me . . ."

That year hardly set me back. My skills usually were ahead of my confidence, but by the time I was 16, in 1971, and Mom came up with the idea of putting Dad, Marty and me together on a line for the Junior Red Wings in a game against the Red Wings to benefit the March of Dimes, the 11,000 who turned out at the Olympia didn't scare me. Our junior team had already drawn 14,000 for a game.

Dad's wrist was really bad by then, and so were the Red Wings. At age 43, he had already decided this was going to be his final season, and this game was meant to be one of the goodbyes. I set Dad up for a goal. Even Murray, who at age 10 made an appearance in the final minutes, was given a penalty shot, and the goalie risked a groin pull letting my little brother score.

For Mom, that night was a culmination of a lot of hard work for a charity with which she and Dad always were involved. For me, it was all business; I just wanted to play well. For Dad, who had long been fantasizing about playing with his sons, it was the fulfillment of a dream.

"When they announced us, it sounded like an Indian line—'Howe, Howe, Howe,'" Gordie joked later. "There was about a 10-minute standing ovation."

He looked at us boys and said, "Wouldn't it be wonderful if it was for real?"

CHAPTER 3

A Silver Lining

"No pain, no gain" is the mantra of strength and conditioning coaches everywhere. Indeed, the first major surgery I underwent turned into the opportunity of a lifetime.

The Detroit Junior Red Wings were down 3–2 against Guelph with less than two minutes remaining in game seven of the 1971 final of the Southern Ontario Junior A Hockey League when I drove the zone, trying to force a face-off in the offensive zone. A guy hit me into the boards and I went in at a funny angle and knew immediately that something bad had happened to my right knee.

They slowly got me up and back to the bench. We pulled the goalie, and our coach, Carl Lindstrom, put me at the point with my brother Marty. We won the face-off and my brother lifted a backhander over three guys, off the screened goalie's back, and into the net for a tie that gave us the championship on a total-points basis. But after the game, my knee swelled up horribly.

I sat out the first two games of our next series, the Centennial Cup eastern semifinal against the Ottawa Rangers, while waiting for the swelling to subside, then played until we were eliminated in the eastern final against Charlottetown, Prince Edward Island. It was believed I had suffered a partially torn ligament that would heal without surgery. But every once in a while that summer, my knee would catch, swell up and lock.

Regardless, I went on with preparation for the next stage of my hockey development: Junior A in Canada. Canadian kids graduating from midget-level hockey (ages 15 to 17) were subject to the Ontario Hockey Association draft, but as Americans, Marty and I were free agents. So the two of us got in the car on our own and went off on a recruiting tour, Mom and Dad believing our decision should be uninfluenced by them.

First stop was in Toronto to check out the Marlboros. Tommy Smythe, the grandson of former Maple Leafs owner Conn Smythe and the operator of the junior team, took us up to the Smythe cottage about an hour north of Toronto, where we had a nice dinner, met the family, and then spent the next day around Maple Leaf Gardens.

From there, we drove to St. Catharines and Kitchener to hear similar spiels. All the cities were great, and the people were nice everywhere we went, but the Marlies were run as well as probably half the teams around the NHL today. On the two long trips to Sault Ste. Marie and Sudbury, they flew—only in a DC-3, but still pretty nice for junior hockey travel. So we headed home with our minds pretty well made up.

Because we were two typically long-haired, bell-bottom-clad teenagers of the '70s, traveling alone, we were waved over by U.S. customs officials at the border in Windsor, Ontario. After no drugs were found in the car, they started searching our belongings. One officer opened a suitcase in the trunk, found a pill bottle and said, "Ha! We got you now." Marty, who was running track, said, "Those are my cleats for running on asphalt." Two other pill bottles yielded sets for running on ash and cinder.

Now they were getting frustrated, as were Marty and I. We must have been there for two hours until they went to a third suitcase, saw Gordie Howe's name on it and asked, "Where did you get this?" We said, "That's our dad." The guy said, "Why didn't you tell me? You guys can go." Boy, were we pissed.

By the end of August, my knee hurt so much that they operated, discovering the damage had been to cartilage, not ligaments. Instead of taking out the entire cartilage, they did something new, snipping off just the ends, but orthopedic surgery techniques were a long way from what they are now, four decades later. Today's scar would be two pinholes, but in 1971, mine was five inches long and I was going to need two to three months to heal. So Marty went off to the Marlies without me.

Like surgery, rehab then also was archaic. I went home with instructions from the doctor and basically just rode the stationary bike. At Olympia Stadium, Red Wings trainer Lefty Wilson let me use the whirlpool. My goal became to get back on the ice by December 20, when the 1972 U.S. Olympic team made a stop at the Olympia to play the Junior Wings. That game lit up like neon on our schedule. And I hit the bike hard and made it into the lineup.

They beat us 6–1 and I was so out of shape, I think I sweated off ten pounds. But I guess I did well enough. About three weeks later, my mother got a call from the Olympic team coach, Murray Williamson, inviting me to try out for the team, which would be playing in the Winter Games at Sapporo, Japan, in February.

Mom didn't want me missing a lot of school for nothing, so she tried to get Williamson to guarantee me a spot. He said he couldn't do that, so she turned him down. But when she explained the situation to me, I told her I wanted a shot. If it didn't work out, I would be back in three weeks and I could make up the schoolwork without much problem.

She could see how much it meant to me, so she changed her mind. Off I flew, at age 16, to Bloomington, Minnesota, and the U.S. Olympic team's camp at the Metropolitan Sports Center.

There was another left wing they wanted to take a look at, Tom Peluso from the University of Denver, but Murray Armstrong, the Denver coach, balked about some things and Peluso never came. So I didn't have any direct competition, but players had been in and out of the lineup since the team began playing exhibition games in September, so

I still needed to earn my spot. Since I had been playing for only a few weeks, I had a lot of conditioning work to do.

I was nervous, of course. But at any level, I always felt at least a little bit of tension about performing, and I already was accustomed to playing against older guys. I had never lived with any, though, except a few nights in hotel rooms at tournaments. Before my first practice, Williamson told me I was going to share a house with three guys from Boston: Robbie Ftorek, Stu Irving and Dick McGlynn. McGlynn had a deal with the Amateur Hockey Association of the United States where they were refunding him part of his rent to put up guys who were coming in for tryouts.

Williamson told me I was going to get $150 a week in meal money. I told him I would be fine on $50, but he said I could do whatever I wanted with the $150. Wow. Where was I going to spend all that? And regardless, moving in with those guys turned out to be priceless.

Ftorek was only 19, but even 19 seemed old to me at the time, probably because Robbie was so mature, intense and also kind. He took care of me, always pulling me along if he was going to do something. Stu had served in Vietnam, landing in helicopters with a gurney to rescue the wounded. First week he was there, the guy running next to him had his leg blown off—just what I wanted to hear, of course, being only a year and a half away from having to register for the draft. When Stu—who had his dad ship him four hockey sticks and a box of pucks he would shoot against sandbags in the steamy Mekong Delta—got the call that the red tape had cleared, the strings had been pulled and he could go try out for the U.S. Olympic team, he packed his bag and sat at the airbase for 24 hours waiting for that plane. And if he didn't make the team, he was going to have to go back.

Unlike Stu, who was a quiet guy, McGlynn was a character. On the way home after my first practice, Robbie and I were in the back seat as Dick drove down an exit ramp on a Minneapolis freeway. Suddenly, he announced, "This is the wrong exit," put it in reverse, and now we were going backward up the ramp, me looking out the back window and ducking, certain a car going 65 miles an hour was going to hit us, or maybe worse, my mother would pull up and take me home. All I remember thinking was, "Yeah, she really would not approve of this."

Since the team was in the last month of training camp and we still had a few games left on the exhibition tour, my roommates had canceled the phone at the house. Whenever I had to make a phone call, I had to borrow Robbie's car, drive down the street to a phone booth and start slugging in all the coins I had. In late January in Minneapolis, it was so cold that, one time, the phone stuck to my ear.

Dick warmed me up a few times at the Burnsville Bowl, where, in the spirit of welcoming the new guy and because Robbie never drank and Irving barely did, McGlynn would take me along. When Mom and Dad came into the locker room after an exhibition game in Saginaw, Michigan, Dick froze.

"So you're Dick McGlynn?" Dad asked. Concerned that I had told my father about the fellowship at the Burnsville Bowl and backing up on an exit ramp, Dick was very relieved when Gordie said, "Thanks for taking care of my son." It was after that game that they told me I had made the team. I went home to get some clothes before we practiced for a week in Colorado Springs to accustom ourselves to the elevation at Sapporo, and then it was on to Tokyo for a week to get used to the time change.

I remember lying in my hotel bed, watching *Bonanza* dubbed into Japanese while Robbie wrote a letter to his fiancée. Next thing I knew, the whole room started to shake and the TV fell off the chest of drawers and smashed on the floor. Earthquake! They said it was just a tremor—some tremor—so I walked down the stairs and was amazed to find, outside the hotel, a seven-tiered, fenced-in, golf driving range about 100 yards long, right in the middle of the big buildings of crowded, bustling downtown Tokyo.

Another time, I was walking and saw people gathered in front of a McDonald's. Somebody was giving out french fries, which apparently were new there. All the people were staring at them, and some wouldn't touch them, so I said, "Hell, I'll eat them," and grabbed some while all these Japanese people stared at me. I'll bet you didn't know that, in addition to all my hockey credits, I introduced the french fry to Japan.

I remember how clean the country was, the friendliness of the people and also their tiny size. Two girls on the street who knew English asked me how old I was. When they told me they were 23 and 24, I would have sworn they were 12.

We played exhibition games on two consecutive days in Tokyo, one against Poland and the other against Czechoslovakia. Both were located where the swimming had taken place in the 1964 Tokyo Olympics, so there was a diving board over one end of the rink.

I remember Williamson saying before the Czechoslovakia game, "I want to rough these guys up, really want to put it to them," and so we did. We took a lot of penalties and they beat us 4–1, but we kept coming and sent the message the coach wanted.

Williamson remembers me getting hit pretty hard in the head in the Poland game and, in the days before there was any protocol about suspected concussions, being impressed that I continued to play. I don't remember anything about it, so does that mean I was concussed?

We flew to Sapporo, a city on the northern island of Hokkaido, which was no little village then and has more than a million people today. The athletes' village was pretty Spartan, with four-person units, two to a bedroom. Again my suitemates were Ftorek, Irving and McGlynn. We were on the second floor, above a big snowbank, and one day as we gathered for a run in the area outside, I freaked my teammates out by jumping from the window instead of using the stairs. McGlynn says that was pretty much the only time he remembers me acting 16 since I had joined the team.

Outside the village, there was a train to the downtown area, where I went three or four times with Robbie and once by myself. This was eight months before terrorists murdered members of the Israeli Olympic team at the summer Olympic Games, so there wasn't a lot of security.

After winning a surprising gold medal in 1960 at Squaw Valley,

California, the USA had finished fifth and sixth in 1964 and 1968 respectively, so we weren't supposed to have much chance at a medal. But I could see we had some talent. Henry Boucha was the best scorer on the team, and my linemates, Keith "Huffer" Christiansen and Tim Sheehy, were good offensive players too, as was another forward, Kevin Ahearn.

Our best player, though, was the goalie, Mike "Lefty" Curran. He came in only a week before the Olympics, even after I did. My job was going to be limited—run around and create havoc, be what they called in those years a clock runner—so it wasn't like I needed a long run-up. But a goalie?

Apparently, during the World Championships a year earlier, there had been bad feelings between Curran and Williamson when the goalie wouldn't play with a knee injury. Coach has said that he thought Lefty was a party guy, something Williamson didn't need for a three-month pre-Olympic tour. And that was the reason the coach had planned all along to kiss and make up just before the Games. I was thinking, "Wow, we already have two goalies. How can they do that?" But I could see why the coach still wanted to take him to Sapporo.

Opening ceremonies for those Games weren't nearly the production they are today. They used the speed-skating oval and we walked in wearing our blue three-quarter-length leather coats and leather-soled shoes, trying to remain upright on the ice on the way in. We complained about how cold it was in the rink and then walked out, happy to get it over with, even though our Olympic experience threatened to be extremely short.

Because the U.S. had finished last in Pool A, composed of the best teams in the world, at the World Championships in 1971, we had to beat the Pool B winner, Switzerland, in a one-game qualifier just to get into the Olympic tournament.

Williamson has told interviewers he was rarely nervous, but was a wreck going into that game. We jumped up early 2–0, but their goalie, Gerard Rigolet, had 40 saves after two periods and the Swiss tied the game 3–3 early in the third. Sheehy responded a minute later to relieve the tension, and then my roommate Irving scored and we won, 5–3, a game that really could have gone either way.

Our reward was a contest the next day against Sweden, which dominated us 5–1. We had two early goals wiped out for having men in the crease, but, had they counted, I doubt it would have made any difference. The Swedes had guys like Inge Hammarstrom and Thommie Bergman, who would be among the first European players to play in the NHL, and probably were the third-best team in the tournament after the USSR and Czechoslovakia.

But my teammates had beaten Czechoslovakia, our next opponent, twice before that loss in Tokyo, where we had played them really tough—actually, pretty dirty.

So when they came out for the only game between us that really counted, the Czechoslovakians had guys pulling up in the corners—clearly intimidated, I thought. But they scored early on the power play and were so skilled they outshot us 19–4 in the first period. Huffer Christiansen scored on a two-man disadvantage, though, to get us out of that period tied 1–1, so there were still plenty of reasons to believe we had a chance.

Williamson threw a tirade in the locker room to wake us up, and it worked. Ahearn scored to put us ahead, Lefty stood on his head again through a 20-shot period, and Craig Sarner and Frank Sanders added goals. Holy shit, we were up 4–1 on the way to winning 5–1, thanks to 51 saves by Curran.

It was one of the biggest upsets in Olympic hockey history, but as a 16-year-old kid, what did I know? And back in the States, where they were 14 to 17 hours behind, they knew even less. NBC was televising only 37 hours of the entire Olympics and showing only a few minutes of our games at weird hours. The three times I called home from a phone center they had set up in the village—it would take 15 minutes to get a call through, just a huge pain in the ass—my family knew whether we had won or lost, but not a whole lot else.

I don't know how much NBC showed of our next game, against

the USSR, but in that case, the less the better. Valeri Kharlamov—what a player he was—scored one of the goals in the first period to put them up 2–0 on the way to 5–0, and omigod, they weren't even breathing hard. I had never seen them play before, and I was in awe.

We were chasing them the entire game, then got frustrated and started taking penalties—really trying to hurt them, because we hated them like we thought Americans were supposed to hate the Soviets in 1972. We lost 7–2, never really having had a chance, so it was hard to say we stunk out the place. Actually, the Russians did that, literally.

All the teams would take the bus back to the athletes' village from the arena after a game to shower and eat. But the Russians would take off their skates, put on their shoes and then run—they were always running, practically everywhere they went—back to the village. There, they all took off their equipment and put it in a pile, where it stayed until the next game. Then they would come to the cafeteria without showering.

So as soon as you smelled something odd, you would turn your head—and sure enough, the Russian hockey team would be entering the room. Even worse was when you played against them and had to line up for a face-off. They and their equipment were rancid.

One day later, our next opponent, the Finns, smelled much better; they just didn't play hockey as well. Sarner scored from the top of the face-off circle just 15 seconds into the game, and though Finland came back to tie it, we dominated from the second period on, winning 4–1 to even our record at 2–2 and keep ourselves in the medal hunt, even though we had gotten killed by both the Swedes and the Russians.

There was no medal round at the Olympics in those days, just a round-robin. So after beating Poland, the weakest team in the pool, 6–1, in our final game, it came down to this: if Finland upset Sweden the next day, we could win the bronze. And if we got that big break and the USSR beat Czechoslovakia, we probably were going to get the silver.

Whatever happened, our tournament was over, so most of us went out to enjoy ourselves. The Swedes and Finns are big rivals, and there was a lot of pressure on Sweden, but I can't say we were optimistic. I was so impressed by the Swedes, who had tied the Soviets 3–3, and we had beaten Finland handily.

But go figure, the Finns scored two goals—within two minutes and 15 seconds—fairly late in the third period and hung on to win 4–3. Just like that, Sweden had gone from second place to fourth and we were guaranteed at least third, pending the result of the final game, which had become a contest for the gold medal between the Soviets and the Czechoslovakians. Robbie grabbed me to go watch it. And probably because it had only been four years since the Russians invaded Prague and shut down all the Czechoslovakian reforms, it was the dirtiest game I ever have seen. It was incredibly brutal, stickwork everywhere.

When Yevgeny Mishakov was called for spearing in the final minute of the Soviets' 5–2 victory, Vaclav Nedomansky, Czechoslovakia's best player, fired the puck into the USSR bench. I couldn't believe what I was seeing—or our good fortune. We had won the silver with a 3–2 record, and the Czechs settled for bronze because of their head-to-head loss to us.

Of course, it helped us that the Canadians, annoyed that their NHL stars hypocritically weren't eligible to play in the "amateur" Olympics against paid players from the Soviet bloc, didn't send a team in 1972 or 1976. Did I care, though? About an hour after the USSR–Czechoslovakia game, there was 16-year-old Mark Howe, pointless in the tournament, on the medal stand, silver hanging around his neck.

Ever since I joined these guys in Bloomington, my main concerns had been not to tarnish my father's image or do anything that would reflect badly on my country. I looked at the tournament pretty much like I did any competition—as a means to my real goal, a career in the NHL. But as I watched the American flag go up, I suddenly could feel the pride washing over me, even overpowering my annoyance about how incredibly long the Soviet anthem—they only play the one of the gold-medal winner—kept going. We thought it would never end. But that was the only thing in those three weeks that didn't go incredibly fast for me, the youngest medal winner in Olympic hockey history to this day. It was a whirlwind, and I wish I remembered more about it.

I do have total recall of the great lesson I learned. Williamson had given me a role and I had fulfilled it. While Murray was kissed by the Russian coach for beating the Czechoslovakians, he must settle for my ongoing thanks for being so positive with me. I was conscious of people thinking I was on the team for publicity purposes—Robbie remembers once having to talk me into doing an interview with NBC that I didn't feel I had earned. All the players were great and never treated me as a kid—or more specifically, as Gordie Howe's kid.

And it turned out even the Russians weren't so bad after they had showered. Following the medal ceremony, the interpreter they had hired, a Canadian named Aggie Kukulowicz, brought me to a room where some of them were partying.

The $60-a-week Junior A pay in Toronto would have made me ineligible for the Olympics, but the Russians were taking money out of their pockets to show everybody how much their federation was paying them for winning the gold medal. They also were filling these little hotel glasses with vodka and drinking it like I drink water. I was hoping they had a beer somewhere, but it was all vodka. They got me to drink one, and I choked.

So I ended up meeting a few of their guys, but don't remember their names. They were headed off to go play somewhere two or three days later to begin preparation for the World Championships. I was thinking, "Wow, they just won a gold medal—for these guys, like winning the Stanley Cup—and they are playing again three days later."

As far as I knew, my first international experience was over. The next day, the souvenirs I had bought with about half of my $500 per diem—a chess set for my mother, bookends for Dad, a calculator for me, T-shirts for a lot of people—were with me on the team charter headed home. We dropped some people in Anchorage and then flew to Chicago, where Dad—coming from I don't remember where—had timed his stop to meet me and we flew home to Detroit together.

I had missed about two months of school, but the teachers, who had given me advance assignments, were great about letting me make up my work. Actually, I had been hitting the books, at least until we got to Colorado. Most of the teachers, knowing I was a pretty good student, gave me a week to review and then combined all the tests I had missed into one. The teacher of my course in government told me to do an essay on what I did while I was in Japan—easy enough.

A couple weeks later, there was a Mark Howe Day at Southfield-Lathrup High School, with Mom and Dad attending the ceremonies in the auditorium. I showed a few people my medal, and that pretty much was it for this conquering hero—back to playing for the Detroit Junior Red Wings for the rest of their season.

An experience like I had never really ends, though. Thanks largely to McGlynn, that team has stayed almost as tight as it has healthy. After 40 years, we have lost only two guys, Frankie Sanders and Wally Olds, both to cancer, and the attendance at the reunions held almost every year has been amazing. Unfortunately for me, they have had these get-togethers at playoff time, when I am busy scouting. But in 2007 I happened to be in Potsdam, New York, for a hockey camp run by my son Travis when the team had a reunion in Lake Placid. So I made my first one. Except for the players I later faced in the WHA and NHL—Boucha, Ftorek, Curran and Sheehy—it was the first time I had seen a lot of those guys since 1972 and it was great fun. I made it to a second reunion in Florida three years later.

Williamson believes our team was good enough to have beaten the 1980 miracle team that won the gold at Lake Placid and caused our silver medals of 1972 to be too quickly forgotten. But that upset of the Russians in 1980 was so unbelievable, and the impact of the Olympics had grown so much even in just eight years, I understand how we got a little lost to history. It doesn't really bother me.

I think the silver medal meant more to a lot of my teammates, most of whom were 24 or 25 years old and at the pinnacle of their careers. I was 16, a tiny little kid just out there banging bodies who saw good competition as a stepping-stone to the NHL and the Stanley

Cup. That's where I grew up wanting to play and the trophy I wanted to hold.

That said, I have my medal framed in my house, mounted on a blue crushed-velvet background, looking pretty great, if I must say so myself. I really don't keep many of my trophies and awards displayed. So that tells you how truly I value my Olympic experience.

CHAPTER 4

The Marlies and Me

During the year I spent rehabbing my knee, winning an Olympic silver medal and concluding my last, abbreviated, season with the Detroit Junior Red Wings, the Ontario Hockey Association had begun a draft of American players. When the London Knights selected me, I no longer was a free agent, as my brother Marty had been 12 months earlier.

In order for me to join him with the Toronto Marlboros, a deal had to be made. For my rights, Toronto dealt center Dennis Maruk and defenseman Larry Goodenough—Marty's best buddy on the Marlies—to London.

"Way to go, Mark, you just got my best friend traded," said Marty.

Blood is thicker than my brother was letting on. He only wanted to bust my chops. Still, I felt a little added pressure. Goodenough and Maruk were good players who would go early in the second round (20th and 21st overall, respectively) in their NHL draft years. The Marlies also had just lost three players—Billy Harris, Steve Shutt and Dave Gardner—who had been selected within the first eight picks of the 1972 NHL draft.

I couldn't replace all those guys, but as loaded as that team was, it had been upset in the playoffs by Peterborough. So it wasn't an impossible act to follow, and we still had plenty of good future pros. My teammates Glenn Goldup, Bob Dailey, Wayne Dillon and Paulin Bordeleau would all be first-rounders or high second-rounders, and Bruce Boudreau, Peter Marrin, Tom Edur, Kevin Devine, John Hughes and our goalie, Mike Palmateer, were guys who would play well in either the NHL, the WHA or both.

None of my new teammates seemed to really blame me for the trade. The son of a Canadian icon never heard any anti-American stuff, either, even though there were not many Yanks in the OHA at that time. Dailey was a good captain of a really great group of guys, and I had a few strong days early that built my confidence. When you prove something to yourself, in general you're also proving it to other people, which helps you become accepted. So does keeping your mouth shut until you've established your worth, which is the way I had been brought up.

There were good players at every level I had played. But the talent always proved deeper at the next stage, and my jump to Major Junior A was the same. Our team, while probably not as star-studded as it had been the year before, was deep enough to roll three lines and play six defensemen, which took pressure off me, too.

We had enough toughness, including that provided by Marty, to keep opponents from wanting a piece of Gordie Howe's next. But I also had ways of taking care of myself. When a player from Oshawa took a run at me, I announced on the bench to Devine, "He's going down!" Kevin thought on the next shift he was going to see me drop the gloves, which really would have been a sight to behold. Instead, I cranked up a slap shot off the guy's leg and put him out of the game.

All in all, my adjustment to the top tier of Junior A was fairly easy. Even when Marty had trouble getting out of bed, was diagnosed with mononucleosis and went back to Detroit for five or six weeks, I didn't find myself homesick. There were a number of Sunday afternoon games that, coupled with usually having Mondays off, enabled Marty and me to drive home Sunday night and return to Toronto either late Monday or early Tuesday.

My anxieties went away quickly, except for one. I forget who the veterans grabbed for the first traditional rookie shaving, but having seen the butchering they performed on Marty the previous year, I schemed to avoid that—well, not at any cost, but by actually putting a price to it. I put the word out that I would get $10,000 or some absurd amount from Marlies management if the players shaved me. I guess I wanted my teammates to fear getting yelled at by management if they cost the Marlies $10,000, but I believe it was a complete coincidence when, later in the year, word came down asking players to desist from that particular hazing practice. It might have died an overdue death on its own, but regardless, they never got me.

There were no deals to be struck on my real contract. It left me $10 a week in spending money after the rest went to the people who billeted Marty and me—Rita and Dick Tanner, who lived in North York, a 20-minute drive from Maple Leaf Gardens in the Cougar XR-7 my mother and father had bought me for my 16th birthday (Dad had a deal with Lincoln-Mercury).

My high school in Michigan had allowed me to take a senior government course in 11th grade, so I really had no specific requirements remaining for a diploma. I needed just two general credits. I don't remember what I took, except that it was pretty basic. Marty, who was in Grade 13—a year of college preparatory courses offered in Ontario schools—was in both of my classes for only two weeks. Never much of a student, he thought school was a waste of time and just stopped going. Whenever anyone asked where he was, I would say something like "Oh, he's not feeling well" or "He hurt his foot in practice." After about a month of this, I began to run out of excuses and became tired of having to make them.

Although I was still in 12th grade, it was stuff I already learned in the States, so classes were easier than ever. What proved to be most difficult was waking up in the morning to attend school after road games. When we flew back from a weekend trip to Sault Ste. Marie, arriving at something like 3:30 a.m., I was just too tired to go to classes on Monday morning and ended up missing two tests. I went in on Tuesday to learn that both teachers had given me grades of zero.

I had been getting marks of 90 or above in each class, so I wanted to take makeup tests. But the teachers were annoyed that other Marlies had made it in and I hadn't, so they refused. I said, "Screw you, I quit," which was not the brightest thing to do, even if I knew I wasn't going to college.

Before I joined the Marlies, the University of Denver, the University of Michigan and Michigan State University had all wanted to recruit me. But when people kept telling my parents I had to get out of Detroit for my hockey development, they didn't mean to play at an NCAA school. Back then, American colleges weren't considered a proving ground comparable to Canadian junior hockey.

There wasn't a clear value to my finishing high school, especially since I thought they should have let me make up those exams. They weren't working anything out with me the way the teachers in Michigan did when I went to the Olympics. Between that and running out of excuses for my brother, I had had enough.

The only reason I ever thought twice about quitting—or even considered going back—was because I didn't want to disappoint my mother, who, like my dad, wasn't happy with my decision. I hid it from them for a while, and don't remember exactly how they found out. But when they did, they said, "If you're not in school, you can't sit around all day waiting for practice and games." So I started working on the broom crew at Maple Leaf Gardens, where both the Leafs and Marlies played.

The Gardens was mopped and swept every day, whether there had been an event the night before or not. It had to be the most spotless building in hockey. But that was great, because some days it didn't take very long to turn clean into cleaner. Being in the building meant that when the hockey sticks were delivered for the Leafs and Marlies, you could call dibs. We would take them to the boiler room, soften the blades and then curve them around doors.

The job and its perks filled my days, but unfortunately, not my stomach. The Tanners were really nice people, but I wasn't getting enough to eat there. So after practice, which would run until something like 4 to 6 p.m, Marty, Boudreau—whom I was dropping off on the way home—and I would stop off at Biggies Burger or Super Subs.

The Tanners liked meat well done—not my taste. And they also ate early. Since we were showing up late for mealtime, they naturally wondered where we were. I didn't want to embarrass them by saying I wasn't getting enough food, but of course they reported my absences, so Jimmy Gregory, the general manager of the Maple Leafs, called me into his office and read me the riot act. When my parents, who had been called, came in, I told them the truth: I was stopping to eat. And they said, "That's all it is?" Relieved, they started sending the Tanners steaks and other food, and the problem went away. Unlike the Ottawa 67's and Peterborough Petes, our biggest rivals.

Nearing Christmas, the Marlies were on a pace that would see us lose only seven games the entire year. But when we went on the road, first place still was at stake against coach Roger Neilson's Petes and Denis Potvin's 67's.

We beat them both to take the lead, and all the guys were celebrating because they said they had earned their Christmas first-place bonuses. "What Christmas bonus?" said Marty and I, apparently the only two players that didn't have them in our contracts. This was my first lesson that teams will get away with whatever they can. We must have been unhappy enough for our coach, George "Chief" Armstrong, the Maple Leaf Hall of Famer, to come over and ask what was bothering us. He said, "Don't worry, I'll take care of it." And we got the same $50 everybody else did. That meant a lot when you cleared only $10 a week.

So it was a happy holiday, with a break in the schedule that enabled the Howes to gather at our cottage at Bear Lake. The Marlies had a game scheduled in Toronto on the afternoon of the 26th, so the plan was to leave around 5 p.m. Christmas Day, drop off my younger brother, Murray, and my dad's Town Car in Detroit, where Murray had a game, then continue in my XR-7 for the four and a half hours to Toronto. Unfortunately, there was a really bad ice storm and the roads were so slippery it took us almost an hour to go one exit on I-75.

We turned back to the cottage and called the Marlies to tell them Marty and I probably couldn't make the game. They said we were about the ninth and tenth players to call in and kind of implied that we wanted an excuse to take an extra day off at Christmas. As it got colder through the evening and snow started to cover the ice, we thought the roads might have become more drivable. My parents, who were hockey people, understood that you had to get to your games, and we had already turned around and come back once. So they trusted our judgment.

We left around 1 a.m. and were maybe an hour and a half into the three-hour trip down I-75, where the road bent to the right somewhere just south of Bay City. I was driving with the cruise control set at about 78 miles per hour, which was not only over the 70-mph speed limit, but way too fast for conditions. The car started to fishtail, first sliding maybe a foot to the right, then a foot and a half, then more as I fought to control it. We ended up going into a spin.

Things happen fast when your heart is trying to pump its way out of your chest, but I remember shouting, "Hold on!" Murray, in the passenger seat, grabbed my arm. I closed my eyes, waiting for the impact . . . and nothing happened. We just came to a rest.

My first thought was, "Oh good, I didn't ruin Dad's car and we're not in trouble." But then I got out and looked. We were on this little bridge that crossed a stream about 20 feet down. The passenger side was hanging off the bridge, resting on the guardrail. Marty, who had been sleeping in the back, could get out the driver's-side door, but I was so worried about the car falling off the rail and plummeting that I got back in to give the left side of the car 190 more pounds and had Murray crawl over me to get out through my door.

There were no cell phones in those days. In the middle of the night, in the middle of nowhere, with no cars on the road during a storm, we had to wait for about an hour until somebody came by. A truck towed the car and they took us someplace we could call our parents, who, after hearing the phone ring at that hour, were just happy we were okay.

When you looked at the car, there was only a tiny bit of visible damage to the door—I remember, at the garage, Dad asking what was wrong with it. But underneath, one of the exhaust manifolds was ripped off and everything was obliterated. The door beam had prevented the guardrail from coming through the front seat—and probably through Murray and me, too. Instead, the car climbed the rail and rode it for about 75 feet, saving us from falling into the stream.

We were really fortunate, for better reasons than the Marlies no longer having reason to doubt that we'd tried to make the game. I learned an important lesson about being more cautious, although I don't think I became the totally careful driver I am today until my son Travis was born and I thought about him growing up without a father.

I don't remember, but I'm guessing the Marlies won the game. We were a deep team and not really dependent upon intensive preparation. The coach, Armstrong, was a fun, nice guy, who at practices pretty much had us do east-west (pickup games) early in the week and then focused more on game preparation as the week went on.

Maple Leaf Gardens owner Harold Ballard was excused from the halfway house where he was serving the final months of his sentence for fraud and tax evasion to lend his smiling face to the Marlie team picture. Who wouldn't have wanted to be associated with one of the most dominant junior teams of all time? When we beat Ottawa, Potvin's team, in the league semifinals, I remember thinking that even though he had outscored me in the regular season (123 points to 104) and this child in a man's body was going to be the first player taken in the NHL draft that year, he had been with his junior club for five years and never gotten as far in the playoffs as I probably would in my first.

Peterborough beat us 6–3 in the opener of the eight-point league final. Because about half of our players had been on the team the

Petes upset the year before, we were really playing uptight. So even though we were leading 7–2 in game two, when Jimmy Johnston high-sticked Palmateer late in the game, Chief said: "Well, I think it's time for a brawl. Who is going to lead us?" Goldup, my linemate—who'd already taken on Bill Evo—flew over the boards and we had a full-on bench-clearer. A few minutes later, Neilson put his five toughest guys on the ice and all 12 players on the ice got into it.

After we came in from the warmup the next night, Chief took off his hat. "I guess all you guys have heard that I got fined for what happened last night," he said. "I don't have that kind of money because I am not very *edumacated* and I have to find a way to pay that fine. So get your money out of your wallets."

All the guys were looking at him like he had to be kidding, but Chief said: "*Now*. Get up and give me your money." Dailey had more than anybody because he had the best job, as a gofer in the team's office. He emptied the $200 he had in his wallet into the hat, which was passed around like a collection plate at church.

Chief then took the money out, stuffed it in his pocket, put his hat back on and said: "Wow, I feel much better. Let's go win the game tonight." The guys cracked up. It got us all loose and we out-shot the Petes 35–20, though we had to settle for a 3–3 tie. It was one of his best speeches. And I don't even remember whether he kept the money or not.

Game four, won 6–3 by the Petes, was more subdued, but when we met back at the Gardens, tempers rose again. Peterborough had a tough guy named Bob Neely. Turned out he didn't play so tough in the pros, but in this series he had one arm in a cast, which he didn't mind using to lay a beating on opponents. In the second period, he and my brother Marty squared off. Neely took hold of Marty's jersey with his good hand and was all set to start whaling on him with his cast, but Marty grabbed onto it and refused to let go. Neely then went over to give Colin Campbell a hand in his bout with Goldup, and as the third man in he got thrown out of the game—but not before he took on a few fans in the rinkside seats.

Following the loss in game four, we had a team meeting where we recognized that we weren't skating the way we did when we played our best hockey. In game five, big Bob Dailey opened and closed the scoring in a 5–0 shutout victory, and we finally took the lead in the series by winning game six, 5–4.

A win or a tie in game seven, played on a Saturday night at Maple Leaf Gardens, would give us the series. Before a sellout crowd of 16,485, the Petes jumped ahead 2–0 in the first period and took a 4–2 advantage into the second intermission. Twenty-four seconds after they added a fifth goal, Marty and I set up Goldup to bring us back within two, and at 10:17, I scored on the power play to make it 5–4. With about two minutes to go, Peterborough defenseman Jim Turkiewicz closed his hand on a loose puck in the crease and we were awarded a penalty shot.

Armstrong called everybody over to the bench and asked, "Who is going to take the penalty shot?" Guess he wanted to hear some confidence from Bordeleau since, by rule, the shot had to be taken by somebody on the ice at the time of the infraction and he was the obvious choice. Paulin said, "I'll score," faked the goalie out of his jock and put the puck in the net, tying the score at 5–5 and giving us the series, eight points to six.

So it was on to the Memorial Cup at the Forum in Montreal, against Medicine Hat, the Western Hockey League champions, and Quebec, the Quebec Major Junior Hockey League titlists. Quebec's star was Andre Savard, who would have a 12-year NHL career. The Remparts also had two big-time 16-year-old prospects in Buddy Cloutier and Guy Chouinard, but lost to us in the opener, 5–2. The three-goal margin put us in great shape on the goal differential that would determine the two finalists if all three teams were 1–1 in the round robin, and that really helped when Medicine Hat, which had Tom Lysiak and Lanny McDonald, jumped ahead on us. Chief reminded us we didn't have to win, just keep it close, which took the pressure off as Medicine Hat held on to win, 3–2.

We thought we would see Medicine Hat again in the one-game

final, but the Tigers lost to Quebec, 7–3. So for us, it was again Quebec, which jumped up 1–0 on a power-play goal scored while I was in the penalty box.

It was my obligation to make good, right? When I went in on a breakaway, somebody had thrown a program on the ice, but I sidestepped it and shot across the distracted goalie's body and under the crossbar.

We were in charge after that. I crashed the net, scoring another goal, but even though I suffered a hip pointer that would affect me halfway through the summer, we won painlessly, 9–1. And with five points in the final game, I was named the Memorial Cup MVP.

Dad came into the locker room to congratulate my teammates and me. And Mom, waiting outside, was soaking in the praise, too. She would joke about how much of her life was spent standing outside locker rooms, but I think it's fair to say that she never put idle time to better use than on the night of May 12, 1973. Among the compliments she received about her two sons was one from Bill Dineen, the coach of the Houston Aeros of the World Hockey Association, which had just completed its first season. The family knew Bill from his five years playing for the Red Wings.

Every pro team had scouts and executives at the tournament. But I was two years away from being eligible for the NHL draft and Marty had a year to go himself, so I was assuming nobody was there to check us out for anything but a future file. That didn't bother me, because I thought I needed more time in junior. But the 20-year-old minimum age for the NHL draft irritated my mother.

When Dineen praised her boys' performance, Mom seized the opening. As she wrote in her book *My Three Hockey Players,* she asked Dineen, "If you had a son who played the piano and you had sent him to the best conservatories in Europe, and he was good enough to play at Carnegie Hall at age 19, would there be a rule prohibiting him from earning a living?" It wasn't the first time Mom had made that case to practically anybody who would listen. Dineen apparently was tuned in, so she asked if the WHA also was in cahoots with the junior leagues with this minimum age. Dineen said that, as far as he was aware, the WHA had no such restriction.

This may not have been only my mother's brainstorm—to this day, Bill is deliberately vague as to whose idea it actually was. But the next day, on the train to Toronto for the WHA draft, he discussed the idea of selecting me with his right-hand man, Doug Harvey, who'd been a Hall of Fame defenseman with the Montreal Canadiens. Jim Smith, the Aeros' president, took it to the lawyers, who felt the team was on firm legal ground to draft and sign me.

I knew about none of this. Five days later, as Mom and Dad were at their door, ready to leave for a benefit art auction that Mom chaired on behalf of the Arthritis Foundation, the phone rang. It was Harvey telling them the Aeros were going to draft me in the first round the next day.

Before leaving, Mom called Marty and me at the Tanners' in Toronto, where we had stayed for the banquet celebrating our championship. I was the only one home because, having gone out the previous night with Kevin Neville, our backup goalie, I had already enjoyed all the festivities I could handle. We drank Newfoundland Screech, a brand of rum, and it made me sicker than a dog. My throat was killing me so much I couldn't talk. I'll bet I had alcohol poisoning.

So when Mom reached me, the Screech was a bigger reason for me to be speechless than the news that I was about to be the number-one pick of a team that, to the best of my recollection, I had never heard of. I knew there was a World Hockey Association, but didn't know much about it.

"What about Marty? Didn't they say anything about Marty?" Mom remembered me asking. "I'm not going unless they take him, too."

Harvey had not mentioned Marty, but the next day, after the Aeros drafted me in the first round, causing a big hubbub, they also took Marty in the 12th round. "Why don't you take Colleen, too?" yelled Bobby Hull from the table of the Winnipeg Jets, whom he had joined a year earlier, a signing that had been huge in getting the league off the ground.

My throat and head were still Screeching, so I didn't make the Marlies parade. Everybody assumed it was because I didn't want to take questions about the WHA, but I probably couldn't have answered them anyway. All I knew was that my head still hurt and that I wanted to return to the Marlies for another year, not go off and play for some team in—*where?* Texas?

By the time Marty and I got back to Detroit, NHL president Clarence Campbell had apparently called Dad and laid this guilt trip on him about how we would damage not only the NHL, but also junior hockey by signing with the WHA. According to my mom's book, Dad called back a day later to tell Campbell he couldn't ask his kids to deny themselves an opportunity to make a living and asked if the NHL would put money in escrow for us until we got drafted at age 20. He likely knew the league would say no to that. And Dad probably already had something else in mind anyway.

Mom called Gerry Patterson, a businessman and agent who had advised Dad on an endorsement contract, and invited him to the new house we had moved into in Bloomfield Hills. Marty and I were told to stay close if we were needed, and as I recall, we were in and out as they were discussing contract strategy.

Marty says he was in the room, but I know I wasn't when Dad famously blurted out, "I wonder what they would offer for the three Howes?"

That shocked both my mom and Patterson, but she knew my dad was serious almost from the start. After having retired at age 43 because of an arthritic wrist that was almost as painful as the condition of the once-proud Red Wings (by 1973, they had made the playoffs one time in seven years), Dad had grown miserable in a do-nothing Detroit front-office job. The team, now run by GM Ned Harkness after the players had signed a petition to get rid of him as coach, had gone out of its way not to make Dad a part of any hockey decisions. A promised position with team owner Bruce Norris's insurance business never materialized, and practically all my father did was attend community functions on behalf of the club.

According to her book, Dad had told Mom that his office was the "mushroom room where they keep you in the dark and every now and then come in and toss a little manure on you." Dad's office was so small, they moved into another whenever they wanted him to pose for pictures. But because complaining was never Gordie Howe's style, neither Marty nor I knew how deeply unhappy he was.

Mom, who sometimes stuck up for Dad when she thought the club was taking advantage of his off-ice time and who organized functions like overnight ski trips for the wives while the Red Wings were on the road, irritated Norris. She wrote that, drunk one time at a post-playoff team party, the owner accused her of having "affairs," not that she ever told anybody about the insult but her husband. Norris sobered up and apologized. But Dad's relationship with the organization was troubled.

Of course, it was not as troublesome as trying to return to the ice from a two-year absence at age 45 with an arthritic wrist.

I had proudly attended Dad's jersey retirement ceremony on March 12, 1972, at the Olympia, an event so big that the vice president of the United States, Spiro Agnew, attended it (Dad had previously met President Richard Nixon at some dinners). There wasn't a dry eye in the place when the Number 9 banner went up. Dad had played 25 seasons, won four Stanley Cups, six MVP awards and six scoring titles. It seemed there was nothing left for him to do in hockey.

But there was. When he had told Marty and me one day, on the way home from one of our games, "Keep it up and we'll be teammates someday," Dad was not completely joking. Neither was he kidding when he played with us for the Junior Red Wings against the big club in a 1971 March of Dimes benefit at the Olympia that Mom had organized. Afterward, he said to reporters, "Wouldn't it be something if it was real?"

In 1973, no athlete had ever lasted long enough to play with a son professionally. (It would be another 17 years before Ken Griffey Jr. joined his father in the lineup for 51 games with baseball's Seattle Mariners.)

Suddenly, Dad's fantasy had turned into an opportunity. Mom and Dad stayed up most of the night talking about it. Dad recalled that when he dropped the idea on Dineen, there was a stunned silence before Bill said, "Hell, yes." Bill, meanwhile, always maintained that he knew all along there was no way we would be coming to Houston without Dad.

So the Aeros placed Gordie Howe on their list of protected players. And Mom invited Dineen, his wife, Pat, Harvey and Smith—the GM who really was a business guy—to Bear Lake to talk about making this happen. They flew to nearby Traverse City, where, in a hotel conference room, Smith and my mother put proposed contract figures in envelopes and exchanged them.

"Gee, I think yours is higher than ours," Smith laughed when he looked at Mom's. I wasn't in the room, but Mom said it cut the tension. So off everyone went, making the 45-minute drive to Bear Lake, where Mom grilled Pat about living in Houston and Dad went up this 25-foot-long water-ski jump that was about four feet off the water—and slipped. Instead of letting go of the rope, he just held on and it dragged him until he fell over the end into the lake.

I remember Jim Smith saying, "Oh Jeezus." But Dad got up, no problem.

After a visit to Houston, where they took us to a suite at the Astrodome for a baseball game and we read that the city had passed Detroit as the most unsafe one in the U.S.—had to be us, right?—we were back in Bloomfield Hills with the contracts in front of us.

The total package for the four-year deals for the three of us was $1.9 million. That was $1 million for Dad; $500,000, including a $125,000 signing bonus, for me; and $400,000, including a $100,000 bonus, for Marty.

Dad's $250,000 a year matched what Hull had gotten from Winnipeg a year earlier. I don't know if that was important to him, but a contract of that size surely represented to him ultimate and overdue respect. When Bob Baun, a veteran of the Leafs, had joined the Red Wings from Oakland in 1968, he had taken Dad out and revealed his salary, which was larger than Dad's $70,000 a year. Baun wanted to wake up the greatest player in the game to the fact he wasn't paid like it. After having been told for years he was the highest-paid player on the team, Dad had felt really betrayed by Norris.

To keep my father—who made $100,000 in 1970–71, his final season—from going to Houston, Norris said the NHL would double the $50,000 the Red Wings were paying him to essentially do nothing, but that Dad would have to work a lot harder. As if he hadn't been saying all along he wanted more to do. So while it surely was difficult for him to leave Detroit, not so waving goodbye to the Red Wings. I remember clearly the excitement in our home because this deal was going to happen, and I was fighting with myself to share in the joy.

Marty, who had already played two years with the Marlies, has said he would have gone to Houston for a "large sandwich." He wanted to be paid to play hockey, finally. Murray was good with it because that's his nature, even though, to continue his hockey education, he would be staying behind to live with our good friends—and youth hockey sponsors—Jeannie and Chuck Robertson and their son and four daughters . . . all of whom, I had noticed, were cute and blonde.

Cathy, rarely easy, was really bitter about leaving her friends. And I still had reservations about having had only one year in Major Junior A.

My father took me aside for about a 10-minute talk. "You are being offered $125,000 just to sign—$25,000 more than I ever made for a whole year," he said. "And you haven't played a game." Right, I thought. That was the problem. I wanted to make sure I was ready to earn that kind of money. "The only way you get better is if you play against people better than yourself," Dad said. "You already are up near the top of the junior leagues, so you are going to learn faster playing in the pros against people who know how to play.

"And what happens if you have a serious injury? It will hurt your earning power. I know what these leagues are like, and I have seen you play. You're fine. You are not going to have a problem."

"Okay," I said, before Dad added, "And if you don't want to sign, I'll break your arm and sign it for you."

That's his kind of humor, so surely he was kidding. Probably. Two months earlier, I don't think I had even heard of the Houston Aeros. Now I was one.

CHAPTER 5

On Top of the World in Houston

As nervous as I was about playing professionally at age 18, I was quickly reminded that it wasn't life and death. On the way to Texas, Marty and I almost killed our little dog Skippy.

Mom and Dad were already in Houston. We were driving down two of the family cars and our beloved dog, which my mother's mother, a collector of strays, had given to us. We were in the late-summer heat of Arkansas when we decided to stop for lunch at a Holiday Inn. We got quick sandwiches and couldn't have been in there more than 12 minutes, but stupidly, we didn't crack the windows of the car. When we came out, Skippy was limp and lifeless over the hump on the floor.

We couldn't think of anything else to do but run back into the hotel and put his head under water in the bathroom near the lobby. He didn't respond, so we got back into our cars to blindly look for help, while I held poor Skippy in front of the air conditioning vent, hoping for a miracle. We couldn't find a vet—I think it was a Sunday—but we saw a hospital and ran into the emergency room with this limp, soaking-wet 15-pound mutt.

"We can't treat a dog," they said, but they gave us directions to a vet, and we were on the way there when all of a sudden Skippy began to perk up. This had to be a good 15 minutes from the time we brought him out of the bathroom at the hotel, but by some miracle he was fine. So we kept on going as if nothing had happened, and Skippy lived happily ever after in Houston.

Initially, I wasn't so sure *I* would. First, there was the big media tour that the WHA and the Aeros sent us on that seemed like a waste of time to Marty and me. Usually, interviewers asked us each only one question, just to be polite, and the rest of the interview was all Gordie. I finally spoke up after a few weeks of this, and Dad, who hadn't wanted us to feel left out, said, "Fine, go home."

The old man—*our* old man, actually—trying to make a comeback at age 45 had become the bigger story, but the few articles I read still wondered how good these teenagers could be and questioned whether our family act was a gimmick. When training camp opened at the Ice Haus in suburban Houston, the only thing on my mind was proving I belonged.

Prepared by being on the ice almost 12 hours a day for six days a week at Dad's four-week summer hockey school in Detroit, I came out flying for the first session. Not helped by the 104-degree outdoor temperatures or the salt pills that teams stupidly thought in those days were better for you than water, I promptly lost eight or nine pounds and was horrible in the afternoon session. Add in the pressure I was putting on myself, and back came the migraines I had suffered from as a kid. By day three, they were so bad I recall missing practices.

Coach Bill Dineen, prompted by Dad, came over one day and said, "You've made the team. Just relax." Those few words made all the difference in the world to me and eased much of my anxiety. My father already was looking out for his boys, even though he was having big problems of his own. As a result of functioning for two years as—for lack of a better job description—the Red Wings' Chief Eater and Greeter, Dad had put on, by Mom's estimate, 12 pounds consuming banquet food. After performing a physical, Bob Bailey, the doctor who had done my knee surgery two years earlier, okayed all of Dad's vitals. In a time when players needed off-season jobs and few worked out year-round, Dad tried to get ready by running a little at Andover High School near our home, and since we were trying to build up one side of the beach at our cottage, he shoveled wet sand for days. But those preparations and the 50 games a year or so he played for the Red Wings alumni team couldn't prepare him for a training camp at age 45. It would be hard enough to come back after two years away at 25 or 35. So once I got over my dehydration and started rocking and rolling, I finally lost enough of my preoccupation with myself to realize, "Wow, Dad really is having a hard time." And because I had never seen him struggle before with anything, it scared me.

"Dad's face got red as a beet," I reported to Mom. "I was afraid he was going to have a heart attack."

It was Marty who told her, famously, that Dad "turned interesting different shades of blue." But of course, Gordie Howe would never complain. Mom, also frightened by what she was hearing from us, told Dad, "You're the one who has to say if it is too much." As she later related in her book, *My Three Hockey Players*, all he did was raise an eyebrow, which would suggest he was concerned, too.

When Dineen suggested that Gordie skate with us only once a day, Dad insisted, "No special treatment." He said the two-a-days would either make him or break him. After about a week of bare improvement, all of a sudden it was there, semi-miraculously. Dad was going through things with ease, suddenly the only guy on the bench at the end of a shift not sucking wind.

"You found it today, didn't you?" I asked him on the car ride home. The old magic showed up just in time for our exhibition tour, for which a lot of tickets had been sold. The first three league games were going to be on the road, too, so it was something like a 25-day trip.

"How do you pack for that?" I asked Dad.

"Don't know, never had to," he said.

Madison Square Garden, home of the WHA's New York Golden Blades, was the first stop. "Hey Maaahk, better go back to school," some fan yelled at me during the warmup.

As a sort of showcase, the format was to play one period each against three different teams. Dad and I were in the starting lineup for the first period against the New England Whalers, and who am I lined up against for the face-off but Tommy Webster, who had stayed at our house while playing five games for the Red Wings a season earlier.

"You nervous, kid?" Tommy asked.

"Shit, yeah," I said, but then set up Dad for a goal at 21 seconds. I never asked if he was more relieved than I was, but I do know the five-minute ovation he got at our next stop, Cobo Arena in Detroit, had to be a thrill. Dad, ultraprotective, went to my aid against 170-pound J.P. LeBlanc of the Los Angeles Sharks and dropped him with a right hand.

"Aw, I'm just a tired old man," he told reporters after another dustup with New England's John French. But there was nothing modest about his mounting back pain.

I scored my first professional goal at Vancouver in my third regular-season contest. When we returned to Houston for the first home game, Dad, who had been increasingly stiff during the trip, agreed to a promotional skate for the Aeros at the Galleria shopping center but then paid for it the next morning by not being able to get out of bed. He landed in traction at Sharpstown General Hospital the night before our opener.

How was it going to look if he couldn't play? He called Mom from the hospital the next morning, saying he was coming home and planned to suit up.

"Welcome to Howeston" was on a banner draped on a downtown skyscraper near the Sam Houston Coliseum, home of the Aeros. Only about two-thirds of its 9,200 seats were occupied when, dressed in white jerseys with powder blue lettering and trim, Number 5 (Marty), Number 4 (me) and Number 9 (who else?) skated out onto the ice with our new teammates. After an exhilarating warmup in front of the exuberant fans, we headed back to our locker room, Dad in the procession ahead of Marty and me.

Suddenly, my brother pointed at the back of Dad's jersey. Marty kept saying, "Look at this! Look at this!"

On the nameplate, they had spelled Dad's name "Goride Howe."

The trainers amended the problem before we went out for the start of the game. The reporters had not noticed. Meanwhile, the fans failed to realize that goalie Gerry Cheevers of the Cleveland Crusaders stoned us 2–0. We left the ice to a standing ovation.

"Don't they know we lost?" I grumbled to Dad. I just hated to lose but eventually came to appreciate that what Houston's new hockey fans lacked in education, they made up for in enthusiasm.

One night, after a brawl against the Minnesota Fighting Saints, a fan jumped on the Saints as they left the ice at the end of period. He was brought into our training room—there was no first-aid room at the Sam Houston Coliseum—cut quite badly across the chest, probably from a skate blade. But it was nickel beer night at the arena, and it was obvious this patron was feeling no pain.

"C'mon, team, let's go!" he yelled as he was being stitched. "We're going to kick their asses!" We just looked at him and had a good chuckle.

Those Fighting Saints lived up to the first part of their nickname. And their fans stayed in character. During a brawl in Minnesota, I was paired off safely with Murray Oliver, who had been such good friends with Dad as a Red Wing that my youngest brother is named after him. We were just standing there, watching players beat the tar out of each other, when Murray suddenly yelled, "Watch out!" He saw a guy in the stands throw a 40-ounce bottle that shattered on the ice, thankfully without hitting anybody.

The only assault I remember in our arena was the nightly assault on our ears by fans blowing horns. It went with the ambiance of a place that had opened in 1937 and was pretty much a cockroach-infested dump, although it hardly was the only building in the south where you would find those "varmints." But the Sam Houston Coliseum had been good enough to host the Beatles in 1965, so it was swell enough to be the home of the Aeros. It was intimate and had a good playing atmosphere, even if it wasn't the friendliest place to shower. Those cockroaches were big.

Attendance would improve that year (from 4,616 to 6,811), but you still had to look behind the high school football scores to find the Aeros' results in the Houston *Post* or *Chronicle.* The WHA had no national television deal in Canada or the U.S., and our local package was, as I recall, about five road games, but I don't remember ever feeling out of the hockey mainstream or wondering what I was doing in Texas. My teammates instantly made it feel like home.

The Aeros were a really good group of guys, handpicked by Dineen, an excellent judge of talent and character. After playing for the Red Wings, he'd had a long run in the minor-pro Western Hockey League (he'd only retired two years earlier) and signed a lot of players he had played against in that league and respected.

The year before, Dineen had ridden a circus elephant in a downtown parade to promote the new team, and gotten sprayed. "My kids thought it was hilarious until they had to smell me in the car on the way home," he said. It could have happened only to Bill Dineen. Affable, rambling and confused like a fox, he was hockey's Lieutenant Columbo, persistently, politely and accurately surmising the cause of any team problems. Largely because of him, there weren't many.

When the Aeros sat around having beers after a loss, we used to talk about feeling bad for Bill. Until I played for Paul Holmgren in Philadelphia 15 years later, Foxy Dineen—so named because he had "missed the odd curfew as a player"—was the only professional coach I ever played for who inspired guilt in his players.

We were behind him because we felt he was behind us. If the fish were biting late in the afternoon, he would move up practice to 9 a.m. so the fishermen on our team could be casting by noon. During hunting season, he would move practice to 1 p.m. so the sportsmen could be out before dawn. His only rule was that you couldn't golf the day of a game. And whenever you did play, you were supposed to use a cart. So life was pretty simple as long as you were winning. And we were winning, even if the Aeros' 18-year-old so-called prodigy with the famous name on his back wasn't exactly setting the WHA on fire.

Since Marty was bigger, stronger and a year older, he adjusted much faster than I did. Dineen knew what he was doing and did not use me on the power play or give me more than I could handle until January, when I began to show him I felt more comfortable.

At first, Dad tried too hard to help by passing the puck really softly to me. They were beautiful passes, flat and on the tape. But after having told me years before that the puck was like a piece of cowshit during fly season—"the softer it is, the more flies are attracted to it"—feeds were arriving to me at the same time as the defensemen.

After about two weeks, I told him, "Dad, you are going to have to pass the puck harder or you are going to get me killed." Not an easy thing to say to Gordie Howe, but he agreed. Our chemistry, good from the start, got that much better. Dad's back problem didn't rematerialize, and everything was turning out beyond his wildest hopes.

The two years away from hockey had given his arthritic wrist, the official reason for his retirement, an opportunity to heal. Regardless, he had the highest pain tolerance of anyone I ever played with. I remember him once scorching his hand by mindlessly touching the boiler coil while making our pre-game meal. Dad melted the skin off the back of three fingers that afternoon, then put on his hockey gloves that night with no bandages or anything to cover his raw, exposed burns. I thought, "How can he do that and not show any pain?'"

So any physical problem had to have been a secondary reason for his walking away from the game after 25 years. The Red Wings were a mess, from the front office to the ice, and the joy of playing had been sucked right out of him. The Aeros, and the culmination of the dream to play with his sons, made him a little kid in a candy shop.

"This isn't what hockey really is like," he told me one day early on in Houston, while sitting with me in front of our lockers. "It's not what I have experienced. This is a great group of guys, the coach is fun, the owners are fun, and we're winning. I'm really enjoying myself."

From mid-January on, when I really began to feel I belonged at that level, the pleasure was all mine. The center between us was Jim Sherrit, a fireplug type who knew enough to move the puck to Dad and go to the net, opening things up for the Howes. I brought speed to the line, so Dad would tell me to just get in there, get the puck to him and get the hell out of the way to an opening somewhere. Generally, I was the guy doing the shooting.

I read off my father—and he read off me—better than anybody with whom I ever played. With Dad having such obvious vision and skills, you would think anybody could have played with him. But I watched him with Bobby Hull at all-star games, and the best left wing and right wing of all time had no chemistry at all.

We had it, though I'm not sure genetics made the difference. It was just one of those natural, wondrous things. We ended up playing on the same line for six years, and I remember yelling for him to give me a pass two or three times at most. I don't think he ever had to yell for me, either. When there was only one place you could go with the puck, he would be there, the same way I would try to be in that hole for him. Obviously, I don't put myself in the same class as my dad, but we thought about the game the same way.

Sure, he had lost a step at age 45, but Dad still had deceptive speed. I was quicker for the first few strides, but when I was up to full flight, he was right there. Because Dad would be doing the hard work in the corners and I had the acceleration to get back quickly, I ended up being the backchecker on the line. But that was easy, just as everything was playing with—still—the world's strongest man.

Especially in our first year, before I got bigger and stronger, it helped having Dad's physical presence on my line. He didn't have a fight in the regular season and playoffs that entire year, but I don't think that was due to any self-respecting goon thinking it was bad form to challenge a 45-year-old man. It was because Gordie Howe's reputation preceded him. Even Billy Goldthorpe, one of the craziest guys ever to put on a hockey uniform, wouldn't mess with Number 9.

"[Goldthorpe] yelled, 'You aren't going to play forever, old man,'" Minnesota coach Glen Sonmor told Ed Willes in *The Rebel League*, a history of the WHA. "'And when you retire, I'm going to get your kids.'"

Sonmor also said that one time Goldthorpe, seated on the bench, yelled out at Dad, "I'm going to cut your fucking head off." Dad stared so hard that Keith Christiansen, my old Olympic teammate sitting next to Goldthorpe, shouted, "It wasn't me, Gordie! It wasn't me!" That's the kind of respect—well, fear, actually—Dad inspired.

Apparently Roger Cote, this guy on Edmonton who played with a toothpick in his mouth, didn't get the memo, but he soon got the message.

Cote had my brother down one time in a game at Houston and was rubbing Marty's jersey back and forth across his neck, making his skin raw in the process. I couldn't get there because some Oiler was holding me, but I heard Dad, standing over them, telling Cote, "Let him up."

Cote looked at Dad and said, "Fuck you." So Dad reached around, put two fingers into Cote's nostrils and pulled.

"Okay, I'm up," Cote said from his knees, bleeding. I'm watching this, thinking, "Who would ever think of something like pulling a guy up by inside his nose?"

At a 9 a.m. New Year's Day practice during one of our years in Houston, Don Larway, hung over like most after a team party, walked into the locker room with an empty beer can he discarded into the trash. This must have really irritated Dad even before Larway got sloppy with his stick and accidentally cut Marty in the face. When Dad saw that, he tried to put his stick down the throat of Larway, his own *teammate.*

"What the hell are you doing?" guys yelled at Dad.

"Anybody else want to mess with me or my kids?" Dad said. "Let's go."

He didn't have any takers. Actually, he *never* had any takers. The fact that he had only 46 penalty minutes that first year in Houston was a reflection of how few players wanted to risk retribution by taking the puck—*his* puck, the way he looked at it—away from him.

There were some real meatheads in our league. Minnesota especially collected them. The Aeros didn't need any because our tough guys—our first defensive pair, Poul Popiel and John Schella; our captain, Teddy Taylor; Glen Irwin; and Marty—could both play and take care of themselves. Of course, we also had the best combination of toughness, skill and power in the game's history leading by example.

Six feet tall with an inseam of 27¾ inches, Dad had these little tiny legs that lowered his center of gravity. And his upper body was so powerful that when he went into the corners, he won the battles; it didn't matter how big the guy was. I won some pucks with determination, but there were guys so big that there wasn't much I could do. Not so with Dad against bigger players. Even battling against two of them, half the time he still came out with the puck.

When he got it in scoring position, he knew what to do. Not only did Dad have really quick hands around the net, but the goalie had no idea where the puck was going because Number 9's shots from the slot and beyond never were telegraphed. They were incredibly swift and accurate, too. When I was playing midget at age 12 or 13, Dad would come to our practices, put some pucks at the hash mark and one-hand them right under the crossbar. Just incredible.

It was a thrill to have a living legend on our team. And having it be your dad just made it that much more special. His first year in the WHA, Dad deservedly won the MVP. He was the best player, bar none, and might have been the next year, too, when Bobby Hull got the award.

People would argue that because Gordie Howe was 45 or 46 years old, the competition in our league had to be subpar to the NHL. But I vehemently disagree with any belief that the WHA was a league of floaters. Our teams didn't have the depth of NHL clubs, and outside of Cheevers—and, from our second year in Houston, Ron Grahame—there was a big drop-off in the level of goaltending. But for the first two seasons in Houston, wow, was Dad ever good—so much better than he had probably been in his last five years in Detroit.

Dad's opinion is that Bobby Orr was the best player ever because he revolutionized the game to bring defensemen into the offensive play. For me, the most gifted was Mario Lemieux and the most creative was Wayne Gretzky. But if you put all the categories together, to me, Dad was the greatest player of all time. And I might be prejudiced, of course, but I also believe there never has been a better father. Or teammate—even if he is your father, too.

If I had to catch his attention on the ice, I would call him Gordie. It was also Gordie in the locker room—where, actually, a lot of the time we called him "Go Ride" after the way they misspelled his name on his jersey for that first home game.

It became Dad again at home or whenever he got hurt. One day at practice, he hooked skates with center Andre Hinse, went headfirst into the boards and was knocked unconscious. When he came to, practically the first thing he remembered was that Mom had been on him about wearing a helmet. "Call your mother and tell her anything but that I hit my head," Dad told me. So of course, the first thing out of my mouth when I reached her was "Dad hit his head today."

Here was a guy who in 1950 needed a hole drilled in his skull to relieve hemorrhaging after a collision with Teeder Kennedy of the Leafs had sent Dad headfirst into the boards. That time, there was a chance he might die. This time, poor Andre only wanted to die. But after that first week of camp, Dad did not give us reason to worry about him. And I think Marty and I returned the favor by not causing any angst for him, including off the ice. Thanks to his always-incredible grace, having your father as your work and travel mate never became awkward.

After the first regular-season game we played, a 4–3 win in Los Angeles, I went out with Marty to have a couple of beers and walked back into the hotel with some girl under my arm. Oops, there's Dad in the lobby with some people he knew. 'This is my son Mark," he said to them, kind of laughing. He never brought it up again.

Back then, a number of players I knew in the game drank pretty heavily—mostly beer, but heavily nevertheless. Sometime during that first year, I was out with teammates who were pretty hung over the next day at practice. So in one of the very few unsolicited pieces of advice Dad ever gave me, he said: "I know you are only 18, but you need to figure out how long you want to play this game. The way you take care of yourself now is going to make the difference. These guys leading a harder life at 27, 28, 29, their careers are going to be over when they hit 31 or 32, and their marriages soon after." But I never felt I was being watched or that I couldn't be myself. Or that I felt obligated to spend time with a lonely old man on the road. I would say about half the time, we would go our separate ways.

There were practically no such things as charters in the WHA. We would get up in the morning to fly commercial, so after the games, a lot of people Dad knew from business, past and present, had the opportunity to see him. If he was free, Dad would let it be known he would be at a certain steak house and teammates could join him, no obligation. And he absolutely meant it.

We had an older, more established team that pretty much hung together when we would go out, even at home. Dad, never much of a drinker, only came the odd time. At first, when players were discussing their social plans, guys joked, "Can she bring her mother for Gordie?" And he would laugh. But Dad wasn't coming with Marty and me to discos, even if he did own a leisure suit.

Besides making goals, our time together was spent doing crosswords on buses and planes. On off-days, we would play golf. And of course, he resumed being Dad at the colonial home my family had bought at the end of a cul-de-sac in Houston's Memorial section. Dad was so fascinated to find cattle and horses in the yard of a house in the neighborhood that he drove friends and interviewers over to see them. We put a pool and practice putting green in our backyard and bought a trampoline, too. It was quite the place for the $250-per-month rent Mom had decided to charge Marty and me, mostly to make the point that we could now afford it.

And we could. Dorothy Ringler, Dad's secretary in Detroit, had been fired by the Red Wings immediately after his departure. Mom brought her to Houston to deal with family business matters. Dorothy showed me a bank statement with $90,000, my signing bonus after taxes, and I had already made the one purchase I planned: a $6,500 custom-made van to go fishing. As a kid, my neighborhood snowblowing business had well taught me the value of a dollar, so did I really need that lesson reinforced by my landlord-mother? Mom countered with an offer for me to buy the groceries instead. I chose the rent. Colleen Howe didn't raise a dummy—I knew how much I ate.

This growing boy grew up quite a bit on the ice over the second half of the season. I was named to the second All-Star team at left wing behind Bobby Hull and won the Lou Kaplan Trophy as rookie of the year, beating out my teammate Hinse. We were neck and neck for points most of the year, but because he was 28 and had been playing pro in the Western Hockey League for six years, Andre had kept telling me he hoped I would win.

Believe it or not, Dad had the first four-goal game of his career that year in Houston, against Los Angeles in December. They called it a Texas hat trick because, of course, everything had to be bigger there. In March, he took a shot in the foot that caused a stress fracture. So when Dad reached 100 points, he shut it down for the final eight games of the regular season. He still finished third in the league in scoring behind Mike Walton of Minnesota and Andre Lacroix of New York/New Jersey.

The Aeros won nine of our last 13 games to win the Western Division by 11 points over Minnesota. In the playoffs, we swept Winnipeg, came back to beat Minnesota in six after falling behind 2–1, and reached the final against Whitey Stapleton and Ralph Backstrom's Chicago Cougars, who had shocked the defending champions, New England, in the first round.

The International Amphitheater—a smelly dump by the stockyards, but boy, I loved the ice there—had been booked for a production of *Peter Pan* during the Cougars' series against Toronto, forcing it to be played at the 2,000-seat Randhurst Twin Ice Arena, adjacent to a mall in Mount Prospect. (Chicago Stadium was booked for the Blackhawks' run to the Stanley Cup semifinals.) I guess nobody expected the Cougars to beat Toronto, either, because the Amphitheater's maintenance crew had dismantled the building's temporary ice plant. It was back to the mall for the final.

Hey, this was the WHA. In its first year, Philadelphia had its home opener canceled when the ice cracked into big chunks during the warmup, and Ottawa, in a rent dispute, moved to Toronto for the playoffs—and stayed there. In the second year, New York wound up in South Jersey, playing in the tiny Cherry Hill Arena, which had a hump in the middle of the ice and no locker rooms for the visiting teams, forcing us to dress at the motel. So a championship series being played before 2,000 people—at least it was sold out—was just another chapter.

I didn't care if we were in a slushy parking lot; I wanted to win that title. Since I hadn't been a big factor in the first two rounds—Dad and our good second line of veteran guys, Larry Lund, Frank Hughes and Hinse, had carried us—I probably was uptight.

The night before game one, Dineen gathered us at our headquarters at the O'Hare Airport Marriott for an 11 p.m. meeting. I thought that essentially was our curfew. But after Bill talked about what we had to do the next night, he said, "I know it's a lot to ask of you guys, but if you are going to go out and have a couple more drinks, would you please try to be in by 12:30?"

I went back to my room thinking, "I can't believe guys are going back out," and then proceeded to sleep about 20 minutes the entire night; I was so worked up. The guys who had a couple of nightcaps slept great and were by far our best players in the first two games.

Stapleton, who had been a really good defenseman for the Blackhawks, was a tough guy to get the puck past, but only the first game of the series was close. We wrapped up a sweep in Houston and our captain, Taylor, carried the Avco World Trophy around the Sam Houston Coliseum ice.

After the series, we went to a big party at the Whitehall Hotel. A few days later, we were on our way in limos from the noontime downtown parade to a public meeting with Mayor Fred Hofheinz when our car ran out of beer. We stopped en route at a local bar to replenish our stock and arrived just as the presentation ceremony was ending. Sorry, Mr. Mayor.

Dad, who nine months earlier hadn't been known well enough in Houston to be elected dogcatcher, had put the town on the hockey map. I was the proud rookie of the year in a league that had been virtually unknown to me on my draft day, and Marty had played his way into joining us on the Team Canada roster for the second Summit Series against the Soviet national team, coming up in September.

Our family had taken enormous risks to undertake this "publicity stunt." Dad could have appeared feeble and greedy, tarnishing his legend. Marty and I might have looked like teenagers playing against men. Mom had not only left her baby, Murray, behind in Detroit so he could continue his hockey education, she had also moved away from the city where she had spent her entire life. And it could hardly have worked out any better for all of us.

CHAPTER 6

The Summit of Frustration

My scouting career wouldn't begin for another 23 years. But in 1972, when Alan Eagleson, the executive director of the National Hockey League Players' Association, organized the first series between Canadian professionals and the so-called Soviet amateurs who had dominated international competition since their first Olympic title in 1956, I had some firsthand knowledge on the subject.

Knowing how good the Soviets were from having played against them only eight months earlier at the Olympics, I told Dad the eight-game series would be close, Canada winning something like five games to three, and I remember he chuckled.

I explained to him about Valeri Kharlamov, whom I had seen take a puck out of the air from the corner of the rink in Sapporo, bounce it off his stick numerous times as he circled behind the net and, without letting it hit the ground, bat it into the net while being cross-checked from behind. I also warned him of Valeri Vasiliev, a defenseman with great mobility, balance and vision who I thought was as good as any blueliner I had seen in the NHL, next to Bobby Orr.

We watched game one on September 2, 1972, from our cottage. Dad's chuckles seemed about to turn into big belly laughs from all the Howes when Phil Esposito put in a rebound after just 30 seconds.

Paul Henderson put Canada ahead 2–0 at 6:32. The rout seemingly was on, in addition to the joke on me, until Canada practically never had the puck again for the rest of the first period. The Soviets scored (Yevgeny Zimin on a cross-crease pass by Alexander Yakushev), and I remember Vladimir Petrov tied it on a shorthanded goal after he outskated everybody from a face-off in their end.

In the second period, Kharlamov went around Don Awrey like he wasn't even there, putting the Soviets ahead. Eight minutes later, he scored again. Yakushev—big, strong and with the long stride and wicked shot of a young Frank Mahovlich—embarrassed some gasping, out-of-shape Canadians going into the slot, and by the third period, a rout was indeed on, only it ended 7–3 for the Soviets.

Hadn't I told 'em? But my crystal ball, remember, had called the series 5–3 for the Canadians, and they pulled it out 4–3–1 by winning the last three games in Moscow, the final one with a rally from a two-goal third-period deficit. Paul Henderson's series-winning goal with 34 seconds remaining is still largely remembered as the greatest moment in Canadian sports history.

After that, organizing another series two years later was begging for an anticlimax. But thanks to Bill Hunter, the Edmonton owner and a driving force in the creation of the World Hockey Association, it would be our league's turn.

The Soviet team, with its brilliant puck movement and joyless, robotic demeanor, had changed little in two years. Kharlamov, whose ankle had been broken by a Bobby Clarke slash in Moscow to turn the 1972 series around, was back, as was their own version of Clarke, crafty Boris Mikhailov, and big-time talents like Yakushev and Alexander Maltsev. By now, these guys were almost household names in Canada.

So were Bobby Hull and Gerry Cheevers, both of whom had been uninvited in 1972 because they had "defected" to the WHA. This time, they would get to play, like my (unretired) dad and me, which was incredibly exciting.

Because Dad is Canadian, I had dual citizenship that enabled me to play for Canada, kind of neat after performing for the U.S. at the Olympics. But having grown up in the States, it was representing the WHA that excited me, along with the opportunity to be in the locker room at the training camp at the old Edmonton Gardens with superstars like Hull and Mahovlich.

I remember telling Hull, who had massive wrists, that I would do anything for a set like his. He said he would happily trade them for my legs. "No deal," I laughed.

Billy Harris, who had coached internationally before becoming coach of the Toronto Toros of our league, went with a more experienced lineup that didn't include Marty and me for game one in Quebec City. So after Hull scored his second goal in the third period to pull out a 3–3 tie, I was surprised that I got to dress two nights later in Toronto.

Dad hit me with a rinkwide pass at the blue line and I pulled out the great Soviet goalie, Vladislav Tretiak, with a fake and fed Backstrom for a tap-in on the first goal. I was so excited that when I joined in the scoring celebration, my overexuberance got the best of me—and Dad, too. I apparently damaged some of my father's rib cartilage, so he had to come out after the first period.

Not very patriotic of me—unlike Tom Brown, the Canadian junior referee who worked the game. He missed a Soviet goal that quickly went in and out of the net. Ralph Backstrom, who still had speed at age 36, and I killed penalties well and our team won 4–1 while Cheevers's father-in-law, who was sitting in the stands in Toronto, was suffering a fatal heart attack.

Thus, Cheesie missed game three in Winnipeg to attend the funeral. Dad, who still was sore, and four other guys from the winning lineup in game two who were healthy also sat out as Harris, true to his word, continued to play everybody. Cheevers's absence, however, left no choice but to go with Smokey McLeod, our goalie with the Aeros. It was a tough spot for McLeod, or anybody. He was bombed 8–5, Canada having to score three of the last four goals to make it appear even that close.

Cheevers and my father were back for game four in Vancouver. With Dad tying the game 1–1 and Hull's hat trick in the first period, we led 5–2, only to begin to take mindless penalties, mostly because our brains were locked in Cold War principles of the '70s. Had to hate those Russians. Even though Ralph and I again did a good job killing the penalties, we lost all our momentum and the dirty Commies scored twice late to pull out what for us was a hugely disappointing 5–5 tie.

We should have been up 2–1–1. Instead the series was 1–1–2 going to Moscow, with games in Sweden and Finland in the interim to help us adjust to the time difference and the larger international ice surface. We beat Finland big because their goaltending broke down, then attended a postgame banquet in Helsinki where Hull, attempting to be a goodwill ambassador as usual, got up and announced how beautiful Sweden was—except we were in Finland.

"Oh, dear Lord," we were saying as Bobby just about cleared the room with that one. Never mistake a Finn for a Swede, or vice versa. They will not appreciate it.

When we got to our huge Moscow hotel after a long—and, we suspected, intentionally harassing—delay at the airport, we opened our bags and it was like a tornado had hit. Somebody had gone through everything, and who knows what they took out.

The survivors of 1972 warned us about the USSR's bad food options and we had brought our own steaks, but the Russians boiled them. *Yeeecch.* The only way to make the beef edible was to pour on the ketchup we'd brought with us, but it didn't show up for several days.

The Russia Hotel had something like 3,000 rooms, because they were the size of closets—with no actual closets, just four hangers on the wall. And we were given no keys. When you got off the elevator, somebody sitting at a desk would open your door.

It's not uncommon in older hotels to find rust in the water. Normally, it quickly clears up if you let it run, but at the Russia Hotel the longer it ran, the dirtier it got. Apparently, they didn't have goosenecked pipes, because the bathrooms smelled from the backup. And the water the maids used was so dirty nothing ever really got clean.

Mahovlich, who had played in the 1972 series before signing with Toronto of our league, warned us about hidden listening devices in our rooms. We never knew for sure, but they were filming just about everything we did. Since we were so far behind them in training methods, what could they possibly have been learning from us? Our paranoia set in, sometimes with good reason.

A few members of the traveling party—no players that I remember—were subject to sudden knocks on the door and searches of their quarters. A couple of our younger players hooked up with girls and weren't in their rooms 10 minutes before the doors busted open and armed guards grabbed the women and yanked them out.

And that was far from the only reminder we were in a police state. On every corner, there were soldiers with guns. After practice and games, there were barricades from the rink door to the bus, with all these people watching, likely because they had never before seen anyone from North America.

There was a boy, about 10 years old, waving at us, and when some players held up the offer of some chewing gum, he snuck under the barricade and ran toward the bus. Just as he got there, military police threw him on the ground, cuffed him, and within about five seconds, they had taken him off in a car with his mother still standing there.

Luzhniki Arena had a huge scoreboard, with the game info in English at one end and in Russian at the other. Otherwise, the building had no more color than the rest of Moscow. Every once in a while, you would see a young girl wearing pink or red, but otherwise it was gray interrupted only by black.

Dad and I each had a goal in game five. Mine came in the final two minutes of a 3–2 loss in which we had only 16 shots on goal. A pattern developed where we would score a goal to get back in a game, then one of the little leg spears the Soviets liked to give out would cause one of our guys to retaliate with a blatant two-hander. Their player would lie down, the ref's arm would go up, and if they didn't score on the power play, we still would lose momentum. Only Cheevers and our penalty-killing kept us from being blown away.

Obviously, we weren't as good as the NHL team in '72. But we had a really talented core of French-Canadians, including veterans Serge Bernier and Andre Lacroix, plus young guys like Rejean Houle and Marc Tardif, soon to become the best player in the WHA. Backstrom, Dad and I made a good line, and Hull scored seven goals in the series. But Harris kept changing the lineup to get everybody in—maybe while in Russia, you do as the collectivists do?—and we really lost our discipline in Moscow.

I don't know if what we experienced with the meals and lost luggage was just bureaucratic incompetence or deliberate harassment. Probably, it was some of both. When Hunter complained, our treatment got a little better, except by the referees.

In game six, I had set up Dad for a tip-in and we were down only 3–2 in the second period. We were playing our best hockey since the game in Toronto. I was in the box for cross-checking Boris Mikhailov when the Russian referee had his arm up to call a penalty on Vasiliev, who had fouled Bruce MacGregor. Vasiliev then threw a punch and, even though MacGregor only held on, they both got five and the original penalty disappeared almost as fast as that Russian kid who wanted the chewing gum. The Soviets scored on the power play and went on to win 5–2.

After the buzzer, Ricky Ley bloodied Kharlamov, causing the crowd to whistle in disdain and prompting Russian coach Boris Kulagin to comment after the game that Ley should have been subject to arrest for committing an assault.

To our players, the mental picture of a Russian jail was not an inviting one. I remember trying to get my bearings after a rock-solid hit from I-don't-know-who near our bench. "Over here, over here," I heard teammates yelling at me. I had enough sense remaining only to get my arm out so somebody could pull me in.

Surely, I was concussed. Still, I don't recall having to be cleared by our doctor to return. In those days, if we thought we could keep

Gordie and Colleen, poolside on their honeymoon in Hollywood, Florida, 1953.

I lived the first four years of my life in this home on Stawell Avenue in Detroit.

Marty and me with Mom's family. From the left: Colleen, Great-Grandmother Ovens and Grandma Margaret.

With Mom and Marty, 1958.

Christmas 1958 with Aunt Elsie, Uncle Hughie and Marty.

Five-year-old Marty and four-year-old me, dressed against the fall chill, in 1959.

We moved to Sunset Boulevard in Lathrup Village, Michigan, when I was four.

Swimming with Gordie and Marty in Florida.

Marty and me in front of Dad's fireplace trophy wall in our Lathrup Village home.

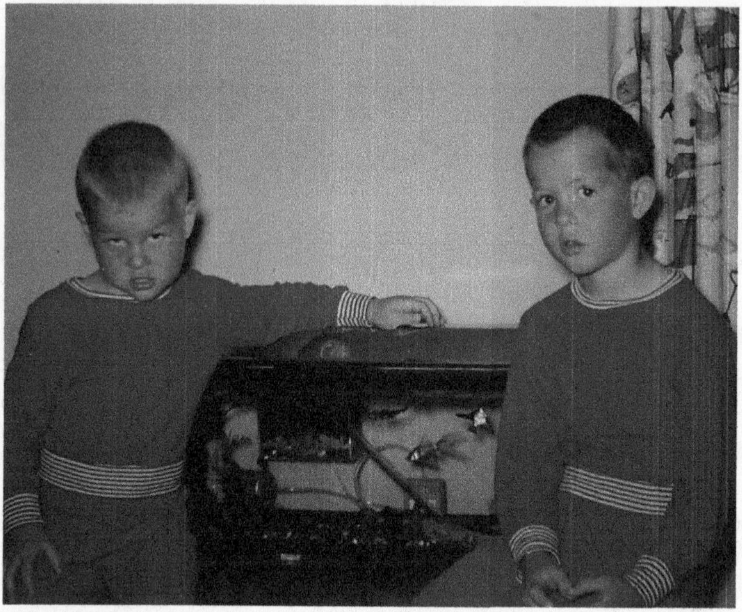

With Marty and the fish tank *before* I broke it.

Marty and I built our snowman with arms made from broken hockey sticks.

Dad's parents, Ab and Kate Howe, with my sister, Cathy, and brother Murray in Lathrup Village.

Posing with Dad and a tarpon at the Philpott family home in North Miami Beach, Florida.

Sitting on Mom's handmade winged wheel mosaic table in my Number 9 attire.

With Dad and Marty at Camp Weegeewa, near Parry Sound, Ontario.

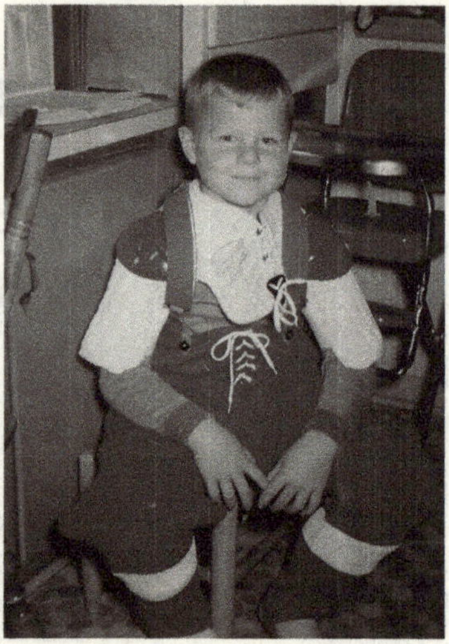

Having donned my equipment in our Lathrup Village home, I'm ready to go to practice.

Gordie Howe Hockeyland, in St. Clair Shores, Michigan. Mom and Dad took out a second mortgage to help build the first permanent rink, other than Olympia Stadium, in the Detroit area.

Our well-dressed family in Lathrup Village, 1965.

The Howes wearing Lathrup Beaver sweatshirts in 1967, the only year all four of us attended the same school.

On my Honda 90 at Bear Lake, Michigan, in 1968.

Gordie and Colleen with their best friends in hockey, Bill and Edna Gadsby.

Ecuador, 1969, with Marty and Gordie after I pulled in a 328-pound black marlin.

Colleen and Gordie at our Bear Lake cottage.

playing, we just did. But I still know our medical care was well ahead of that of the Russians. During one of the games in Moscow, I had just finished a line change and was at the end of the bench, 15 feet from theirs, when a Russian player hobbled in with a charley horse. Their doctor—or whatever he was—slid back the player's pad, pulled out a needle and jammed it into the guy's leg—*right through the sock!* And he went back out for his next shift!

In game seven, I redirected a J.C. Tremblay setup for a goal, Backstrom tied it at 4–4 in the third, and Hull scored at the buzzer to win it for us—or at least we thought we'd won until Brown, the Canadian referee, waved it off, even though the red goal light went on before the green light that was supposed to indicate time had run out.

After Backstrom's goal, the Soviets pretty much had been playing for the tie because it clinched the series. Hunter, feeling screwed as we all did, threatened to take us home early, but he cooled down and realized that it was as bad an idea as the one floated by the Soviets. They said if we continued to play dirty, they'd pull themselves off the ice.

The Soviets sort of did for game eight, not dressing four of their best players—Vasiliev, Tretiak, Mikhailov and Vladimir Petrov. We lost 3–2 to drop the series 1–4–3, disappointing because we probably could have won every game but the one in Winnipeg.

We gathered in one of the hallways of the massive hotel following the final game, drinking beer and taking towels and toilet paper from our rooms to give to people from our delegation who had Russian friends and relatives who couldn't buy those things. Team Canada felt like it had triumphed because, unlike our victorious opponents, we got to return home to North America.

First, we had to go to Prague, where we snored through a loss against the Czechoslovakian national team, then flew back on the charter to Toronto and scattered for our WHA training camps.

Back in Houston, Marty and I were fighting too much over stupid stuff, so I moved in with my teammate Rich Preston. It was a rare time in my life that I didn't have Marty for a roommate, but eventually I would get a better one. And I don't mean Preston, as good a guy as he was.

Through Marty, who was dating Mimi Poe, the sister of a Houston record store owner by the name of Larry, I made the acquaintance of a woman named Ginger Lowery. One day, I was on the balcony of the place I rented with Preston, looked down at the pool, and there was gorgeous Ginger, who—small world—lived in the same complex. Mighty neighborly of her, she had recently broken up with Larry, who said it would be fine if I asked her out.

Fine also described the way she looked and the way we hit if off. An heir to the McFadden family fortune, a big name in oil, she had done some modeling and ran a boutique with her half-sister, a job that didn't tie her down. In the summer, when I was off, she could pretty much pick up and go as she pleased, and so could I, despite my new business venture: when Larry's partner wanted out of the record store, I bought 50 per cent of it for $10,000.

Mom thought the investment was modest enough to be worth a shot. And I was determined to be no absentee owner. Hockey travel permitting, I'd not only spend a day a week at the shop, but also try to stop by three or four other times. I loved music and, having watched a hands-on Mom in her various ventures, understood that to run a successful business, you needed to be there. Plus, in the strip mall where the record store was located, there was a great barbecue place where I could combine a little business with pleasure.

One day, my teammate Frank Hughes was in our store. A customer asked for his autograph. A hockey fan and record buyer—music to my ears! The guy wanted it on a Mac Davis album, which seemed a little strange, but I thought the guy didn't have any paper handy. Frank obliged.

"Why didn't you sign your real name?" the fan asked.

"I did," said Frank. Turns out, the guy thought Frank was Mac Davis, live and in person at Southwest Records and Tapes.

Unlike Mac and Frank, the 1974–75 Aeros didn't completely resemble our WHA champions of the previous season. Our top two lines and defensive corps were intact, but we had added four players—Rich Preston, Terry Ruskowski, Don Larway and a talented goalie, Ron Grahame. Thanks to Dineen's Colorado connections, Grahame had been signed out of the University of Denver and was coming up after a season with our farm club, the Macon Whoopees (any long-time hockey fan knows I'm not making that up).

We called Grahame "The Reverend" because he could have been one. He never swore, and . . . well, I was about to say he never drank, but to make a round of golf competitive, once in a blue moon we'd bet that if he won, I wouldn't have a drink for month and if I won he had to go out with me and knock one back.

One time we had an extra day off in Cincinnati, where I won the match and took him out that night to pay off. He kept ordering different drinks, hoping one would taste better to him than the last, but he hated them all. After six or seven tries, the sips were adding up, and here was the Reverend, actually tipsy.

Marty said, "Dad has to see this," so we took Ronnie to my father's room, where the Reverend talked some trash, and it was hilarious, although I'm sure it wasn't funny for him the next day. It would have been a lot easier on me to not have a drink for a month, no doubt.

We improved our win total by five that season. During the first round against Cleveland, I was open in the slot and hot, one-timing these setups under the crossbar, scoring eight goals against Cheevers. In the handshake line, he said to me, his Team Canada teammate, "Congratulations. Great series. But if you shoot one more puck near my head I'm going to chop yours off."

"Ohhhkay," I said, and moved on, thinking, "Thanks for the warning." We swept San Diego, then Quebec in the final, winning the last two in Quebec City. After scoring 22 points in 13 games and playing much better than in the previous year's playoffs, I was so exhausted that I was resting my head on Dad's shoulder as they readied the Cup presentation. Maybe Larry Hale was tired, too. As we were getting off our commercial flight home the next day, he dropped the Avco Cup on the tarmac and it broke into three pieces.

As well as I had performed, I still wasn't the playoff MVP, and deservedly so. Grahame had been sensational all year, especially in the playoffs, with a .941 save percentage and 2.00 goals-against average in all 13 games.

Counting our Memorial Cup championship with the Marlies, this was the third league title in three years for the Howe boys, but that string couldn't last forever. As WHA teams folded, rosters were merged and a smaller league grew even stronger by signing up more talented 18- and 19-year-old prospects not yet eligible for the NHL draft.

One of them was our high-energy winger, John Tonelli. Bill tried him between Dad and me, which didn't really work. The kid's game was just to take the puck to the net, so his only assists came if you could get to his rebounds.

John was tireless, though. He hung a heavy bag from a tree in the backyard of the apartment he rented in the same complex as four other Aeros, and in an era where off-ice workouts were in their early stages, he pounded that bag all day. He was a great kid who already was proving capable of killing opponents with tenacity.

He wasn't our only workhorse. For the third straight year, the line of Ted Taylor, Gord Labossiere and Murray Hall remained productive, and our second line of Andre Hinse, Larry Lund and Frank Hughes was as consistent as ever.

While Hughes was no Mac Davis, he did score 40 goals twice and have another claim to fame: he married Debbie Lawler, the Flying Angel, who once jumped 16 trucks on her motorcycle and drew a challenge from Evel Knievel. She lost, but Debbie had a hubby who consistently found the net.

Lund, who worked toward earning a law degree during most of his years with the Aeros, was a big body, strong on face-offs. Hinse, according to Dineen, was the best player never to play in the NHL, and I probably agree. He skated and thought the game quite well, but having average size and not being very physical, Andre didn't have that one outstanding attribute that an NHL team would be looking for.

But while we certainly didn't own any guys with 25 years of NHL experience besides Dad, we had players who had been there, like our top defensive pair, John Schella and Poul Popiel. Schella was a big body who would drop the gloves every once in a while, and he played a very responsible defense; Popiel was a little nastier and highly competitive at everything he did, even in card games on the planes. He gave us good point production on the power play, too.

The Aeros' defense, including Marty, benefited hugely from the teaching of Doug Harvey, who, as long as he lasted, basically was Dineen's staff. Harvey, a seven-time Norris Trophy winner who probably was the best defenseman ever before Orr came along, fought bipolar disorder and the bottle all his adult life and fell off the wagon in Houston.

Years later, when I was playing for Hartford, Dave Keon and I were walking down the street back to our hotel near the Forum when we passed a guy sleeping on the sidewalk. "Hold on a minute," Keon suddenly said, after we took a few more steps. We went back and he said, "That's Doug Harvey."

Dave pulled out $250, asked me for the same and we took him to the hotel and Keon told the clerk, "Give this guy a room until the $500 runs out."

That was the last time I ever saw Doug. The Canadiens hired him a few years later in one last attempt to save his life, but he died in 1989 of cirrhosis of the liver.

As young guys like Preston, Tonelli, and Ruskowski developed, I believe our third team in Houston was the best one. But the league, and especially Winnipeg, also had gotten better.

Ulf Nilsson and Anders Hedberg, two dynamic and fearless Swedes, had given Hull a new lease on life when they joined the Jets in 1975–76. By their second year together, that line was unstoppable. I never respected anybody more than I did those two for the consistent physical abuse they took and ignored. And their fellow Swede, defenseman Lars-Erik Sjoberg, dished out more than he took and moved the puck brilliantly.

Even our path to the final against Winnipeg was more difficult than the previous two. Playing our first year in the 15,000-seat Summit, we finished 1975–76 with the same point total (106) as the previous season and jumped up 3–0 in the first round against San Diego before having to squeak by, 3–2 in game six.

In the next round, New England beat us 6–1 in game six, and we were hanging on to a 1–0 lead in game seven with about two minutes remaining and a face-off just outside our blue line. Dad, who was playing center with Preston and me, looked over before he took the draw and gave me this little eye gesture, looking up ice.

He always was rubbing his nose and blinking—players in the NHL used to call him "Blinky," although not to his face—so I think I was the only one on the ice who picked up on it.

Any other time in that situation, I thought defense all the way. But he looked at me as if to say, "Here's where I want you to go," so when the puck was dropped, I took off. He pushed it forward and I went in on a breakaway and put the series away. To me, it was the quintessential goal I ever scored with him, both because of its importance and the chemistry between us that it demonstrated.

In the final, we lost the first two games at home on late goals by Hull and, after losing game three, 6–3, we were trounced in game four, 9–1, with Nilsson and Hedberg combining for eight points. It was ugly. I wasn't used to losing, not that I ever really became accustomed to it. But the crowds and atmosphere of that series—between a two-time defending champion and a powerhouse upstart—had hype and a big-time feel to it.

Helped by a base of oil company transients from Alberta, filled in by Texans who had fallen in love with hockey, the Aeros were averaging about 9,000 a game and drew about 15,000 for each of the two games of the final played at the Summit. Whenever there was speculation about the two leagues merging, the Aeros, playing in the nice new arena we were sharing with the NBA Rockets, figured to be in on the plan.

By then, my sister, not a happy camper in Houston, had finished high school and gone back to Michigan to live with her future husband, Danny Greer, whom she never had wanted to leave. When Cathy moved out, Mom wanted to downsize, so we bought three townhomes in the same development—one for her and Dad, one for Marty, one for Ginger and me. We were headed for marriage a year later, with reason to believe we would live happily ever after in her hometown. But the business of hockey intruded.

She'd high school, and gone back to Michigan to live with her future husband, Danny Green, whom she never had wanted to leave. When Cathy moved out, Mom wanted to downsize, so we bought three townhomes in the same development—one for her and Dad, one for Marty, one for Ginger and me. We were headed for marriage a year later, with reason to believe we would live happily ever after in her hometown. But the business of hockey intruded.

CHAPTER 7

Disconnected in Connecticut

There was trouble in paradise by 1976–77, the fourth and final season of the contracts we had signed with the Houston Aeros. Team members had not received the $10,000 bonuses owed to us for making it to the WHA final the previous season. While my mother successfully fought for ours, I'm not sure all the other players ever received them.

Paul Deneau, the founder of the franchise, had been gone since our second year in Houston, and the new local owners, fronted by George Bolin, must have needed that bonus money to make ends meet. When the season started, management asked all the players to defer some of their pay, and according to what was leaked to the newspapers, everyone agreed but the three of us. We said no because a lot of our money already was deferred.

My mom, who had really become the first female player agent, met with Bolin several times to reach a deal to keep us in Houston, but if the Aeros weren't going to get us on the cheap, they didn't want us at all. Worse, Bolin clearly resented dealing with Mom, belittling her to the point where one time she walked out. After she left, they announced they were ready to make another offer. Marty said, "Why don't you write it down on real soft paper and then shove it up your ass."

Marty's next paycheck was held by Bolin, pending an apology that never came. Marty was paid regardless, but Bolin had the LeRoy Neiman painting of Dad taken off the wall of the office they had given him as the playing team president, claiming it was the club's property.

The Aeros' best offer for my ongoing services was $125,000 a year for either one or two seasons, minus any signing bonus this time. That amount was the same annual salary I had signed for in 1973, before I averaged 37 goals and 77 points a year and helped bring the franchise two championships.

Mom publicly suggested it was doubtful we would be back for a fifth season, and while members of the team never said anything directly to our faces, anonymous quotes appearing in the papers indicated they thought we were holding the future of the franchise, and their jobs, hostage. Since we all had no-trade contracts to keep the Aeros from getting cheaper players for us, I guess we were.

These were painful turns in what once had been a beautiful relationship. I was marrying a Houston girl and hoping to play someday for a Houston NHL team that was run by Bill Dineen. But an agreement-in-principle on an NHL–WHA merger announced in March 1977 would fall through because a few hard-line, old-school owners like Toronto's Harold Ballard still resented that the new league had escalated player costs. It was becoming problematic for the Aeros to survive long enough to make it to the NHL.

Dineen held the team together, signing a good goal scorer, Morris Lukowich, who had been a third-round pick by Pittsburgh of the NHL. Other young guys like Terry Ruskowski and Cam Connor stepped up with solid years. Again, we had as much depth as any team in the WHA, but in that league, 25 guys—including minor-leaguers—was pretty much what a franchise had under contract. When the Aeros grew short on defense about halfway through the season, Dineen switched me to the blue line.

Bill had other reasons for moving me. I was coming off a separated shoulder, and he thought that with my speed, playing defense would make it easier for me to skate away from hits. He also could increase my ice time.

I was surprised, but I remembered back when Carl Lindstrom, my midget and Junior Red Wings coach, had idly told me one day at age 14 that I would someday be a "great NHL defenseman." I thought that was nuts. Except to use me at the point on the power play, Lindstrom never had acted on it; neither had George Armstrong with the Marlies, nor Dineen in my first three seasons with the Aeros. But, always knowing what to do, Bill paired me with Poul Popiel, our best defenseman, whose veteran presence guided me all the way through the playoffs.

Even though Frank Hughes (who had scored 40 goals twice for us), John Schella (Popiel's normal partner) and both Dad and I all missed significant chunks of time, our team entered the postseason with the same 106 points as the previous year.

We had too much talent for Edmonton, whom we beat in five, but not enough again for the Jets. As we were eliminated in game six, 6–3 in Winnipeg, I don't remember reflecting about our Aeros days being over, probably because I was still hoping for a miracle to keep us in Houston. But the chain of events that would take us away from there already was irreversible.

In December of that season, Mom had received a letter from John Ziegler, the attorney for the Red Wings and owner Bruce Norris, asking for a reconciliation that would bring the Howes back to Detroit.

Mom wrote in her book *And . . . Howe!* that she and Dad were moved to tears at the thought. If only it were that simple. When I had become eligible for the NHL draft in 1974—the NHL had lowered the age limit to 19 for that one year, with the stipulation that underage players had to be taken after the first round—the Boston Bruins had claimed my rights with the 25th-overall pick. The Canadiens then selected Marty, who was 20, in the third round.

Dad was a complete free agent, but in order to get us all to Detroit, Boston or even Montreal, trades would have to be struck.

Mom's conversations with the Red Wings must have started out promisingly, because they made a future-considerations deal with the Canadiens for Marty's rights. Ziegler wanted to bring Mom and Dad to Detroit to discuss a role for him in the organization. But on the day in March when she and Dad were supposed to meet with Norris and Ziegler, the Red Wings organization suddenly announced it was replacing GM Alex Delvecchio with Ted Lindsay.

Dad and Ted had been linemates on the ice and inseparable off it in their early Cup-winning days in Detroit. But when Lindsay was traded to Chicago immediately after fronting an attempt to form a players' association, he felt the movement had failed because my father, the best player in the game, had not pledged his support.

Dad never wanted to rock the boat with authority or speak poorly of friends. But the rare time Lindsay's name would come up, I can remember my mother not having very nice things to say about him. When Ted had been quoted a few years earlier as saying the WHA couldn't be much of a league if its MVP was a 45-year-old man, Lindsay certainly was not acting like a dear old family friend. Dad, who had encouraged Ted in his comeback to the Red Wings in 1964 after four years out of the game, had to feel hurt at having his successful return dismissed by his once-best friend.

Business is supposed to be business. But the way Lindsay responded to the speculation about us coming to Detroit sounded personal.

"I'd be interested in a package as long as Colleen didn't try to run my hockey club," he told the *Windsor Star*. "I'd want Gordie off the ice, though. I want people here to remember him as he was."

Lindsay also insisted that the Red Wings, who remained as terrible as when Dad retired in 1971, were in no condition to give up the number-one pick Boston wanted for me. But this made little sense. At age 22, I already was an All-Star in a major league, and most scouts thought I would have gone no worse than second overall behind Denis Potvin had I been eligible for the NHL draft in 1973.

It was obvious that Ted wanted no part of the Howes. Lindsay has since blamed all his negativity on being the mouthpiece of Norris, saying the owner didn't want us back. But Ziegler had expressed a belief in his December letter that Norris wanted reconciliation. John withdrew from the negotiations when he became president of the NHL that summer, but all the signs were positive until Lindsay was hired.

Whatever really happened, it was clear we weren't welcome in Detroit. The Bruins, however, were stepping up. GM Harry Sinden flew to Houston, met with all of us and offered me $225,000 a year for five years, way more than what the Aeros had proposed. The Boston owners, Max and Jeremy Jacobs, were offering Dad a position with one of their other businesses (Mom wrote that it was with Ramco Steel; Sinden recalls it being with a travel service in Detroit), but there never was any interest on the Bruins' part to keep Dad on the ice.

That was not the case with my mother's hole card. Howard Baldwin, the president of the WHA's New England Whalers, had received a call from Bolin partway through the season to try to engage the Whalers in dealing for us. I guess Bolin thought he could make things so uncomfortable that we would waive our no-trade clauses, which wasn't going to happen. But when the season ended and we were free agents, Baldwin told us his team would have a playing offer for Dad, too, if negotiations with the NHL teams didn't work out.

I was dying to go to Boston. The Bruins had won two Stanley Cups in the decade and been to two other finals, including one just that spring. My offer from them matched what they were paying Jean Ratelle, their top center, and was only $10,000 below the salary of Brad Park, their best defenseman.

Their acquisition of Marty's rights from Detroit was not likely to be a problem. And even if the teams couldn't make a deal, I was confident my brother was a capable, top-four-caliber defenseman who would land on his feet.

I had wanted to play in the NHL for as long as I remembered. And I was almost there. But according to my mother, the Bruins suddenly said they wouldn't guarantee five-year contracts like Ray

Rozanski, who had been negotiating for the Jacobs brothers, had said Boston would.

Jack Kelley, the Whalers' general manager, and Dave Andrews—Baldwin's right-hand guy—flew out to the Calderone-Curran Ranch near Jackson, Michigan, where my parents were involved in the Polled Hereford breeding business for a time. Andrews and Kelley spent two days talking to Mom and Dad, and then sent for Baldwin to close the deal. He flew out in time for dinner, and made his offer that night.

I would receive $200,000 per year, less than I would have in Boston, but for 10 years, deferred over 15. Marty's total package was for $1.2 million and Dad's, from what I remember, was for $250,000 a year as a player, reduced to $100,000 once he left the ice for a front-office position.

Mom called me in Houston well after midnight, gave me the numbers, and expressed her concern that all the Boston money wasn't guaranteed. She also said that Hartford's was the only playing offer for Dad, which made the structuring of the Boston deal a secondary concern by far.

A decision to end Dad's career really was in my hands. I told Ginger I couldn't do that to him and called Mom back quickly to tell her to take the Whalers' offer. She walked back into the other room, where Baldwin, Kelley and Andrews were waiting, and told them we had accepted their offer.

Baldwin, fearing the Bruins would swoop back in and change our minds, quickly scheduled a press conference. But we weren't going anywhere else. I was disappointed but unwilling to elect myself the most selfish person in the world by going to Boston. Marty, too, thought it was the best thing for all of us, and a good night's sleep wiped the slate clean for me. By morning, I looked forward to joining the New England Whalers.

The Howes had just completed a deferred deal with Houston that had caused problems, but the Whalers, bankrolled by insurance corporation money, seemed secure. Baldwin, who had once been the Philadelphia Flyers' ticket manager and was still tight with owner Ed

Snider, had been a driving force in merger talks, so the Whalers were a good candidate to be taken into the NHL. As Mom reassured me, I still was only 22 years old and would get there sooner or later.

A 10-year deal left the probability you would be underpaid after five, but that also made you more tradable if you wanted out. The deal made me one of the better-paid wingers in the game, and being commensurate with other players of my ability is all I ever really desired. The no-trade clause I received also gave me some control, which was important in a time of franchise upheaval. As it turned out, the Aeros lasted one more year before all their players were dispersed, many to Winnipeg.

"I'm not ever going to Winnipeg," Ginger once vowed to me.

"That's two of us," I told her.

The newly wed Mrs. Howe was good to go to Connecticut, though. Five weeks after Marty had walked down the aisle with Mary James—whom he had met at a party to which he had been invited by my record-store partner, Larry Poe—Ginger and I were married on July 9, 1977, at the Palmer Memorial Church in Houston.

As Marty's best man, I had zealously guarded my big brother from any pranks at his wedding, so how was I paid back? During the reception at the Warwick Hotel, Marty asked for my room key to "put some presents there," and I was dumb enough to give it to him. He crumpled about 20 bags of potato chips under the covers and then short-sheeted us.

Yes, Ginger too. My brother short-sheeted my bride on her wedding night.

By then, she had been around enough hockey players to be unfazed. Off we went early the next morning for five days at Lake Tahoe, five in Honolulu and five in Maui, where no one at any stop got possession of our room key. A week after we got home to Houston, Ginger called me upstairs to announce she was pregnant.

Having always wanted kids while I was young enough to be active with them, this news only extended my honeymoon. I had one with the Whalers, too. From a season-opening victory in Houston—as many friends as I had there, it's always important to get back at your former team—we went on to a 15–1–1 start.

Hot as we were on the ice, however, the New England locker room proved frosty. Our introduction to Whaler camaraderie was so stunning it seemed like a prank to Marty, the ultimate prankster, and me.

When defenseman Ron Plumb, just picked up from Cincinnati, was invited out by a few teammates after a home game for a bite and a few beers, he asked Ginger and me to come along and we had a nice time. The next day, Plumb told me that after we left, he had been told: "We invited you, not the Howes. Don't ask them again."

One time on a road trip, three or four Whalers got into a cab, and Captain Rick Ley and Brad Selwood shut the door on Marty saying, "Ride by yourself."

We weren't the only outcasts. Forty-two games into the previous season, the Minnesota Fighting Saints had folded and been merged with the Whalers, so we had joined an already-divided dressing room.

Dave Keon, Johnny McKenzie and Mike Antonovich had all played together in Minnesota and stayed on the same line in New England. Johnny was an old pro with a wicked sense of humor, and Antonovich, a gifted player, was a jubilant kind of guy and a good golfer—except on the April day his new $1,000 set of clubs didn't save him from a rotten round. When he dumped his second shot on the 18th hole into the water, Mike drove his cart to the edge of the pond and, one by one, threw every club in his bag into the drink.

We had been at the 19th hole for some time when we noticed Mike's absence, followed by a sighting of somebody in the pond on the 18th hole. There he was, retrieving his clubs in what had to be about 40-degree weather.

One season, Antonovich, who played at about 170 pounds, came in looking three months pregnant at 192. Keon walked up to him and said, "Don't talk to me until you get down to 170." He then told the coach, "Don't put him on my line." The day Antonovich got down to 170, Keon walked up and said, "Let's go to lunch."

That was Keon: stubborn, principled, ornery and demanding at age 38. But he was great with me, and I needed someone to be great with me. The New England guys froze out the Howes, and to this day, I have no idea why.

As always when moving to a new team, I was shutting my mouth and doing my own job. Once you get your feet in the door, you can gain your personality back a little. But there wasn't a chance to do that in Hartford, which was bewildering and upsetting after leaving a Houston team where everybody had each other's back. Ley didn't like the Howes, and that set the team's agenda. And how much can you love a place when a team does that to you?

Most of the chill was targeted at Marty. I was playing on a line with Dad at center and Tommy Webster on right wing, and we were all in the top 10 in the WHA in scoring. But then Tommy, one of the better finishers I ever played with, suffered a herniated back disk that would turn out to effectively end his playing career, and the Whalers tailed off from their hot start.

After playing for Bill Dineen, George Armstrong and Carl Lindstrom, New England wasn't the same atmosphere to which we had become accustomed. There were more benchings for mistakes, a lot of screaming by an often red-faced Jack Kelley, and about as much togetherness on the ice as there was off it. As Marty said, a Whaler's way of communicating was "I had *my* man" after a goal was scored against us.

Coach Harry Neale worked the players hard every day, including the guys pushing 40 and beyond: Dad, Keon and McKenzie. That took its toll. So, perhaps, did a sense of displacement when the roof caved in on us, literally.

On January 19, we were leaving Edmonton on our way to Winnipeg, when we learned the roof of the Hartford Civic Center had collapsed from the weight of a snowstorm in the overnight hours after a University of Connecticut basketball game.

I remember players speculating that the owners would collect the insurance money and fold the franchise, but Baldwin flew into Quebec City, where we finished the trip, to tell us they were making arrangements to play in western Massachusetts at the 8,000-seat

Springfield Civic Center, 28 miles from downtown Hartford. So began my five-hour commute for every home game.

I liked living in Connecticut a lot more than I ever enjoyed playing for the Whalers. We had a place in Avon, down the street from a great golf course, Bell Compo, and there was excellent fishing nearby on the Farmington River. After Detroit and Houston, I enjoyed a smaller city. But for as long as were going to be playing in Springfield, I was on the wrong side of Hartford, a good 75 minutes away from our home rink, a pain in the ass when you had to go to the morning skate, then home, then back to the game.

One time, in a snowstorm strong enough to cancel the morning skate, I left my house at 2:30 p.m. and didn't get to the arena until 7:45—fifteen minutes late for the start. Turns out only about eight players were there and the game had been pushed back to 9 o'clock.

The lighting in Springfield wasn't the best, making it look smaller than its 8,000-seat capacity. The building didn't have much character, but the ice was good and the boards fast, so I guess it served its purpose, even though there were more Bruins fans in Springfield than there had been in Hartford. I remember beating Boston—after we moved to the NHL—and the fans booing us.

One more move of one more team—though ours was temporary—remained the modus operandi of the WHA. By the 1977–78 season, Calgary, San Diego and Phoenix were gone, leaving an eight-team league that was more competitive than ever. I guess Birmingham, which had moved from Toronto, needed to sell more than just hockey, because the Bulls collected the baddest asses in the game—Frankie "Seldom" Beaton, Serge Beaudoin, Dave Hanson, and last, but certainly not least, Steve "Demolition Derby" Durbano.

As had been the case in Houston, the Whalers' tough guys, Al Hangsleben and Jack Carlson, also could play a regular shift, and in Carlson, we really had the ultimate weapon. Jack, the brother of Steve and Jeff, who essentially played themselves as the Hanson brothers in the movie *Slap Shot,* had been on a call-up with the Minnesota

Fighting Saints when it was being filmed in Johnstown, Pennsylvania, where the Saints had their farm club. Dave Hanson became the third brother in the film.

While Jack never gained Hollywood stardom, we had enough scenes in the WHA to create our own movie. When Durbano came onto the ice a couple of minutes into one of our games with Birmingham, Neale tapped Jack on the shoulder and said, "I want him." Jack went onto the ice and, as soon as the puck was dropped, the gloves went off and he pummeled Derbie.

They did their time in the box, but Coach wasn't done. When Durbano came out the next time, Neale tapped Jack on the shoulder and said, "I want him again." This time, Derbie wasn't going to drop his gloves, so Carlson slapped the stick out of Durbano's hands and beat on him for a second time.

When they came out of the box again, Harry still wanted more blood. At the next Durbano sighting, there was another tap on the shoulder for Jack.

We won the next face-off and scored. Durbano fished out the puck, shot it at the referee, received a game misconduct and, before leaving, skated by our bench saying, "Ha ha, can't get me again!"

Because of our 15–1–1 start, 29–30–4, our record for the rest of the season, was enough to hold off Houston for second place behind Winnipeg. We played with no sense of urgency. Neither was nature in any rush to have Ginger deliver our first child before the playoffs.

In those days, there was no such thing as paternity leave. And, especially during the postseason, missing games was unthinkable. There was no baby yet when we flew to Edmonton after winning the first two playoff contests at home.

We had just finished the warmup prior to game four—I always gave it one or two more laps after the buzzer sounded—when I saw the timekeeper flailing his arms, trying to get my attention. "You have a son," he said.

Travis Gordon Howe—the namesake of Colonel William Travis, commander at the Battle of the Alamo, and of a hockey player you might have heard of—had come into the world. I still have no idea to this day how the timekeeper knew. I had checked in with Ginger a few hours earlier from the hotel—no cell phones in those days—and her water hadn't broken.

"Hey, Grandpa!" I said to Dad, congratulating him on his first, too, as I ran around the locker room with the news. I was on such a cloud nine, I must have had six breakaways in the 9–1 win that put us up 3–1 in the series. My skates never touched the ice, but the puck never touched the net either. I think I hit four posts, settling without the goal for my son that I had wanted in the worst way.

There were no direct flights from Edmonton to Hartford, and we didn't land the next night until 7 p.m., which got Dad and me to St. Francis Hospital no earlier than 8 o'clock. I held my son—and Gordie his grandson—for a total of 30 minutes each. Then I drove home to Avon to repack for the possibility of game six back in Edmonton.

It took 75 minutes to get to the hotel in Springfield where the team was staying, causing me to miss the 11 p.m. curfew by five minutes. I got fined. I don't remember if it was $50 or $100. But 25 cents still would have put a bad taste in my mouth.

We won the series the next night to save us the long flight back to Edmonton, then put away Quebec in five, with Danny Bolduc doing a great job of checking Quebec star Marc Tardif. Winnipeg, our opponent in the final, still had more weapons than anyone in the WHA, but one in particular—Kent Nilsson—made our goalie, Al Smith, paranoid. Nilsson had a wicked one-timer from the point that Al would scream for us to cover before it could be launched.

His concern was understandable. But with Lars-Erik Sjoberg at the other point and Ulf Nilsson, Anders Hedberg and Bobby Hull lurking, we had to choose our poison, which we swallowed hard. We lost in four straight in Ulfie and Anders's farewell to Winnipeg. They were about to sign with the New York Rangers.

Harry Neale also received an NHL offer from the Vancouver Canucks and took it. Sadly, the Aeros had folded, although Bill Dineen insists their last ownership had the money to wait out the merger and just didn't want to spend it. So Dad got Jack Kelley's okay to ask Bill if he wanted to coach New England, and he accepted.

We received one more gift via Houston. The Jets, with a sudden glut of Aeros, traded Andre Lacroix—who had helped fill the void we had left behind in Houston with 113 points—to us in August 1978. He was coming off his sixth straight season of 100-plus points—with four different franchises. Teams always were moving or folding on him.

Dad, back on right wing with Lacroix between us for the Whalers' 1978–79 season, was still defying time with almost a point a game until he took a shot off his foot. He kept playing on it until a second x-ray showed the fracture, and then, with the cast on, he shot a 75 on the golf course, claiming the plaster acted like an anchor and steadied him over the ball.

Even without Dad for 22 games, Lacroix helped me to 107 points, making 1978–79 my best offensive year. Although Andre had other limitations, he was the best passer, other than Dad, I ever regularly played with, equally adept on both his forehand and backhand at feeding me these nice little saucer passes as I broke to the holes. He created time and space for me on the ice and shared time and space with me as a roommate.

So I mean it as no slight to little Andre when I say that, in January of 1979, I got to play with the best center ever—Wayne Gretzky—on a line with the best player ever, Gordie Howe. Safe to say, it was one of the most memorable experiences of my life.

The WHA All-Stars played Moscow Dynamo—usually the second-best club team in the Soviet Union—in a three-game series in Edmonton. I didn't get there until late in the afternoon of game one; I was in Houston because Ginger's father, Art Lowery, had passed away from cancer that had been missed by too many doctors until it was too late. I excused myself after the viewing to get to the game, and to this day I remain grateful that Ginger and all her family understood. I'm the only person in the world who ever got to play on a line with Gordie Howe and Wayne Gretzky.

Wayne's foreword in this book tells you how much the opportunity to play with his boyhood idol meant to him, too. I was kind of along for the ride, but loving it just as much. With a nagging back injury, I didn't even play that well in game one, but I had a goal and two assists as the line combined for seven points. When I was named player of the game, I got booed because the fans wanted it to be Wayne, and I think they were right. I was the third wheel.

It was the same deal playing with Wayne as it always had been with Dad. You might box yourself in the corner, but both of them always were in the right spot to be your outlet. It was hard to ever be in a bad place playing with those two. And if you were anything close to being open, you had to make sure your stick was on the ice, because the puck was coming. In game two, Wayne and I each had goals in our second straight 4–2 win on the way to a three-game sweep.

What I remember most about Wayne at age 17 was his playmaking, of course. But boy, was he competitive, hungry and determined to score on every shift. Here was a player 32 years younger than my father, with the same skills and mentality.

If only the Whalers had made an attempt to be on the same wavelength. After enjoying three games with two of the three best players who ever lived—Bobby Orr would be the other—it was back to Hartford, where Dineen was getting the same reception we had received the previous season. Unlike in Houston, where Bill could bring in guys he wanted and who wanted to play for him, many Whalers thought he was a bad coach, not much for Xs and Os, and more about managing people.

A playoff spot was never in serious jeopardy, but we had won only six of the last 19 when Bill was fired by Kelley with nine games to go, and replaced by assistant coach Don Blackburn.

By then, there was another major distraction. On March 29, a couple of days before Dineen's dismissal (they made him director of scouting), the NHL–WHA merger finally got pushed through. The Montreal Canadiens, owned by the Molson brewery, had fought the acceptance of the Quebec Nordiques (owned by their rival brewers,

Carling-O'Keefe), claiming an intrusion on their territory, but bowed to a threatened beer boycott and changed their vote to provide the required three-quarters majority for the NHL's acceptance.

The NHL teams wanted to reclaim the good players they had drafted but who had signed with the WHA. So for their $6 million entry fee to the NHL, each of the four surviving WHA teams—Edmonton, Quebec, Winnipeg and New England—would be able to protect two skaters and two goalies. (I believe the only reason it was two goalies instead of one was because the WHA didn't have many the NHL wanted.) They would have to fill out the rest of their rosters in an expansion draft.

Because I was sure to be protected by the Whalers, I didn't face the uncertainty of the majority of my teammates. But I was a little cynical about all the angst over their upcoming displacement. If we were so talented that NHL teams were going to reclaim 10 or 12 of our players in the expansion draft, shouldn't we have been higher in the standings than fourth?

We had to hold off the fifth-place Cincinnati Stingers and Robbie Ftorek to get home ice against them in a best-of-three preliminary round. Ftorek was the second-leading scorer in the league after Quebec's Buddy Cloutier. Gretzky and I were neck and neck with Kent Nilsson for third.

Robbie had been my mentor and friend at the 1972 Olympics, but he had not been so kind to my brother. Being only five-ten, 155 pounds, Ftorek's method of buying himself some room was to put the puck just off to your side, then take his stick and run it up by the side of your head. In a game on December 30 at Cincinnati, Ftorek had similarly jumped in the air to avoid a Marty poke check and nailed my brother with his stick, causing a concussion, breaking his cheekbone, scratching his cornea and putting him in the hospital for a couple of nights.

On one of those nights, Dad and I visited him. We were getting ready to go home, when my father asked Marty if there was anything he could do or bring.

Marty said, "I was hoping—"

Dad cut him off. "You don't even have to ask," he said.

So, during a game against the Stingers in Springfield in the final week of the season—Cincinnati needed the points to make the playoffs, while New England still had a chance to move up to third place and receive a bye into the semifinals—Ftorek grabbed a missed shot that had rimmed out of the zone and appeared to have a breakaway until Dad came from the other side of the rink. Just as Robbie was getting ready to shoot, my father took his stick and turned it over so that the blade was facing up, not down, and delivered a one-hander right across Ftorek's face, cutting him really badly.

If somebody did that today, he would be kicked out of the league for two years. Dad got just five minutes for the worst thing I ever saw him do. We killed the penalty, won the game and beat Cincinnati in both home games of the best-of-three preliminary series to move on.

We were the underdogs in the semifinal round against Gretzky and the Oilers, who had finished 15 points ahead of us during the regular season. I still was having back problems and contributing nothing offensively. But by winning every home game, we got to game seven in Edmonton before they put us away with four goals in a 10-minute stretch of the second period and won 6–3, Gretzky completing the series with 15 points.

"We died like rats," said Blackburn, who on the last shift of the game used Dad with Keon and McKenzie, explaining afterward that Canada should have a chance to say goodbye to Gordie Howe, just in case this was going to be it for him.

Winnipeg, restocked from its loss of Hedberg and Ulf Nilsson by the influx of my old teammates from Houston, then beat the Oilers for the last WHA championship. I was happy for the Jets. But as the deepest team in the league, with players the NHL wanted, Winnipeg was going to get ripped apart in the expansion draft. Intact, the Jets would easily have been an NHL playoff team and, with a couple more defensemen and an elite goalie, a Stanley Cup contender.

They were that good. So was our league at the end.

Excited as I was to finally be going where I had always wanted to be—the NHL—the passing of the WHA hit me with sadness and a great deal of pride. Wacky though it often was, the league not only dramatically advanced the salaries of players, it improved the game by opening its arms to so many skilled Europeans.

The WHA gave me a chance to play for six years, no mere cameo, with my father—who, despite winning four Stanley Cups and six MVP trophies in the NHL, says playing with his sons was the biggest thrill of his career.

The NHL refused to recognize the 208 goals and 504 points I scored in the WHA, but I kept counting them in my career totals. During the 1986–87 season, when I was playing with Philadelphia, my upcoming 1,000th point was not noted in the Flyers' press notes. But when coach Mike Keenan learned about the milestone and congratulated me for it on the bench in Chicago, I was moved.

Somebody was remembering the WHA.

CHAPTER 8

The Net Result: Goodbye, Hartford

In junior hockey, I had competed well against many players who were having success in the NHL. Still, when the merger with the WHA finally came, I couldn't help but wonder how good I was going to be in the league where I had always wanted to play.

I suspected this step up would be like every other I had taken—the higher you went, the deeper the pool of good players. But this time, I was entering the best league in the world with everyone watching, which brought another level of intrigue and, of course, pressure.

You would read and hear absurd things like "Wayne Gretzky will not do well in the NHL." Those of us coming from the other league knew we hadn't been playing against chopped liver, so predictions like that were motivational fuel. But to prove how good the WHA had been, we would have to do it individually. The Edmonton Oilers, Winnipeg Jets, Quebec Nordiques and my renamed Hartford Whalers came into the NHL with rosters that were very different from our last WHA season.

Wanting to get in and start making money, the newcomers bent over and took the harsh terms. The NHL teams, desiring many of the players they had once drafted but had been unable to sign, were allowed to reclaim those players. Then, each incoming franchise was permitted to use "priority selections" to take back a grand total of two skaters and two goalies

Through this process, the Whalers kept winger Jordy Douglas, goalie John Garrett and me. Through a side deal with Montreal, they also held on to defenseman Gordie Roberts. Winnipeg, the last WHA champion, had much more to lose than Hartford and was ripped apart.

With that business completed, the four WHA teams took part in an expansion draft of players the NHL teams didn't want. Our GM, Jack Kelley, reclaimed (from Toronto) right wing Blaine Stoughton, who had come to us the previous year when Indianapolis folded. We also kept Mike Rogers, who scored 72 points for us in our last WHA season, plus some 50-year-old guy who had scored 19 goals the previous year despite missing 22 games. Dad, granted an exemption from the draft because at his age he had earned it, was going back to the NHL after an eight-year absence, which seemed to excite everybody but Kelley and the Whaler team doctors.

Kelley told my dad that one of the physicians wanted him to sign a waiver. The issue was dropped when no problem was found with Dad's heart, but then the Whalers came up with a new way to try to break it—sending my brother Marty to Springfield of the American Hockey League in the first round of cuts.

Marty's conditioning couldn't have been an issue. He had been running five miles a day to get ready. "We're going to use five defensemen, and he is not in our top five," said coach Don Blackburn, who then talked about moving me to the blue line.

My first game in the NHL, a 4–1 loss in Minnesota, was played on the wing. Two nights later in Pittsburgh, when Dad scored his first NHL goal since 1971 to a big ovation, I still was a winger. It wasn't until I walked into the visiting locker room in Buffalo on the night of the fourth game and saw my name in the defense pairs on the chalkboard that I became a defenseman.

At first, I didn't believe it. I had skated on wing at the morning practice. Thinking it was a mistake, I erased my name. "Who's messing with the blackboard?" said one of the coaches when he came in.

To say that the switch had been hinted at for more than a month does not mean I had a clue what to do on my first shift. My partner—I don't remember who—pinched and suddenly, Lord help me now, I was solo with Gilbert Perreault, one of the great one-on-one players in the game's history. Fortunately, he lost the puck and I laid on it, then made it back to the bench out of breath from being so nervous. We lost the game only 3–1, so I guess I didn't disgrace myself.

Two nights later, when I scored my first NHL goal on my good Houston friend Ronnie Grahame and we beat Los Angeles 6–3 in the home opener for our first win, I was on defense forevermore. Nobody taught me anything about playing the position. It was learn as you go. As a forward, I had always thought defense first anyway, so I just relied on my instincts to read the play. When, inevitably, I made mistakes, a lot of times my speed would allow me to catch up.

There were a lot of pictures taken that year of both Al Sims, who became my steady partner, and me around the opposition goal, waiting for rebounds. We were both puck-moving types who took advantage of good opportunities to jump into the play. Although we were a decent pairing, I would have been better off with a stay-at-home partner.

I knew one very well, and he had been banished to Springfield without a real look because the Whalers were convinced Marty had a bad attitude. My brother is an easygoing guy, a fisherman whose nickname was "Foggy." But when he stepped on the ice, he always was competitive. There was no way Marty wasn't at least a third-pair defenseman on that team. "Half my reason for playing is gone," Dad told reporters sadly.

The other half welcomed the opportunity to play 30 minutes a game on defense instead of 22 on the wing. I again remembered

Carl Lindstrom, my midget and junior coach in Detroit, predicting that I'd one day be a great NHL defenseman. And isn't the coach always right?

Don Blackburn, my first NHL coach, operated like Bill Dineen—more people-oriented than systems-oriented. Chalkboard diagrams were not going to save us from having to play 25 of our first 40 games on the road, so scheduled because the Hartford Civic Center wasn't going to reopen until February. We had won only once in our last 17 games when the Whalers went to Detroit on January 12.

Dad's return to the city where his legend was forged would have been that much more special if the schedule maker had gotten us there a little earlier. The Red Wings had played their first 12 home games that season at the Olympia as the new Joe Louis Arena was being readied. But in whatever arena Gordie Howe played his first NHL game in nine years, Detroit was still *his* town. John Bell, the PA announcer, got only as far as "Number 9" before he was drowned out. The ovation had to last five minutes, long enough to embarrass Dad, who just kind of skated in small circles as it went on and on.

This was such a special occasion that the Whalers even recalled Marty—mostly so they could get a picture of the three of us playing together on the first shift. I was on right wing with Dad at center. Blackburn put my brother on left wing with insulting instructions to come off immediately after the face-off, but my father told Marty to stay on for the full shift anyway. The game was spent in an unsuccessful attempt to set Dad up for a goal, but our 6–4 win gave him a lot of joy and got the team going.

Next game, one day short of two years after the roof collapse, we moved back into the remodeled and expanded Hartford Civic Center and beat Pittsburgh. The backlog of home games helped us to a 14–7–2 run.

Dave Keon, at 39, still was productive. Rogers, a good puck-possession player, complemented grinder Pat Boutette and Stoughton, a supreme sniper. Stoughton didn't like the rough going and wasn't much into backchecking, but if you needed a goal, he was lethal.

When we were getting ready to pull our goalie, he would say, "You know where to find me." That meant at the red line, and when you got it to him, he scored.

Dad still knew where the net was, too, even at age 51, but he was getting no time on the power play, where he could have helped us the most. Regardless, he became the most recognized fourth-liner ever, getting standing ovations everywhere.

The biggest hand of all was in Detroit again, on February 5, when the Red Wings hosted the All-Star Game. Dad couldn't figure out what to do this time, either, again skating around in small circles, blinking back tears, finally going over to crack a joke with Lefty Wilson, the Red Wings' longtime trainer, before Bell, the PA announcer, cut the cheers short at four minutes by introducing the anthem singers.

Sid Abel and Ted Lindsay came out to drop the first puck, but Wales Conference coach Scotty Bowman, who broke down some resistance in the league about Dad being named by threatening not to coach a team without him, should have taken a big bow. Stoughton, the Whalers' obvious All-Star who was bumped to get Dad there, said he understood. The show was about Gordie Howe.

When he shot a good first-period scoring chance right into goalie Tony Esposito, the groan from the crowd drowned out the groan of Tony, who was injured making the save. Dad, who set up a goal by Buddy Cloutier in the third period, showed he could still put some zip on the puck.

Obviously, his legs had slowed. It hurt him that season to no longer be playing with my speed and our chemistry. His hands were still good, though, and if I were coaching that team, he would have been on the power play, positioned in front of the net. Even greater testament to Dad still belonging in the NHL at age 51 than the 15 goals and 41 points he scored that season were the 10 goals that Nick Fotiu tallied as my father's linemate. Like Dad said, Nicky could run into you on a two-man breakaway.

Fotiu was dangerous to be around for another reason. He got so worked up that just about every practice he threw up.

One time that year against Montreal, Guy Lafleur, the best player in the game, came over the boards, so Blackburn took Fotiu and my dad off to get another matchup. Lafleur scored regardless. Five minutes later, Blackburn changed Fotiu again to have somebody else against Lafleur; he scored a second time.

When the coach made that change once more, Nicky, so upset he was shaking, charged our bench. I thought he was going to hit Blackburn, but instead he went up the tunnel to the locker room, and then home.

"How could we do any worse than two goals against on two shifts?" he asked me when he came back a day or so later, probably following a conversation with Blackie. Nicky just wanted to do what he could to help the team, including creating laughs and putting people in their place.

Sims, once Bobby Orr's partner, had been picked up from the Bruins in the merger draft. Everything out of Al's mouth was about Boston this and Boston that.

"Don't be in love with a team that didn't want you," we told him, but once a Bruin, always a Bruin, I guess; he kept it up. One day, during a layover in Chicago on the way to Detroit, Nicky said, "I've had enough of this." He called ahead to our hotel at the Renaissance Center and left a message at the front desk, saying, "This is Al Sims's agent. Please have him call me when he checks in. He's been traded back to Boston."

When we got there, Al read his message and ran upstairs to call his wife, his agent . . . everybody. A little cruel, but that was the last we heard about Boston from Al Sims.

In Pittsburgh, where the ceiling of the visiting locker room went up at an angle, Nicky got a 20-foot atrium ladder and a hot glue gun. When somebody who had been bothering him tried to get dressed after practice and wondered, "Where are my shoes?" they were found 20 feet overhead. If there were a Hall of Fame for pranksters, Nicky would have been in on the first ballot.

The Whalers acquired another shoo-in for the Hockey Hall of

Fame by obtaining Bobby Hull from Winnipeg, which had reclaimed him in the expansion draft from Chicago mostly out of spite and were not using him.

Hartford withheld the announcement until the Golden Jet skated out for us against the Blues on February 29 at the Civic Center. It was the perfect night for Dad, suddenly a teammate of his once-great rival and one of his better opposition friends. My father scored NHL career goal number 800 in the 3–0 win over St. Louis.

Two games later, Hull blew one by Buffalo goalie Don Edwards from outside the blue line. Despite some chronic bursitis, it looked like Bobby was going to help us. But seven games later, when he came in from the warmup, someone from the organization called him out into the hallway to speak to him. He took off his equipment and left.

We learned that Claudia Allen, Hull's fiancée, who was pregnant with his child, was in a coma following a car accident that occurred while she was looking for living quarters for them in Connecticut. She lost the baby and was permanently disabled—a horrible tragedy.

We went winless in 10 down the stretch. Nevertheless, 27–34–10 got us to a 13th-place finish in the 21-team league—better than five established NHL teams.

The bigger statement about the WHA was that seven of the NHL's top 24 scorers that season—including me, at number 24—had come from the other league. Gretzky tied Marcel Dionne for the scoring lead (they gave the Art Ross Trophy to Dionne because he had more goals), and I'd been rooting for the guy "too skinny to make it in the NHL" all the way.

For the first two years after the merger, each team in the league played every other club four times—a completely balanced schedule. Division and conference standings were thrown out, and playoffs were seeded according to the overall rankings, 1st through 16th. At number 13, we drew third-place Montreal, winners of the past four Stanley Cups. Talk about the short straw.

Short series, too. After we lost the opener of the best-of-five round, 6–1 at the Forum, we were losing 8–3 in game two when

I gained the zone and threw a backhand pass to Dad, whose own backhander from 45 feet out went through traffic and beat goalie Denis Herron. It was NHL playoff goal number 68 for my father, and I remember thinking that it might be his last one, regular or postseason. The Montreal fans probably thought so, too; they gave him a big hand.

We put up a fight in game three, rallying from a 3–1 deficit on two goals by Tommy Rowe to force overtime. "Be ready, they have a history of scoring fast in overtime," warned Blackburn. *Pfft.* Yvon Lambert won the game after 29 seconds.

So ended my first NHL season. Also, Dad's playing career—not of his own volition. He played in all 80 games that year and scored 15 goals and 26 assists on the fourth line. But when he went into Kelley's office to present a plan to become a player/assistant coach, Kelley said no thanks—the team was going to a youth movement. My father was so upset, he instantly told Kelley to "shove it" and quit.

Kelley clearly was happy about that. The Whalers called a press conference the next day, not giving Dad any chance to change his mind and potentially bring pressure from fans and media. Mom was furious with Dad for surrendering all control over his retirement announcement and breaking his promise that my mother would be the first to know.

He agreed he had blown it, and then, still seething about the turn of events, compounded his mistake at the press conference by telling reporters, "I can damn well still play this game." That only raised the question of why he was retiring.

At age 52, after a mindboggling 32 seasons, 975 goals, 2,358 points, six league championships and seven league MVP awards, it was over. (Why shouldn't I count everything he did in the WHA?)

Kelley had the ignominy that summer of telling both Gordie Howe and Bobby Hull they were finished. Hull, who had come back for the last two regular-season games and the playoffs, asked for another contract and was told no. The Whalers' "youth movement" included Keon, who in 1980–81 came back for another year at age

40—not that we had anyone young and dynamic who should have been playing ahead of him.

Trying to change the culture of the team, Kelley acquired Jack McIlhargey and Norm Barnes, both of whom had just played on a Stanley Cup finalist the season before in Philadelphia. He also brought back 33-year-old defenseman Thommy Abrahamsson, who had played with the Whalers in the WHA days, but Thommy was scared to death and wound up mostly a spectator. The Whalers had a promotion in the game magazine where if your face was circled in a picture of the fans, you would win tickets to the next game. Swear to God, one day Abrahamsson's face was spotlighted—they didn't know who he was. When he and Mike Rogers carpooled, if Abrahamsson wasn't playing, he would flash the porch lights, and then yell out, "Not tonight mister!" and Mike would keep driving.

For scoring, we were pretty much still reliant on the same guys. But following an early-season nine-game winless streak, Stoughton and Rogers were playing well and so was I. On December 27, 1980, we had won our last two games to get to 13–15–7 and had just rallied from a 3–0 deficit to take a 5–3 third-period lead over the defending Stanley Cup champion New York Islanders.

That was when John Tonelli, my old Houston teammate, came barreling down the left wing on a three-on-two with my ticket out of Hartford.

I can't remember which of Tonelli's two linemates—Bryan Trottier or Mike Bossy—was carrying the puck, but my partner (don't remember who) was closing the gap. So at the hash marks, I was turning to cover a pass when Tonelli collided with me from behind.

It was incidental contact, but enough to knock me off balance from full speed. Everything happened in the snap of a finger. But I knew I was sliding into the net with a bad back and I remember thinking, "Absorb the shock with your knees."

My skates lifted the net up, but not off the rods that anchored it to the ice, raising the sharp edge of the metal flange that lay at the center of the back of the goal. I could feel that piece of metal slicing me open.

"The net went into my ass!" I yelled at trainer Joe Altott, the first to reach me. "Cut off my pants, cut off my pants!"

I was certain I had punctured my intestines and was bleeding to death. When I looked up and saw that Fotiu's eyeballs were as big as bowling balls, it scared the hell out me—and my teammates, too. Rogers, on whose arm Altott had arrived, remembers seeing a pool of "black blood" beneath me. They stuffed my wide-open wound with towels, put me on a stretcher and brought me into the training room.

Dr. Vincent Turco, our team doctor, was playing with my toes. "My toes aren't the problem," I said, but he was checking to see if I was paralyzed. I had feeling, which should have been reassuring, but didn't stop my panic. "Am I going to live? Am I going to live?" I asked the doctor over and over.

Dad, who had been watching from the press box, raced to the locker room. On the way down, he told me later, some idiot asked for his autograph. My father was on my left side, holding my hand, when he asked the doctor if he could see the damage.

"You would be better off not to look," instructed Dr. Turco, but Dad insisted, saying, "That's my boy." So the doctor took the towel away. What he saw made him squeeze my hand so hard, I thought he broke it.

"Oh shit," I said to myself.

Dr. Turco did not come to St. Francis Hospital, where I was taken by ambulance, Dad riding along. I was calmer by then, actually pain-free, probably because I had lost three and a half pints of blood and shock had set in, same as it had on the team left at the rink. The Islanders scored twice late to gain a 5–5 tie.

I asked Dad to call Ginger, who had stayed home with Travis to prepare for a team get-together we were hosting on New Year's Eve, and tell her I was going to live. And then I lay there for, I swear, 75 or 80 minutes while they kept changing the bloody sheets before the surgeon on call, Dr. John DMaio, finally came in. Had my mother—who was not at the game that night, either—been at the hospital, she would have gone berserk.

Dr. DMaio started off by apologizing for having been at a family function, and then took the towel away.

"Omigod!" he said, and my heart started pumping again. He said he was sorry, hadn't meant to startle me, but having been told only that I'd suffered a laceration and needed to be stitched, he was now livid. "I should have been told what this was!" he yelled. "I would have gotten down here right away."

They prepped me immediately for surgery. I was on the table for more than two hours as they checked for damage and cleaned out shards of metal. The hole in my body, I would learn, measured three and a half inches at its widest point and was four and a half inches deep.

Two days later, when I was alert enough to have a conversation, Dr. DMaio, who had been an army medic in Vietnam, told my wife, father, mother and a well-medicated me that, considering all the places that metal could have gone, I was the luckiest patient he ever had treated.

Had the flange come in perfectly straight, it would have gone into my spinal cord, probably putting me in a wheelchair for the rest of my days. The sphincter muscle was only slightly torn, saving me a life sentence with a colostomy bag. My hamstring, which could have been severed to end my career, was missed completely, too, and my rectum only scraped.

"Am I going to be able to play hockey again?" I asked the doctor repeatedly. He said yes and that the healing needed to start immediately with me getting out of my hospital bed. I had no strength and was nauseous, but Dad came to my bedside and said, "Grab onto me."

"I'm going to get sick all over you," I said.

"That's okay, do what you need to do. The doctor wants you on your feet."

He held me as I spewed all over him. I don't know what is the ultimate expression of love, but letting an adult vomit on you would be near the top of my list.

Because of the damage to the sphincter muscle, there still was some concern about my bowels. When there was no movement along that front for four days, the doctors and nurses were beginning to threaten me with something much worse than warm compresses on my belly to give me the urge. When it finally began to work, I was warned it could hurt pretty badly because of the location of my cut, so I was terrified.

"I don't want you sitting here while I am crying," I told Ginger.

"Why don't you get your morphine now, then I'll leave and you can go," she suggested. Twenty minutes later, I was in La-la Land, just me and my little call button in the bathroom. Success!

"I'm Mr. Howe," I announced, when they came in to clean me up.

"We know," they said.

"It didn't hurt!" I rejoiced as they helped me back to bed, where I went to sleep.

After six or seven days, with all body parts working properly, I was sent home with one inch of the cut still exposed in hopes that the wound would heal from the inside out, which they said would help prevent infection. My poor wife wiped the wound one time and said that's the end of that—she couldn't stand looking through the exposure. I understood. So I had to look at my butt in the mirror and try to wipe myself in between the multiple showers I was ordered to take each day, all the while barely having enough strength to stand.

I was running fevers and getting so much pain in my legs, I couldn't walk more than 15 or 20 feet without having to lie down. Twenty-five days after the accident, feeling worse and worse, I was told to come back to the hospital.

My temperature was 103 degrees. The doctor said I was obviously infected, which they had been hoping to avoid. The cut went almost all the way across to my right hip, where he lanced me. Instantly, I could feel all this warm, milky stuff running down, and within a minute, I swear I said, "Omigod, I'm hungry," which I was—for the first time in almost three weeks.

On the way home that day, I told Ginger to stop at the first place she saw that had food. Burger King was it, and I believe I had three Whoppers. My conscience was clear about putting on weight from junk food. I was down 20 pounds, from 191 the night of the accident, but at last my healing process was beginning,

After only about a week, I felt well enough to begin skating again. I did that on my own a couple days, and then practiced with the team, which was on what would become a 2–14–4 skid. That wasn't due only to my absence. Rogers was injured, too.

Most of my pain was gone, but the ache of watching our team struggle added to the internal pressure of getting back into the lineup. Nobody pushed me. But nobody warned it was too soon, either. When I think about the strength and conditioning supervision I later experienced with the Flyers and Red Wings, it's amazing the Whalers allowed me play so soon.

Ginger didn't say whether I should or shouldn't. She never interfered with me about stuff like that. I saw my team losing and desperately wanted to get back on the ice.

There was another incentive. I very much wanted to play in my first NHL All-Star Game, scheduled for February 10 in Los Angeles. I targeted February 8 in Philadelphia—43 days after the accident—for my return.

Blackburn said he would use me only on the power play against the Flyers. As I recall, I ended up playing close to 25 minutes. I had wondered whether I was going to be net-shy. Sure enough, on an early shift, I came down the ice and, instead of going to the goalmouth, I chose the much safer path behind the net.

"I'm never doing that again," I told myself, and I didn't. I successfully forced my trepidation away after just one play and set up two third-period goals in a 6–6 tie. But the adrenaline ran out quickly and the fallout from the accident would linger for a long time.

Poor John Tonelli spent six months thinking I was mad at him. There were no cell phones then, but John had left messages with the team that I never received, and of course, I want to thank the Whalers for that courtesy. The first time I crossed paths with him the following season, he approached me and said how sorry he was.

"What for?" I asked. "It wasn't your fault."

I watched a replay of the accident only one time, via a VHS cassette provided by one of my Avon policeman friends who had taped the game that night. I must have jumped three feet off the edge of the bed where I had been sitting when I saw myself sliding into the net.

I took the tape out of the VCR and threw it away. There appears to be no copy of it anywhere today, and that's fine by me. I knew John never intended to injure me.

What happened was a call to action, though. Several months later, when I went to see my lawyer, Barry Krass, about another matter, he asked me how the lawsuit was going. I told him I had not filed one.

Immediately after my accident, the Hartford Civic Center altered its nets by taking five inches off the flange and rounding it. A month later, the NHL ordered its teams to immediately make the same change. But the metal still was protruding, so I thought the alterations were inadequate. And as I went around the rinks, I saw the hazard inherent in the net design.

Over time, the way the goals were slapped onto the ice over their moorings or put into storage on concrete would cause the piece of metal that had pierced me to rise and protrude, even without the net being lifted up. If other players—or my own kids—someday got hurt, I wouldn't have been able to look at myself in the mirror. I went back to Krass, my lawyer.

I didn't want to sue the league. My lawyer's advice was to name the city of Hartford, which owned the Civic Center; the Civic Center Authority, for its poor maintenance of the net; and the net manufacturer, Jayfro, for the design. But, as predicted by Krass, the NHL became a party to the litigation in December 1983, and ultimately, that flange—useful only to deflect pucks up so that they wouldn't fly back out of the net too fast for goal judges' detection—was replaced by a big, heavy pad that had no point. In an era when players would drive the net with little fear of being called for goaltender interference, the game became safer.

I had accomplished my objective. In 1985, I was offered a lump-sum settlement of $70,000, three-fifths of it coming from Jayfro.

The cost to the NHL was only $14,000. I opted for a structured plan of $24,000 a year for 10 years, payments to begin in 1990, when I thought my playing days likely would be completed.

Only by incredible good fortune were they not over in 1980, but getting myself back on track was an uphill climb. I was sadly mistaken that my return could help the Whalers save their 1980–81 season. We didn't win one of the first six games I played. Blackburn was fired and replaced by Larry Pleau, who had been a Whaler from day one of the franchise in 1972–73 and a teammate for my first two years there. Nice guy, Larry, back then.

We were in Washington with five games remaining when Pleau walked into the locker room and said he was not running the pre-game skate.

"I gave [Baldwin] an ultimatum to either fire me or make me GM, too," he announced. "I think I have proven myself."

At that point, we were 4–9–2 since Pleau had taken over as coach, and we ended up completing the year with 60 points, 11 out of a play-off spot. Pleau had proved about as much as I had by coming back too soon, but at least it was summer. I had only gained back seven of the 20 pounds I'd lost, and so I planned two full months of training, starting in July, to prepare myself for the upcoming season.

My schedule was interrupted, however. Five days before the opening of the Team USA camp for the Canada Cup, I was at Ginger's mother's place in Melbourne Beach, Florida, when I got an invitation over the phone from Lou Nanne, the GM of the U.S. team.

I don't remember why he was calling so late. Neither does Nanne. But I said yes, drove my car 1,000 miles back to Hartford, packed my clothes and hockey equipment and caught a flight to Minneapolis-St. Paul. I wanted to compete for my country against the best hockey-playing nations in the world—Canada, the Soviet Union, Czechoslovakia, Sweden and Finland—but I had been preparing to play in mid-September, not early August.

One could measure the progress of hockey in the United States by comparing its Canada Cup rosters every three to five years. Unlike the first tournament in 1976, by 1981 we had a full complement of at least above-average NHL players. We didn't have nearly the scoring power of the Canadians and Soviets, though, which was probably why coach Bob Johnson used me on left wing with Dave Christian, a good offensive player who had been a key to the U.S. Olympic gold medal at Lake Placid the previous year.

Our pairing was a bad break for Dave. I still had little energy or strength and quickly realized it had been a mistake to come. We beat Sweden and upset Czechoslovakia without much help from me. In a 4–4 tie with Finland, somebody on defense got hurt and I made a couple of nice plays filling in, but in the semifinal game against Canada, I was back on the wing.

We were overmatched, losing 4–1. I was extremely disappointed with my play, and wanted to be out of there so badly that I drove home from Montreal after the game instead of waiting for my morning flight. The only thing my participation had accomplished was to remind me I was in trouble for the NHL season.

When I reported to camp, there already were signs Pleau was putting the Whalers in peril, too.

Boutette, who provided the grind for our good first line with Rogers and Stoughton, had gone to Pittsburgh as compensation for Pleau's signing of free-agent goalie Greg Millen. Rogers, who had scored 100 points in consecutive years, was no longer playing with Stoughton during training camp.

"They're going to trade me," Rogers told me.

"C'mon, they can't," I said. "You're too important."

But four days before the opener, Pleau dealt Rogers to the Rangers for defenseman Chris Kotsopoulos and Doug Sulliman. Sulliman was supposed to replace Boutette, but now we had no first line, and since both Garrett and Millen were capable, it wasn't really an upgrade in goal.

Garrett, however, knew his days were numbered. When Pleau said he was going to trade John because he was too friendly with Greg and wasn't competing for his job, John begged the GM not to send him and his elementary school-aged children to French-speaking Quebec. Pleau traded him there a day or two later.

Ron Francis, our number-one pick, obviously could play right away in the NHL, but Pleau sent him back to junior for the first 21 games. So much for the youth movement. The two previous first-rounders, Ray Allison and Fred Arthur, had gone to Philadelphia for 31-year-old Rick MacLeish.

When we won only three of our first 21 games in 1981–82, Pleau was wild to change the perceived country-club atmosphere. He probably thought I chaired the membership committee.

A year earlier, my 30 minutes a game of ice time had been a piece of cake, but now, 18 to 20 had become a killer. I had little power or endurance. Once you lose your upper-body strength, you lose everything, including the push in your legs, and there was no organized training program to help rebuild it.

Most of the players didn't trust the Whalers' medical staff. When I complained about my back problems, which had been ongoing since Houston, to Dr. Turco, he said they were a result of poor posture. When he told me that on the day I had just had a myelogram, I got up from my wheelchair and walked out, eventually finding my own doctor in Port Washington, on Long Island, who gave me injections that helped.

Another time, the team dentist, gracious enough to stay late when a sudden abscess threatened a summer cruise that Ginger and I were departing on early the next morning, worked on me with a cigarette dangling from his lips, the lengthening ash teetering over my wide-eyed face.

Had that ash dropped in my mouth, it wouldn't have been the only bad taste I was being forced to endure. It was the only time in my career I ever knew that the coach didn't like me, and it was turning into my hardest year in hockey for another, more personal, reason. Ginger was having a difficult pregnancy.

After Travis's birth, she had suffered a miscarriage while we were on a cruise. She was hemorrhaging this time, too, spending much of the last six months in bed and making this likely our last child. We knew we were getting a breech baby, which probably meant inducing labor. But with only three road games in a 20-day period from November into early December, I liked my chances of being there for the birth.

At Ginger's last checkup, her obstetrician—a substitute because her regular doctor had suffered a heart attack—said she wasn't dilated. I was happy to hear that. The Whalers, who more often than not flew the day of the game, had decided to take us a night early to a December 2 game in Toronto for dinner and team bonding.

When I got back to my hotel room that evening, the phone message light was flashing. The cesarean-section delivery of Azia (pronounced like the continent Asia) Candace Howe had gone routinely, but Ginger had some post-birthing complications and had to spend about a week in the hospital.

For our daughter's middle name, Ginger honored her sister, who had tragically died from a combination of alcohol and prescription drugs five years earlier. For a first name, Ginger had two requirements—that it be different and practically impossible to abbreviate. At the birth of our first-born, Travis Gordon, she had been upset when my elated mother referred to him as "The Big TG" to a reporter.

I, meanwhile, was compiling names for Pleau, mostly uttered under my breath. He had gone from being a real nice guy to one of the worst I ever met in my life. The fines and threats to my teammates were only making the Whalers worse. By Christmas, we had won just eight games.

As other defensemen failed or were injured, the recall of Marty late in the season had become an annual event. Larry Kish, the coach of our farm team in Binghamton, had learned to rely on my brother and make him feel important to the team. And since it was clear Marty had no future in Hartford, he didn't want to be called up to take Pleau's abuse. It took the heart out of him.

Going around the room in one postgame tirade, the coach/GM told both my brother and winger Ray Neufeld that they "would never play another game in this uniform as long as I live."

Neufeld, a Whaler draft choice in his third year who would become a solid 25-goal-a-year scorer, actually replied, "I don't want to play here; please send me to the minors," even though in Binghamton his salary would be cut in half.

My father wasn't a happy camper in the front office, either, not that he ever complained to me. Because Pleau didn't want him on the ice helping out, practice times and locations—sometimes at the Civic Center, sometimes at a rink in Bolton, Connecticut—were not forthcoming. After I started to give him the right information, Dad was told he couldn't be on the ice.

I didn't understand why the Whalers wouldn't want his wisdom. He had 32 years' worth of advice for anyone who asked. While playing junior in Toronto, I went through a four- or five-game stretch where I wasn't putting points up. So I called Dad, who was in his first retirement, for advice, and he and Mom drove up to watch. I did a lot of good things that game, but still scored no points.

"You're doing the defenseman's job for him, going into his strength," Dad counseled.

"Next time, stay next to the boards and make him commit. If he jumps out early towards you, you can cut inside him. If he doesn't, the worst that happens with your speed is that you carry behind the net and make a play from there."

Basically, he was telling me to move 10 feet closer to the boards. The next game, I think I scored three goals.

I also remember these tips from my father about defending: "Put your stick either under the guy's arm or in front of his face. When the guy flinches, take the puck away. And if you are going to get a slashing penalty, don't just mindlessly whack the guy; hit him on the bone above the elbow pad or on the knee or the ankle. Make the two minutes worth your while."

Who thinks of these things? And who on the struggling Hartford Whalers wouldn't have listened to Gordie Howe? Instead, I had to hear Ricky Ley, who had become the coach of the defensemen after an injury forced him off the ice, reprimand us for being outhit by the Capitals in a game in which we dominated 3–0 late in the first period.

"We've had the puck the whole period," I couldn't help but yell back. "Do you want me to give it to them so we can have more hits?"

I had learned to play defense on my own, with no help from Ley and certainly no understanding from Pleau that I was giving the Whalers everything I had—even if, for most of that season, it wasn't nearly enough.

Hearing rumors and knowing he wanted to get rid of me as badly as I wanted out, I put together a list of my dream destinations—the Rangers, Islanders, Flyers, Bruins—and sat down with Pleau.

I asked why the Whalers wanted to trade me. During the course of the conversation, Pleau said, "We figure you have made so much money in your career, you want to get out of the game. I know some people who can line you up in business and you'll be fine for the rest of your life."

I'm thinking, "Where is this coming from?" Did he think the only way to get rid of me was to talk me into retiring at age 25?

"I don't know if you've looked, but I have a no-trade clause," I finally said. "If you want to trade me, you have to go through me. Here are four teams. Make your calls."

Eventually, I contacted Bruin GM Harry Sinden myself to tell him I would come play for him for a cut in pay. I knew that, in Boston, those were the magic words. Harry called me back a few days later and said, "They want two first-rounders and more. I just can't do it."

"Thanks for trying," I said.

I talked to my dad a few times about wanting out. He said, "The only way to do that is to play well. If you don't, other teams won't want you."

That became my motivation. When my endurance finally started to come back in the final month of the season, it made no difference for our team, which won only five of our last 27 games. But if I played well, it might at least help me. Eight of those contests were against the four teams on my wish list.

At the end of the season, Mom invited Baldwin, Pleau, Marty and me to her home, hoping to clear the air. Pleau denied saying what he had to Marty, promised him a chance to make the lineup next season, and everybody said "Okay" until I said, "No, it's not okay."

When I was younger, I punched holes in walls and kicked doors after losses. I had gotten over that, but not my hatred for losing. I was tired of it, saw the Whalers going nowhere, and couldn't take all the lying, so I said, "Get me out of here."

I didn't hold my breath. Early that summer, Pleau told me he didn't think they would be trading me. I remember saying something like "You'll be sorry you didn't. I'll badmouth this organization to every young player you bring into this team." I was trying desperately to be moved.

In August, just before I walked out my door for a three-day fishing trip with Marty to Montauk, Long Island, there was a message to call the Whalers office. Was this it? Apparently not. When I phoned in, I was told it could wait until I got back. On August 19, I called again and was told to come to Pleau's office.

He told me that if I would waive the no-trade clause, he had a deal with Philadelphia. I was so happy to hear it, I didn't even care to ask who the Whalers were getting.

Pleau gave me the numbers of Keith Allen, the Flyers' GM, and Ed Snider, their owner. I walked down the hall to Dad's office and told him what was happening. He was really stunned. For once, they had kept him out of the loop for a good reason—his son was being traded—and I was ready to do cartwheels and probably was a little insensitive to his feelings. We would be going our own ways for the first time in nine years. But I didn't really feel he would be working for the Whalers much longer.

Allen, a late-season call-up on the 1955 Red Wings team that won the Stanley Cup a month before I was born, knew Dad and talked to him, too, after me. All I had wanted to hear was that one of the best organizations in the NHL wanted me, and when I spoke to Snider, he asked for a second to finish swallowing a bite of his peanut butter sandwich and then put his money where his mouth was.

Because of the deferred dollars in my contract, the Whalers had paid me only $625,000 for the first five years and were passing a balance of $1,375,000 to the Flyers for the next five. Pissed me off. Snider asked if $50,000 from the Whalers would make my anger go away.

"A hundred thousand would be more like it," I countered. We agreed to $75,000, and Snider said it would be taken care of—which I assumed meant he would press Baldwin for the money, which was satisfactory revenge on the Whalers for me.

I also expressed to Snider that I had just taken on a big obligation with a new, yet-to-be-completed home and wanted my family to jump into Philadelphia as soon as I did. Snider said the Flyers would carry the cost of the house until it was sold and make up any potential shortfall.

Jackpot. Sure seemed like I was going where I was wanted. Later, I found out even more about how much. Ken Linseman, whom the Flyers were moving to Edmonton in what was a three-way deal, with Hartford getting defenseman Risto Siltanen—was dating Snider's daughter Lindy.

"I feel like I just sold my son to Siberia," Snider told the newspapers. But it turns out I had been desired by the Flyers for a long time. Snider had asked Baldwin, his former ticket manager, to let Philadelphia know if the Whalers ever wanted to trade me.

Allen, who had three defensemen on his wish list that summer—Rod Langway, Rob Ramage and me—was preparing to walk on the deal because Pleau, who also was getting a number-one pick, wasn't budging on his demands for prospect Greg Adams. Snider pushed Allen to relent.

I called Ginger and told her to go the basement and tell the workmen to stop. We were going to Philadelphia.

Snider was not likely to get as attached to that house as was my wife. She was all upset at first, and on one of the happiest days of my life, I guess I didn't want to hear it.

"You can stay and keep your house," I said. "I'm leaving."

On the way home, I stopped at the Bel Compo Golf Club to tell the pro, Tony Rotondo.

"Wow, you are going near Pine Valley, one of the greatest golf courses in the world," he said. "You gotta get on that course."

Cool. But bitter as I had become in Hartford, I didn't need any more sweeteners to go to Philadelphia.

CHAPTER 9

Flying Low

On the initial face-off on my first day at the Philadelphia Flyers' training camp in Portland, Maine, Ron Flockhart stole the puck from Behn Wilson and scored. Wilson immediately flattened Flockhart from behind and pounced on his back, all the while screaming at him, "Nobody touches my puck!"

Before the session was over, Glen Cochrane put Ilkka Sinisalo, who had just scored on a rebound, into the boards and out for six weeks with a broken collarbone.

The Flyers were beating the tar out of each other *in practice.* Guess I wasn't in Hartford anymore. I was part of a different animal.

My new teammates were pretty friendly guys, as long as you didn't touch their pucks. The only player I previously knew well was Ray Allison, who had been traded to Philadelphia from the Whalers a summer earlier. Bill Barber and his wife, Jenny, picked up Ginger and me at the airport on our first visit after the trade and took us for dinner at Bobby Chez in South Jersey, after which Barber set up a get-together with a few players who lived locally. Bob Dailey, my captain with the Marlies—sadly, about to announce his retirement because of multiple leg fractures he sustained while crashing the boards for an icing touch-up early the previous season—was kind enough to put me up at his home for 10 days prior to the start of training camp.

When I stopped by the practice rink at the University of Pennsylvania in late summer, Pat Croce, the Flyers' strength and conditioning trainer, was so welcoming. He invited me to lie down on the weight bench in my street clothes and see how many times I could lift 190 pounds—I think it was three. Seeing as practically the entire team was there even before official training camp began, I guess Croce wanted to make me one of the guys. Having never seen organized off-season workouts before, this was the new preparation reality for a 27-year-old, nine-year veteran accustomed to doing just his solitary push-ups, sit-ups, wood chopping and stationary-bike work.

From playing against them, I knew that the Flyers, two seasons removed from being in the Stanley Cup final, weren't the fastest, youngest or deepest team anymore. But I could immediately see why they were still good: the expectations of their management and players.

When we won our opener 9–5 over Quebec—I had a goal and an assist and looked pretty snappy in my Cooperalls, the long pants the Flyers had pioneered in the NHL the previous season—Bobby Clarke played that game like it was the Stanley Cup final. I wasn't surprised by that, of course. The year before, after listing Philadelphia to Larry Pleau as one of the places I was begging to go, Hartford played the Flyers, and Clarke was the guy I felt I had to impress. I could skate around him easily, but however far he had to come to catch me, as soon as I made my play, I would get a cross-check in the back. There was no quit in him, and I wanted to prove there was none in me.

Whenever the Flyers went down, they went down hard. After winning five of my first six with them, we were on our way home from a 3–1 loss at New Jersey when Brian Propp chuckled about something in the back of the bus. Seven or eight heads snapped around and gave him a snarly look. We had played pretty well that night, but on a team with Clarke and Paul Holmgren, there could be nothing funny about losing; it was just not acceptable. In Philly, there were some horseshit wins, but never a good loss.

That said, it was no secret around the league that the Flyers' mindset was not always properly channeled. They had given up a league-record 102 power-play goals the season before and lost their first-round series 3–1 to the Rangers. Largely because of injuries—after Dailey quit, Jimmy Watson retired during camp because of back problems—Frank Bathe was the only defenseman left from the team in the 1980 final. I was one of three new parts on the blue line.

Brad McCrimmon, a number-one pick by Boston three years earlier, had struggled after a promising rookie year and been traded to Philadelphia for goalie Pete Peeters. Miroslav Dvorak was one of the first veterans the Czechoslovakian Ice Hockey Federation, trying to discourage the defection of younger stars, had allowed to come to the NHL.

Brad Marsh, a heart-and-soul guy the Flyers acquired the previous year to begin their defensive overhaul, ignored language barriers and became inseparable from Cookie Dvorak, who was an icon in his country but a kid in a North American candy store. He got off the bus from an exhibition game holding a beer in one hand and a cigarette in the other, proclaiming: "Budweiser. Marlboro. Me love America!"

Well-schooled and disciplined like all players from behind the Iron Curtain, Dvorak still had a sense of adventure and humor. One day, he passed up his usual safe-outlet pass, circled the net, tried to stickhandle around a forechecker 20 feet in front of our goal, got stripped from the puck and gave up a scoring chance.

"Cookie, what the fuck were you doing?" Coach Bob McCammon asked on the bench.

"Dipsy-doodle," Dvorak said. "Good for fans!"

That season, some of them were disguised as empty second-level seats at the Spectrum, not the franchise custom. On a team with three future Hall of Famers over the age of 30—Clarke, Barber and Darryl Sittler—the clock was ticking. I had been brought in to help get Philly back on top in a hurry.

Very early, McCammon called in my partner, Glen Cochrane, and me for a meeting. "We just want you to play like you did last year," the coach said to me.

"If I do, I'm going to retire," I said. "If you were happy with the way I played last year, you'll *really* be happy this year."

McCammon, first nicknamed Cagey during his days in the minor pro International Hockey League, then looked at Cocker.

"Your job is obvious," the coach said, and then pointed at me. "Nobody touches him."

"Don't worry," Cocker said as we walked out of the office. "Nobody is going to touch you."

He kept his word. In a game at Los Angeles, a King went to finish his check on me and missed, but a half-undressed Cocker—he always peeled his jersey and whatever else he could get off before he fought—was chasing the guy down the ice. "I didn't hit him, I didn't hit him!" the player yelled. After receiving 15 to 20 body blows a game for Hartford, I was thoroughly enjoying Glen as a partner.

Cocker didn't take too many hits without retaliating. But with him staying at home, and me jumping into the attack when there was an opportunity, we were a good pairing that year.

When McCammon yanked Rick St. Croix after five goals during a rout in Buffalo and put Pelle Lindbergh in net, our decent start quickly turned into a roll. The next night, Lindbergh beat the Rangers, always an endearing act in Philly.

Pelle, a really likable kid, had legs almost as quick as I was to extol to the media the virtues of being a Flyer. Whenever asked, I was so exuberant in my praise of the organization that Jay Snider, Ed's son and the team vice president, called me in. After pledging his support of my lawsuit against the NHL to get the nets changed, which I really appreciated, Jay asked me to tone down my praises. Seems I was hurting the feelings of the Sniders' good friend Howard Baldwin, the Hartford boss.

I hadn't been trashing the Whalers, just talking up the Flyers. But I soon received the money Ed Snider had promised to get me from the Whalers to make up some of what Hartford had deferred for five seasons. My lips became sealed about how happy I was to be in Philadelphia. But I have decided not to carry to my grave the identity of the teammate who, during a Pollyanna gag-gift exchange at Christmas, gave Clarke, 33, a retirement home brochure.

"I don't get it," the proud 14-year veteran demanded to know as my eyes darted around the room to escape detection. "Who gave me this?" I was just the new guy; why did I have to draw the franchise icon? Why couldn't I have gotten Frank Bathe?

It would be absurd for me to take credit for firing up Clarke, the ultimate self-starter, so it probably was a coincidence that, two days after Christmas, his hat trick in Detroit put us into first place in the Patrick Division. With a 3–1 win in Chicago, we finished a perfect six-game trip and stretched the winning streak to 10 before a couple of kicks canned our good fortune.

Or, should I say, practically everybody but Barber's good fortune. First, he missed 14 games with a partial MCL tear, then had the captaincy taken from him because McCammon wanted Clarke—who had given it up when he had become a playing assistant coach under Pat Quinn a few years before—to have the job back. Barber kept plugging. Against the Blackhawks on January 15, he dove to prevent a breakaway and took a skate boot in the jaw, breaking it.

Sometime during that same game, I lost my edge cutting to the net and also took a skate, this one to the back. When I came out for the next period, I felt sluggish, which didn't go away during our win the next night in New York and was worse two nights later in Washington, where our 11–0–1 unbeaten streak ended.

When I got off the bus from Landover after 1 a.m. and went home—we were renting Reggie Leach's place—it wasn't just the pastel-blue toilet bowl that made my urine look funny. When I turned on the light, it was rust-colored. I immediately called the team doctor, Jeff Hartzell. "Drink some water, and if the color turns red the next time, call me," he said. "Otherwise, see you at 8 a.m."

Forty-five minutes later, it was red, so Hartzell told me to come in at 7 a.m. and get some rest in the meantime. Try that when *your* urine is bright red. It turned out that I had a lacerated kidney, causing toxins to build up in my body and sap my energy. Hartzell referred me to a kidney specialist at Pennsylvania Hospital, who ordered me to bed for seven days.

Barber was taking all his nourishment through a straw. Lindbergh was lost to a sprained wrist suffered in a 5–2 loss against the Soviet national team—it was embarrassing how they kept calling penalties on them to keep us in the game—but the Flyers' roll was barely interrupted. Bob Froese came up from the minors to replace Lindbergh and stoned the three-time champion Islanders, 1–0 in Uniondale, New York, on a goal by Sittler.

Darryl's feet had slowed a bit by the time I became his teammate, but at age 32 his preparation and conditioning had him on his way to a 43-goal season, the second-best of his career. After being persecuted out of Toronto by owner Harold Ballard the previous season, Sittler, like me, was thrilled to be appreciated again and in a winning atmosphere. When Pelle returned to shut out the Kings 2–0 in Los Angeles, we were 18–1–2 in our last 21.

But when Lindbergh lost his hair to the rookie shaving ritual during our layover in Southern California, he simultaneously lost his confidence. After giving up seven goals in half of the All-Star Game in Uniondale—four to Gretzky—the cap he wore couldn't hide his embarrassment. It was a typical all-star game—with virtually no checking and the goalie's back left uncovered—but I couldn't console him, and he started to struggle.

I wasn't doing great, either. The kidney laceration had left me lethargic when I returned after four games. Barber had lost weight and was weak, and then his play was questioned publicly by McCammon, the kind of thing that should always be said in private, particularly about a player of Bill's stature.

Cagey had an idea I found beneficial, bringing Ed Van Impe, a mainstay defensive defenseman from the Flyers' Cup teams, onto the ice at a practice. "What could I teach you?" Van Impe asked. "You may win the Norris Trophy this year."

Plenty, I said. For two and a half seasons, I had been relying on my speed and instincts to play defense without learning the fundamentals of the position. Van Impe told me that when it was necessary to back up, you should do it directly to the goalpost. That way, when you pivot 180 degrees, no one can beat you to the net. Eddie also explained that on two-on-ones, the defenseman can dictate who he wants the shooter to be by taking the pass away and trusting the goalie to do his job. Simple, effective stuff, a lot of which had not occurred to me.

McCammon's practices, which periodically included east-west (scrimmages) instead of drills, were not very technical or demanding and started to catch up to us as the playoffs approached and the intensity picked up. When, inevitably, things start to go poorly, there has to be a confidence in a system to fall back upon, which is why good teams still win on bad nights.

When we lost for the first time in four games against Herb Brooks's small, quick Rangers, 8–2 at Madison Square Garden, their speed broke us down. "Nobody hit their Smurfs all night," McCammon complained famously, but as doubts set in and our aggressiveness lagged a little or became misdirected, we weren't in good position to take the body.

We hadn't lost to the three-time champion Islanders in five meetings, but five days after the Rangers loss, our loosening screws fell out in a 9–2 loss at Uniondale to a team that was in the habit of getting better as a season went along. Usually, though, Denis Potvin, Mike Bossy and Bryan Trottier didn't need the help they received from referee Wally Harris to jump up 5–0 after the first period. The calls were slanted like I had never seen before from an NHL official.

"Wally, what's going on?" I asked him before the start of the second period.

"I'm retiring at the end of this season, and this is the last Flyers game I ever will referee," he said. "This team has been on my case for years and I'm sticking it to them tonight, that's what this is. Look at that bench."

I looked over, and Cagey and most everyone were yelling obscenities, even after the 15-minute intermission. I said to myself, "Kind of see what you mean."

In our final 20 games, we barely played over .500 (10–9–1). Still, on the last weekend, one could easily believe we had just become bored with our big lead and knew it was time to put on our playoff faces.

The Flyers called up Dave Poulin, an undrafted center out of Notre Dame who had been signed out of Sweden on the recommendation of Ted Sator, a guest power-skating instructor at our training camp the previous fall. In Poulin's first NHL game, against his hometown Toronto Maple Leafs, Dave scored on his first two shots. We won that one and dominated the Islanders in game 80, so it may have looked like we were going to be okay.

But almost from the first shift of our best-of-five first-rounder against the Rangers, we were in trouble. McCammon, spooked by their speed in two late-season losses, ordered a passive forecheck, which left some of our slower guys flat-footed as the Rangers jumped to a 4–0 lead.

I set up two goals in the 5–3 loss, but was minus-2 and played like it. For almost three months, the effects of the kidney laceration had left me playing nothing like I had been beforehand. It also was my first playoff series in the NHL where we were expected to win, and I probably was too pumped up for my own good. I wasn't performing at the level that either I or the Flyers wanted.

McCammon, who got scolded by Snider privately for not having the team ready and publicly by Clarke for the cautious game plan, took the brakes off us in game two. We were much better, hitting every Ranger that moved for the first 15 minutes and jumping up 1–0 on a power-play goal by Propp. But the Rangers didn't flinch, and two of our mistakes wound up behind Lindbergh, who was in no mental state to stand on his head and save us.

Nevertheless, Sinisalo, set up by Poulin, who was in his fourth game as a Flyer and still by far our best player, tied the game 2–2 early in the third period. We had a chance to even the series and perhaps get our confidence back until, on a simple two-on-two—Cochrane and me against Rob McClanahan and Mark Pavelich—I made the most haunting mistake of my career.

Cocker had McClanahan lined up, but I drifted too far that way. Pavelich, one of the few guys too quick for me to recover against, had the room he needed to take McClanahan's pass, go in alone and around Lindbergh for a deposit.

Pavelich then sprung Anders Hedberg on a two-on-one—hadn't I already lost enough playoff games to Hedberg in the WHA?—and Reijo Ruotsalainen cranked one under the crossbar to make it 4–2.

Tim Kerr, dressing for the first time since February, was almost our secret weapon, having played so little because of one injury after another for three years. He scored and got us back to within a goal. We were all around Ranger goalie Ed Mio in the final minutes, but I missed the top corner by inches just before the buzzer. After consecutive losses at home, we were one game from elimination by a team that had been 26 points inferior to us during the regular season.

There was little confidence, discipline or structure to save us in game three in New York. Lindbergh had to stop two early breakaways as the Madison Square Garden fans waved stuffed Smurf toys. We were code blue, too. The Flyers were down 2–0 when I got slew-footed by Kent-Erik Andersson and went headfirst into the boards.

In the training room, our doctors and Everett Borghesani, the team dentist, were all around me while I was insisting I could play.

"What is 100 minus 7?" I was asked.

"Ninety-three," I said.

"What is 93 minus 7?" was the next question. To count on my fingers was too obvious, so I looked at my skates and tried to envision my toes. That's how screwed up you are with a concussion. Meanwhile, Behn Wilson was standing behind the doctors mouthing "86" and I was mouthing back to him, "What?"

"That's it, you're done," one of the doctors said. I spent the night in a hotel room with Borghesani, who woke me up every hour to make sure I was okay, and then got me home the next day.

I was spared recollection of the gruesome details of our 9–3 loss, but today I still suffer pain from the worst series defeat I ever experienced. Following a 106-point season, we had shown nothing, almost to a man, in losing to an archrival that skated rings around us. Wherever I went in Philly or South Jersey that summer, I felt like a miserable failure. It is tough to walk tall when you feel like you have let yourself, your teammates and your fans down.

Finishing second behind Washington's Rod Langway in the Norris Trophy balloting was neither consolation nor disappointment. The voters got it right. Langway was more important to the success of the Capitals in a turnaround year for that franchise than I had proved to be for the Flyers as we failed down the stretch. I really had played better with the Whalers before my accident, but because I'd been in Hartford nobody noticed.

Snider accused the Rangers of tanking the regular season to get ready for the playoffs while McCammon second-guessed himself for letting Clarke, Barber and Sittler run down. So our age and approach to the regular season became the big issue.

When McCammon got an offer to become coach and GM of the Penguins, Ed Snider decided to push Keith Allen, who had put together the Stanley Cup teams, to a senior advisory capacity and give Cagey both jobs. So, during my second year in Philadelphia, McCammon was on the ice for fewer practices then he had been in the first, which meant more east-west games. In an attempt to have more structured drills, Clarke and Sittler tried to organize them on their own, but Cagey would come out, take the extra pucks away and order more east-west.

McCammon's strength was as a personnel guy. And as we were back in short pants—the NHL had passed a uniformity rule—there was much evidence during the 1983–84 season that our coach was taking a long-term view. Poulin and Ron Sutter, our number-one pick in 1982, were playing a lot, which moved Sittler to the wing and meant Clarke was no longer the number-one center.

A finally healthy Kerr was on a 50-goal pace, leading a depth chart at right wing that included Sinisalo and Rich Sutter—Ron's twin, whom we had picked up from Pittsburgh in a deal for Flockhart. Holmgren had been getting fourth-line time until he was traded (for

Paul Guay) to his hometown North Stars, a nice thing for McCammon to do. He also had just given Paul a contract extension as thanks for his years of service. But not so polite was the failure to inform the traded player before announcing it to the media.

Preferring not to upset the team before the game with Minnesota, Cagey's plan was to tell Holmgren afterward, but, disappointed that he wasn't dressing, Paul didn't stick around. Minnesota GM Lou Nanne leaked the news, and Holmgren received it from his car radio, more egg on the face of McCammon.

Clarkie's best friend on the team was gone. But he had grown tight with Poulin and still had strong followers like Marsh and Sittler. Despite the fact that Clarke led by example and seldom spoke up, it still was his locker room.

Even in his 15th year, Bobby was the first guy to the rink for practice and games. I don't think he touched a drop of alcohol during the season. I would come rolling into the locker room at 5:30, an hour and a half before warmup, and he was fully dressed and ready to go.

Clarke openly questioned McCrimmon's dedication, and there was friction sometimes between the two. When Brad and Proppie, who had been tight going back to their junior days in Brandon, Manitoba. had gone out one night—it wasn't the night before a game—Clarkie didn't like it and let them know. When they went back at Clarke, Sittler chimed in on Bob's side.

I've heard worse in locker rooms, but I've been in tighter ones, too. Still, there never was a shortage of effort on that team. And because Froese played well, we stayed out of long losing streaks even as Lindbergh continued to struggle. In a February game against Vancouver, Pelle tried to clear a dump-in, got his feet tangled and kicked in the tying goal. It got worse on the winning goal, when he fanned on a slower-than-molasses deflection while falling on his backside. Pelle was so screwed up and the fans on him so much my heart went out to him, but he wasn't the only Flyer not playing well.

Both Marsh and McCrimmon endured benchings. I was just average enough on defense to get myself a trial on the wing for 10 games, which I believe was at Clarke's urging. When I didn't do much there, McCammon moved me back to defense.

"What's today's date?" the coach asked me at about the midpoint of the season. When I gave it to him, he said he just wanted to make sure I knew the season had started, his sarcastic way of letting me know he wasn't happy with my play.

I wasn't thrilled about it, either, and I remember Barber, my road roommate, making clear his displeasure with me after I couldn't get out of bed with a high temperature for a February game at Madison Square Garden. He witnessed my vomiting and countless visits to the toilet, but after the game—we beat the Rangers for the first time in nine tries on Kerr's goal in overtime—he let me know I was a Flyer and should not have let illness stop me from playing. Bill was a good friend and leader, wanting me to demand more of myself.

But I wasn't blaming the mediocre season I was having on physical problems. Over the summer, I had recovered from my kidney laceration, but my ice time was being reduced because Cochrane and I were not playing at the same level as the season before. When he took a penalty, I would sit on the bench until he returned from the box. The year before, McCammon would mix his pairs. I thought I would play better with more ice time, but it's not my style to go to a coach and ask.

Clarke caught some kind of respiratory thing and was coughing on the bench. McCammon, determined to have a fresher team going into the playoffs, ordered March vacations for Bob, Barber, Sittler and Dvorak. It wasn't a terrible idea, but Cagey didn't execute it well.

He announced a plan to sit Clarke for five games, then Barber, Sittler and Dvorak simultaneously for four. "It's like arguing with your wife—you can't win," said Clarke, who wasn't scoring but was too proud to admit he could use a break. When McCammon moved up the starting date for Clarke's hiatus to the next game, some members of the press suggested Bob was being banished for speaking out against McCammon's authority.

So the whole thing went over like a lead balloon. Privately, Clarke thought it was the worst thing anybody had ever done to him, and I know Billy, who was playing the best he had in a year and a half, didn't like it, either, no matter how diplomatic he was publicly. Told to use the time away to build up strength in his knee, Barber went to the Poconos and blew it out doing Pat Croce–ordered squat thrusts. Not only was he out for the year, but it turned out Bill never would play again.

To our rescue at the end of a challenging season came five games in the last nine against the Penguins and Devils, who were terrible. We won eight straight and, going into the final weekend, actually had a chance to take the division title that our owner had announced the previous April never was worth winning again.

Snider didn't have to worry about it. In the final regular-season game, with home ice on the line in a first-round best-of-five series against Washington, we got shut down 3–1 by the Caps—a cold bucket of water on a very quiet Spectrum—and finished third behind Washington. It was clear they were a lot better than us defensively.

We had two leads in game one, but couldn't hold them and lost 4–2. For game two, McCammon took Poulin off our big line with Propp and Kerr and put him with Clarke, who put us ahead 2–1, but we broke down again repeatedly and the Caps pulled away to win 6–2.

Before game three at the Spectrum, somebody phoned in a death threat on McCammon. No, it wasn't Clarke. Our trainer, David "Sudsy" Settlemyre, was joking about the peril, so when Cagey took his place behind the bench, we all ducked. It was just a little gallows humor for a franchise about to go down miserably in the playoffs for the third straight spring.

The Caps were up 1–0 when McCammon sent out tough guy Daryl Stanley to attack Mike Gartner. All that accomplished was to give Stanley two extra minutes as the instigator. After Washington scored on the power play, we fell apart again. McCammon's days with the Flyers ended with a 5–1 loss and chants of "Bob must go!"

When Jay Snider, who had become team president that year, asked McCammon to leave the bench and become GM only, Cagey, determined to live down three straight first-round flops, resisted. He and Jay agreed to disagree and McCammon resigned. I think he knew that whenever Clarke retired, whatever role he would take with the organization would leave McCammon's own position untenable.

What I didn't know was that Snider would immediately offer the GM's job to Clarke and that he would accept. Because Bobby had played so well in the playoffs—he was our best player—I was surprised when he took it, but when I thought about it, not really. He was cramping so badly during that series that he could barely walk after games. The price of continuing to play was becoming too high for him.

Among the first calls I received with the news that Clarke was our new boss was from McCrimmon. "Clarke is GM; I had better get serious," he said, and even if Brad giggled as he said it, no joke was intended.

The laughs were on the Flyers every April. Even if this loss had been less shocking than the one to the Rangers the year before, I still was just as embarrassed. The Flyers' streak of playoff losses was at nine. Counting the Whalers' loss to the Canadiens my first year in the NHL, so was mine.

When Jay Snider handed Clarke a list of coaching candidates compiled by Allen and assistant general manager Gary Darling—some of them already interviewed—the new GM knew better than anyone he had to select one who would provide discipline and accountability.

In May, I lifted my head from where it had been hanging in shame to answer the phone. It was my brother Marty. After playing regularly as essentially a loaner from Hartford to a Bruins conference finalist in 1982–83, he was very disappointed when the Bruins and new Whaler GM Emile Francis couldn't work out a deal to keep him in Boston. Marty had played 69 games for the Whalers in the just-completed 1983–84 season. But he had spent enough time in the American Hockey League over the last five years to develop sources.

"You had better be ready," he said. "The Flyers are hiring Mike Keenan as coach. In Rochester, they hated him so much, they signed a petition to get him fired. Good luck to you."

Marty hung up laughing.

The way I was feeling every April, I was ready. I just had no idea what to be ready for, having never seen an act like Mike Keenan's.

CHAPTER 10

Sudden Death

Better to be safe than sorry. After the first exhibition game of the 1984–85 season, Ilkka Sinisalo and I dutifully reported the mildest of groin pulls to trainer Dave Settlemyre, who put us on the excused-from-practice list he gave to the Flyers' new coach, Mike Keenan.

Two minutes later, the door flew open to the training room. "Get your fucking pampered ass out for practice!" Keenan screamed at Ilkka, unfortunate enough to be the first guy in sight.

I quietly dropped my ice pack, scurried out the back exit to the locker room and put on my gear. Suddenly, there was nothing wrong with a little groin pull that a good taping by Sudsy couldn't keep from getting worse. So much for our orders to notify the trainer about every injury, no matter how small. And so much for any comfort zone we had ever known as players.

"Personally, I have experienced a contagious phenomenon whereby the more I win, the more I want to win," Keenan had written in a questionnaire prepared for the coaching candidates by team president Jay Snider. "Nothing short of this objective is acceptable."

Keenan wanted to develop a team that thought like him. That

summer, he sent out a form asking each of us for our goals and our chances of reaching them. I met him for lunch at Kaminski's Bar and Grill in Cherry Hill, New Jersey, and said I wanted to win the Stanley Cup and Conn Smythe Trophy, and put my probability of success at 5 per cent. Since one team wins the Stanley Cup and one person the Conn Smythe every year, that seemed pragmatic to me. So was my request to Keenan for more ice time, because I had handled 30 minutes-plus per game in Hartford.

Mike referred me to a Dr. Steven Rosenberg, a psychologist whose name the coach had been given, to help me build my confidence. I agreed to go and Keenan said I would get my chance to play more, a promise he delivered on immediately by playing me all night in the first exhibition game. Great, I thought. Not so great was playing me close to eight straight nights. Keenan hadn't made that schedule, but he was using it to quickly learn something about each member of a team with a roster of many unknowns.

With Bob Clarke retired to become GM and Bill Barber out for the year following reconstructive knee surgery (he would never play again), the only surviving Flyer who had any playoff success in Philadelphia was Brian Propp, a rookie on the 1980 finalists. The 1984–85 team was largely being written off as being in transition, but I knew young veterans like Tim Kerr, Brad Marsh, Dave Poulin and Ron Sutter were character people. And despite the fact that Philadelphia had traded its first-round pick in 1983 for me, a year later we had three kids from that draft—Bob McCammon's only one as Flyers GM—who showed in camp they could play.

Right wing Rick Tocchet was a fireball, tough and cocky. Center Peter Zezel could shoot a puck. Left wing Derrick Smith was a big body who could skate all day and had good checking instincts. Just before the season, we would add a fourth kid, center-left wing Murray Craven, on a stunning and sad day.

Two nights before our opener, we were celebrating our survival of Keenan's boot camp at Kaminski's. Keenan took Darryl Sittler aside and told him what had seemed all along to be a fait accompli: he would be succeeding Clarke as captain of the Flyers. Darryl was told to prepare a speech to present the next day for the annual face-off luncheon at the Bellevue-Stratford Hotel.

When the program ended without an introduction of Sittler by emcee Gene Hart, the Flyers' play-by-play announcer, I was prepared to kid Gene about screwing something up for once in his life. He never missed anything. I wondered . . . maybe the program just ran long? Sittler, who had a *C* by his name on the team roster at every place setting, told reporters at post-luncheon interviews what a proud day it was.

After the bus ride back to the Coliseum, our practice facility in New Jersey, we got in our cars and went home—all except Darryl, who was called into Keenan's office by Clarke and told he had been traded to Detroit for Craven, the Red Wings' 1982 number-one draft choice, and left wing Joe Paterson. In seconds, Darryl crashed from living one of the best days of his life to having one of his worst. Keenan, who had bought a house in Sittler's development, gave him a lift home, where he sat with Mike on the front steps until Sittler's wife, Wendy, drove up with the keys, wondering why Darryl was crying.

Clarke had wanted to close the deal in the morning, but couldn't reach Detroit GM Jimmy Devellano until after the luncheon had started. That was understandable, but with a trade pending, there had to have been a way to delay the captaincy announcement, particularly one about a player who had done so much for the game. That said, by my 12th professional season, I had come to accept that if these types of things could happen to my dad, all of us were vulnerable. And I knew enough about Clarke after playing with him for two years to have faith that he thought he was doing what was right for the Flyers.

Darryl, who at first told the Red Wings he wasn't coming, called me a few days later to ask about living in Detroit. I knew his daughter was playing hockey, so I told him there were better programs in Michigan than South Jersey and that whatever bad impression visiting athletes received of downtown Detroit, the suburbs were beautiful, with good schools. I didn't really try to talk him into going—your heart has to be in it—but Darryl went and suffered a broken collarbone that limited him to only 61 games and 11 goals for a bad team. He retired at the end of the season. It wasn't the way you wanted it to end for him.

I was only a little surprised the next day when the Flyers named Dave Poulin, beginning his second full season, as the captain. Dave had built a strong relationship with Clarke, was calmer than I was, and proved quickly to be an excellent spokesperson and choice. Brad Marsh, a real Flyer, was a no-brainer for one assistant, and I was proud to be named the other. Without a Clarke, Barber and, suddenly, Sittler, we were definitely not being given token responsibilities for leadership.

Kerr scored late to get us a tie in the season opener at the Spectrum against Washington. Two nights later in Landover, Pelle Lindbergh—told he would be the number-one goalie during his summer meeting with Keenan—stood on his head for a period before I scored to start our comeback to a 4–2 win, earning us three points out of four against the team that had humiliated us the previous spring.

Two nights later in Montreal, we looked pretty much like seven sophomores, three rookies and a few veterans who had been losing in the playoffs for too long, falling 5–2. The next day's "optional" skate turned into a no-pucks, starts-and-stops torture session—Keenan's way of showing us that losing was no longer an option. The next game, we beat Vancouver 13–2.

Keenan's practices generally were not more than an hour, but they were high-tempo and extremely organized. We had our own water bottles, which was a first, but only 10 to 15 seconds between drills to use them. Mike was not really a systems guy, more a pressure-the-puck and don't-you-dare-lose kind of guy. His assistants—Ted Sator, who he kept on from McCammon's staff, and E.J. McGuire, who had been coaching at Brockport State in Western New York when he became an unpaid assistant of Mike's with the Rochester Americans—were two smart guys who provided Xs and Os and played good cop to Keenan's bad cop. McGuire took our pre-game video study to another level.

Keenan pushed more buttons than any coach I ever had seen.

Uncannily, he hit the right ones during a 17–4–5 start that stunned the NHL. We had gotten out of the blocks well in our two years under McCammon, too, but with an outlook refreshed by youth and veterans thriving with new responsibilities, this felt different.

My dad always had said the difference between a 10-goal and a 20-goal scorer was five minutes a game of ice time and work on the power play. I had gone from 24 and a half minutes a game the previous year to more than 32. My new partner, Brad McCrimmon, had recorded the highest fitness score of any player in camp, demonstrating that he had become more serious now that Clarke, never a fan of Brad's work or after-hours habits, was GM.

The Beast—McCrimmon's nickname from his days with the Brandon Wheat Kings, where he was a teammate of Propp's—was a muscular, hairy, tough, stubborn and proud guy who, I was learning, could be a soft puppy on the inside. Having grown apart from Karen, a girl from Western Canada he married too young, Brad acted like he couldn't care less about her. But that summer, he called and asked if we could talk. At a little South Jersey pizza place, Brad confided in me how much it bothered him that he had succeeded at everything in life but his marriage.

In that 1984–85 season, we were good friends becoming better friends, roommates on the road who spent most of our waking hours together. He was straightforward—an ultimate team player on a club loaded with them, and an absolute man of his word whom I could trust with anything. Very early in our partnership, I screwed up to turn a two-on-two into a two-on-one and a goal against. He came back to the bench apologizing for not covering for me after I had been the one who had left him in the cold.

Over beers and in hotel rooms we talked the game, correcting our mistakes, adjusting our plans. If opponents were overly focused on me, I would suck in the forecheckers and Brad would become the puck carrier and join the rushes. Whatever we tried, it was always good to test new strategies in practice against Poulin's line, and if it worked against our best, it would work in a game.

Pouring his heart out at that pizza place, Brad asked if I thought his self-esteem could be raised by talking to my psychologist. It wasn't an easy question for a man's man like McCrimmon to ask. I made the call and Brad felt the sessions helped.

Dr. Rosenberg would put you in a light trance and talk to your subconscious. He recorded our sessions on cassette tapes that I would listen to in my spare time. They were designed to make you feel capable of anything. On mine, I was making passes, scoring goals and blocking shots with five seconds left in one-goal games. He also made me a tape designed to clear my head of racing thoughts so I wouldn't be tossing and turning until 4 a.m.

I continued my visits to Steve periodically throughout my career. A lot of Flyers went to him, including Lindbergh, who was dealing with the cancer diagnosis of his sister Anne-Christine.

If Keenan had gotten a relaxation tape from Dr. Rosenberg, it would have said, "Use McCrimmon and Howe for 30-plus minutes a game." Mike was sparingly playing two defensemen—Doug Crossman (acquired from Chicago for Behn Wilson) and Thomas Eriksson—who had been in the rotation under McCammon, and only spotting the 34-year-old Dvorak.

Keenan used every bit of the depth we had up front, however, to keep us hot. When Zezel was injured, Mike moved Craven to center, and he put away a victory in Boston with a goal. We were winning even though Poulin, a first-year captain who probably worried too much about others and not enough about himself, wasn't playing nearly the way he would. When Dave missed his check and Pelle got beaten on a 40-foot winning goal in Pittsburgh during late December, Keenan criticized players publicly for the first time.

"I don't expect that of a veteran player," he said. "And if you want a comment on the goaltending, theirs was better than ours."

Keenan was mad about the loss, but also wanted us to rally around our struggling captain and goalie. I always tried to help teammates in that way. Though I didn't read the papers much—it makes life less aggravating for a professional athlete—in interviews I would try to praise slumping players. So much of the game is confidence. I tried to do what I could to build it.

We bounced back from the Pittsburgh loss to win our next game, against Washington, and the following morning reported for Christmas Eve practice and our traditional exchange of gag gifts. The 8:30 a.m. start was Poulin's request so that Tocchet, Zezel and Smith could catch an 11 a.m. flight home to Toronto.

After our usual fast-paced 45 minutes, we stepped it up for Keenan's 12-minute aerobic skate. But as a Merry Christmas after a good win and a snappy practice, Mike lined us up for another 45 minutes of starts and stops. "Expect the unexpected," he said when we were finally dismissed, the three kids racing for the airport and most of the players throwing our Pollyanna gifts for each other disgustedly in the trash.

Not pretty. Neither was the 6–0 loss to Washington in Landover on December 26. We had no legs, and according to Keenan in the media, no leadership. The method to his madness resulted in our winning our next two, in Vancouver and L.A. We thought Lindbergh, who had played eight straight with the Washington loss, was getting weary, but the extra conditioning work had gotten him back over the hump.

Even though we wouldn't play again until January 2 against the Oilers, Keenan didn't let us do New Year's Eve in Southern California. Our coach got on the bus, taking us to our team party at Goose Loonies, an Edmonton bar, with a cigar.

"Bet you wish you had a cigarette," he teased Dvorak. The Czech opened his coat to show a carton tucked inside, and the team roared. After Tocchet spent part of the night dancing with his shirt on his head, Keenan came out the next day at practice wearing his jacket there.

Mike, the human being, was a new concept to us. Of course, it didn't last, even after we beat the Stanley Cup champions the next night without me (groin pull) in the lineup. I came back 24 hours later in Calgary, where we rallied from two goals down, only to lose late on a deflection. Keenan ripped Kerr for not scoring.

Timmy came back to net two in St. Louis as we closed the trip with a win. Shutting Keenan up was becoming a preoccupation. For me, so became breathing after Mike Bossy hit me, blowing out some rib cartilage just before we blew a late lead in a January loss at Uniondale. I missed four games.

We had only played .500 for a two-month stretch until we went to Landover on February 9, 11 points back of the first-place Capitals. Kerr scored four goals and I threw the puck across the crease to Propp, who scored with two seconds remaining for an exhilarating 5–4 win.

It jump-started another run, even though McCrimmon was out from a finger broken on a slash by Kerr, who lost it after Beast had playfully stolen the puck during warmup. "These things happen," shrugged a Keenan we did not know.

After getting back within striking distance of Washington, we lost three straight at Boston, Quebec and New Jersey, and blew two leads at Uniondale, one in the final minute. But just when it again looked as though the old Islander pros knew how to close a game and we didn't, Propp sprung Poulin for a breakaway goal in overtime and everything turned our way. We then beat Washington back-to-back to go into first on the way to winning 11 straight.

Keenan still gave us hell when the streak ended in a 5–2 loss at Chicago because he thought we could catch Edmonton for first place overall. He thought right, as he had all season. We won 16 of our last 17 games and stunningly took the regular-season crown. As Pelle would say, "Unbeleeeeeeevable." But not really, thanks to him. Lindbergh—apologizing for losses, never taking credit for victories—was our Bobby Clarke Trophy winner as team MVP.

Even a franchise-record 53 wins would be meaningless, however, if we flopped again in the best-of-five first-round series against the Rangers. We had won all seven regular-season games against a team that, after firing Herb Brooks midyear, had finished with the second-worst record of any playoff team ever. So when the Rangers started to come back from our early 3–0 lead in game one, hesitation set in, and Anders Hedberg tied it 4–4 with 26 seconds left to send it into overtime. Our playoff nightmares were recurring.

Keenan laid into us so many times that I don't particularly remember him blistering us before sudden death, as others recall. But however nervous we were, we had control of the overtime when Ron Sutter knocked Reijo Ruotsalainen off the puck along the end boards and saw me moving in from the point. With Lindsay Carson screening Glen Hanlon, all I wanted to do was put the puck on net. It went through Lindsay, then Hanlon, and the biggest goal I ever scored won game one, 5–4. Relief washed over the Spectrum with the Flyers' first playoff win in 10 tries over four springs. I don't know what would have happened had we lost that game.

We didn't celebrate much on the ice. It was clear the Rangers intended to ruin another of our seasons. In game two, we lost Poulin to a slight knee-ligament tear and we were fighting for every inch of space. Or, should I say, everybody was except for Todd Bergen, a late-season rookie call-up who wanted to be a golf pro more than a hockey player.

Bergen was adept at shooting a puck and turning everybody off with his indifferent attitude. Perhaps this was a good thing that night, when, blissfully unaware of all the hand-fighting going on around him, Bergen flashed through the slot to deflect a Crossman drive from the point to tie the game 1–1, then picked a top corner to put us ahead. With less than three minutes remaining, Sutter, who had checked our nemesis Mark Pavelich doggedly, took Barry Beck wide and fed Sinisalo, who beat Hedberg up the slot to put away a 3–1 win.

Gradually, our confidence picked up as we worked our way through another first-round minefield. Game three in New York was a power-play contest, with the Rangers leading 3–2 when Kerr reached back for a pass intended for me at the point and swept it past Hanlon in one motion. Like a lot of us, the big guy had been fighting it, and that one got him going big-time. He scored again on his forehand, his backhand and on a one-timer from Zezel for four goals in a Stanley Cup-record span of 8:16.

We were ahead 6–3 and just had to stay out of the box, but Beast took a bad angle on Grant Ledyard and took him down at the second-period buzzer. The Rangers cashed the power play, and when Lindbergh got his feet tangled as Hedberg cut in off the wing, it became 6–5. The Garden was going crazy and we faced the longest 16 minutes of our young lives.

Keenan took his time-out and calmly reminded us that we still had the lead. He then put out Sutter, Tocchet and Carson, who created two scoring chances on the next shift, and all the confidence and structure we had built during our 113-point season took over. Lindbergh didn't have to touch the puck again for the next 13 minutes, Craven jammed it out with eight seconds to go, and I had won my first NHL playoff series in a sweep, even if it had been much harder than that.

The first time our Swedish goalie heard the expression "monkey off your back," Pelle looked over his shoulder quizzically. But in any language, we were believing in ourselves and gaining confidence. We beat the Islanders convincingly in the first two games of our quarter-final series, then survived a desperate 27-shot second-period barrage by the proud ex-champs at Nassau Coliseum and coolly hit the empty net for a 5–3 win in game three.

"Who the fuck is Bryan Trottier? Who the fuck is Mike Bossy?" Keenan kept asking us. I had heard of them. When we made Sinisalo's second-period goal hold up for a series-clinching 1–0 win in game five, we had beaten one of the best teams of all time, only one year removed from four consecutive Stanley Cups.

Because the Adams Division had a better head-to-head record against the Patrick, we opened the next series in Quebec, where Peter Stastny beat Lindbergh under the crossbar in overtime of game one. But despite losing Poulin again to cracked ribs, Kerr to a torn knee ligament, and McCrimmon to the most gruesome shoulder separation I ever have seen—the bone took his shoulder pads up past his ear—we bounced back to win the next two games.

Pelle finally let in a couple of shaky ones in a 5–3 game four loss that sent us back to Quebec City tied 2–2. On the plane, he listened to Dr. Rosenberg's relaxation tape and read *Mad* magazine. What, Pelle worry? Keenan vowed that the goalie who had carried us would be ready, and thank God he was, keeping us within 1–0 through two periods in which we did nothing. Rest assured, our coach was not as emotionless as we had been. He took a stick and knocked the water bottles off the table in the middle of the dressing room.

We were accused of being satisfied to have won two rounds and quitting in this one, and then reminded we still had a period to play. I pinched to turn up the puck for a goal by call-up Joe Paterson; Craven put in a pass from Propp; and, with the help of a disallowed goal by the Nordiques that should have counted, we ran out of Quebec like thieves in the night with a 2–1 win and a 3–2 series lead.

We had a meeting before game six to remind ourselves how fortunate we had been. If we needed any further re-energizing, Poulin, killing a second-period five-on-three, stole a D-to-D pass from Mario Marois and soloed to beat Mario Gosselin's glove. I thought the Spectrum walls would come down, and in a sense they did on the Nordiques. We had 19 chances to Quebec's two in a 3–0 win that might have been the best single-game postseason performance by any team I ever played on.

We were almost as good in game one of the final, outchancing the Stanley Cup champion Oilers 17–4 in a 4–1 win, but I could tell Edmonton wasn't ready to play. At the game two face-off, I looked into Mark Messier's big eyes and I remember thinking we were going to be in for a much tougher game. Believe it or not, we had won nine straight against Edmonton, but these were different Oilers, finishing their checks, dumping the puck, canning their fancy plays. They ground us down 3–1 to tie the series.

Wayne Gretzky scored a hat trick on four-on-fours to give the Oilers a 3–1 lead in game three in Edmonton. But we still were making them pay a price. Mark Napier had finished his check on Ed Hospodar and Eddie was protecting himself as defensemen could do back in the day. When he came to our bench, he said, "Look at my stick, but remember we're on TV. Don't laugh." On his blade were four indentations from Napier's teeth. "I got him good," said Eddie.

When the Oilers, still leading 3–1, had a five-on-three, Keenan tried to slow their momentum by pulling Lindbergh and putting in Froese, who had played only half a game in the playoffs. "Good luck to you, my friend," Dvorak bid Frosty, but Edmonton failed to score.

After a reinserted Lindbergh gave up another goal in the second period, Keenan put together a Craven-Tocchet-Propp line and double-shifted it. I scored on Tocchet's rebound, Propp put one in from an angle off Grant Fuhr's hip, and had Rick, who was in alone, not needed to reach back for Craven's pass in the final seconds, we might have tied the game.

Nevertheless, we fell short, 4–3. And even though we jumped up 3–1 in game four, Gretzky and the Oiler power play were sizzling. Poulin was freezing his rib cage so he could play, and Keenan was out of answers. He took Sinisalo and Propp into the adjacent locker room, whose walls didn't muffle the worst tongue-lashing I ever have heard from a coach, and then stopped playing them, even though we didn't have Kerr.

When Pelle took a shot in the back of his knee, Keenan was forced to use Froese in the third period of the 5–3 loss and for all of game five. Good luck to us, my friends. Gretzky circled like a shark in an 8–3 win that gave the Oilers their second straight Stanley Cup.

Getting steamrolled in that final game made us feel pretty crappy, but it was nothing like those first-round losses of the preceding years. We had exceeded expectations and learned a great deal. On the interview day before the series, Gretzky had said there are three seasons—regular, playoffs and finals—and when it was over I understood what he was talking about. No one remembers those Oilers as a great checking team, but, after losing game one, they did everything necessary to win, and now we had a better idea of what was required of us.

Lindbergh won the Vezina Trophy, presented at the awards ceremony by his boyhood idol and mentor, Bernie Parent. Keenan was named coach of the year, but he didn't want our laurels eroding the work ethic, even though we would bring back the same young, hungry team with an upgrade in our skill level—center Pelle Eklund, Ted Sator's tout in Bob McCammon's great draft of 1983. When Ted Sator was named head coach of the Rangers, Paul Holmgren joined McGuire as a Keenan assistant.

Before our 1985–86 opener against New Jersey, Keenan came up to me and said, "After the first period, I am going to come after you, get in your kitchen a little bit."

"What?" I said.

"Yeah, I want some of these young guys to be scared to death, thinking, 'If he goes after Mark Howe, what's he going to do to me?'"

"Yeah, whatever," I said.

Mike played me like three shifts in the first period. So I'm pissed anyway. Then, sure enough, during the intermission he goes up and down me like I had never been done before. Being tipped off didn't keep me from being ticked off. When he finished, I was so furious, I had to vent my anger on something. I went into the bathroom and busted down the new partitions in the stalls. First game, home opener, he practically benched me for no good reason and we were beaten, 6–5.

Two wins later, we outshot Quebec 41–14 and lost 2–1. "You fuckers will pay for this," Keenan announced. Next day, we skated with no pucks for an hour and 15 minutes, and Mike told us that if we ran into another hot goalie, "someone better run him over."

But as we started to blow teams away, the closest thing to a machine of any team I had ever been on, there really wasn't much Iron Mike could say. Beast and I stopped for a couple late ones at Kaminski's after getting off the charter from a win in Quebec City. There we were, after closing hours, talking hockey as usual, when we heard a knock at the back door.

We hid our beers, thinking it was the cops. Worse, it was Keenan. And we had a game the next night. We got up to go. "No, no," said Mike. "Relax."

We stayed half an hour more, at most. The next night, when Brad and I were horrible as we fell behind Los Angeles in the first period, we got the Mike Fright glare, but we pulled away to win 7–4, and Brad and I were pluses on every goal. We went by Keenan's office giggling and laughing like kids. As he always said, winning solves every problem.

With a four-day break coming up between home matches against Boston and Edmonton, Keenan promised us two consecutive days off, an event so rare the team planned to meet for a probable "late night out" after the Bruins game at the after-hours bar in the complex that housed our practice facility.

After beating the Bruins for our 10th straight win, practically everybody was ready to party but Hospodar, who hadn't been playing much and was upset about being in Mike's doghouse. Eddie and I changed plans after the game and went to Kaminski's instead to get a quieter table for a little pep talk. We were among the few Flyers who weren't partying with Pelle Lindbergh until minutes before he lost control of his Porsche, crashed it into a concrete wall outside a school and died.

My call, like most of them that awful Sunday morning—November 10, 1985—came before 8 a.m. It was from Poulin, who was at Kennedy Memorial Hospital in Stratford, New Jersey. He said there had been a car accident, that Pelle was severely injured and that it did not look good. I knew right away that things were bad, but how bad I didn't know for certain.

Dave said he'd call back with more details. I waited, hoping for some type of miracle, but felt down deep that wouldn't happen. I had plans to go to the shore that day to winterize my boat, and had a babysitter scheduled so that I could get Ginger out of the house as well. We canceled the babysitter, whose father was vice principal at Somerdale Elementary School, about a mile from the Coliseum, where Pelle's car hit the wall. Small world.

When Poulin called back, he told me Pelle was brain-dead. I joined my teammates at the hospital, where they put us in a room and we learned that Lindbergh, Ed Parvin Jr.—the son of the realtor who brokered most of the Flyers' home purchases—and an Atlantic City waitress named Kathy McNeal, who had dated Peter Zezel for six months, had piled into the two-seat red sports car with the intention of taking Parvin home. Tocchet and Craven, who shared a place within walking distance of the Coliseum, were going to wait for Pelle and Kathy to return, after which they planned to go out for breakfast.

Two women who had been at the Coliseum saw the Porsche fail to make the 45-degree bend in Somerdale Road at the school, phoned 911 and drove back to tell Craven and Tocchet. They reached the scene as Lindbergh, Parvin and McNeal were being put in ambulances, Pelle only after the Jaws of Life were used to cut him out of his crushed car.

Because they were on the passenger side that stopped against the elementary school steps—not against the wall that took the driver's-side impact—McNeal and Parvin would survive—in Parvin's case, with some permanent disability. But our goalie, whose leg was badly broken, had been deprived of oxygen for too long by trauma to his brain stem and could not breathe on his own.

Dr. Edward Viner, our team physician, explained to us what brain-dead meant. One of the players, I forget who, asked the doctor about Pelle's chances for recovery, and the doctor had to go over it again. We were listening, not hearing.

Pelle's finance, Kerstin Pietzsch, had been woken up at the Lindbergh townhouse by the knock of Voorhees policeman Jack Prettyman, a longtime friend to the players. Lindbergh's visiting mother, Anna-Lisa, was coming down the stairs and burst into tears as Kerstin had to translate for her the devastating news.

At the hospital, Zezel buried his head on Keenan's shoulder and wept. That afternoon, we went to Poulin's house to do nothing but be with each other. I don't remember anybody saying much of anything.

The next day, Keenan decided to practice us. The only importance he attached to it was that we might work out some of the pain, but that was impossible. The goal opposite Bob Froese's was empty, and that was reminder enough. Guys were making mistakes right and left, and Mike didn't blow a single whistle to correct us.

Reality didn't set in for me until Tuesday, when I was taken to the hospital room where Pelle—whose organs his parents had consented to be donated—was lying, hooked up to a monitor, his chest rising and falling. I held his hand. It was warm, but there was no life to it. I accepted he was gone, but not easily. Other than my grandparents, whom I'd seen only about once every five years growing up because they were in Saskatoon and we were in Detroit, I had never before been close to anyone who passed away. This was a guy—and such a good guy—whom I had been with every day during the last three seasons.

When we talked to the media for the first time on Tuesday, Marsh said he was angry with Pelle for throwing away his opportunity to win a Cup with our team on the rise. Crusaders against drunk driving expressed condemnation. I can't say it was misplaced. Pelle's blood alcohol test came back .07 over the .10 legal limit. The skid marks showed he didn't brake until he was 10 feet from the wall, so alcohol obviously impaired his judgment and slowed even world-class reflexes like his. Still, he wasn't a chronic drunk driver; in fact, he rarely drank at all. He did what too many of us have done—turned on the ignition when he shouldn't have, especially to a car with the power of that one.

I would regularly drive at 70 to 75 miles an hour on I-295 on my way to practice. Pelle would shoot me a smile as he passed, shifting and spinning his wheels at 85. I was fascinated with the ridiculous horsepower in that car and used to ask him if he would trade for my Mercedes for a day. In fact, I hoped he would agree to that swap in return for my taking him to Egg Harbor that very week to look for the new boat he was in the market to buy. I don't know if he would have agreed. That car was his joy.

As one numbing day turned into another, we nevertheless had a game to play—against Edmonton, of all teams. If anybody was thinking about hockey that week, there was the great consolation of having not traded our unhappy backup, Froese, who was better than a lot of teams' starters.

The first word Bob received on the Sunday morning was that Pelle had suffered a broken leg in a car accident. His first thought was "I'll get to play now." He was beating himself up over that when he also remembered joking with Pelle, just the previous week, that if anything ever happened to him, he shouldn't worry because he—Bob—would take care of the gorgeous Kerstin.

"Frosty, he knew you were kidding," I consoled him. But it got worse for Bob. His emotional pain turned into physical discomfort when he took a shot in the groin at practice the day before the game.

That afternoon, almost everyone in attendance at the Old Swedes' Church in Philadelphia was sobbing when Poulin, in the best eulogy I ever heard, described a love for life so strong that it made Lindbergh's teammates envy as much as love him. "We laughed about his ways, but he managed to see and do a great deal more than most of us ever will," said our captain. "If he wanted something, he got it; if he wished to go somewhere, he went.

"We remember Pelle for his wide grin, his ever-present bubble and zest for conquering the world. Anything Pelle did, he had to be the best at. And through his exuberance, he was able to transmit this will to his teammates. He wasn't happy unless there was something on the line. He won games by himself, and by so doing gave us the confidence to develop that winning attitude."

In his pew, Froese was in increasing agony. At home, he passed blood. This was unbelievable, on top of incomprehensible. We wouldn't have Froese for the game against the Oilers, either. We were calling up Darren Jensen, who had one game of NHL experience. It was a terrible spot for Jensen, but frankly not that much harder than for any of us. Poulin had been conducting group therapy, encouraging us to open up about our fears of not being able to function. When the Oilers arrived in Philadelphia, Gretzky said he didn't know how *they* would, either.

Edmonton had asked if we wanted a postponement, but we had to get on with our lives at some point, and our fans needed to say goodbye. The Spectrum boards were whitewashed of advertising. A sign on the facade of the upper deck read: "Get Pelle's Name on the Cup. It's His Last Chance." By coincidence, Lindbergh's picture was on the tickets that night, so the ushers didn't tear them, only marked them on the back with an X.

With Pelle's number, 31, shining from the scoreboard message board, Gene Hart conducted a pre-game ceremony that he introduced as a celebration of Lindbergh's life. Parent told 17,007 grieving friends how he regretted never telling Pelle how much the teacher admired the pupil. Then we had 15 minutes in the locker room to get ready to play.

It's hard for athletes to admit there are times when they are preoccupied by their own little issues. There have been only a couple of games in my life when I was totally distracted by another thought. I remember so little about that contest.

I'm told it started a little tentatively until Hospodar started driving the Oilers crazy, as usual, with a cross-check of Kevin McClelland, then I sent in Poulin and Propp on a shorthanded opportunity. I scored a goal off Andy Moog's glove to put us up 1–0, but I don't recall it. I only remember shedding a few tears on the bench when everything from the last five days, the rush of the game, the goal, and our lead just came out of me.

During the second period, I pulled a groin and was done for the night, but I have no recollection of that, either. I know Jensen made some saves, that we kept going to the net like we had been trained to do in good times and bad, and that we won, 5–3, doing ourselves as proud as in any game during the Keenan era, when there were a ton of them worth celebrating.

Without Froese or me, we won in Hartford two nights later. Keenan was so appreciative that he helped the flight attendants serve the meals on the short charter home. When the Islanders jumped up 4–1 on us the next night, we came back to win 5–4, our 13th straight victory.

"I don't believe these guys," said Keenan. But maybe it wasn't so surprising. Teams that lose a key player become more dangerous for a while if you have the right structure in place to compensate. Plus, the games probably became an escape from our grief.

In our next match, the Islanders jumped up 5–1 at Nassau Coliseum and we still got it back to 5–4 before losing 8–6. Froese returned—as did I—in a 3–0 shutout of Hartford, and though everybody expected us to hit the emotional wall, by mid-January we were 33–11–0.

As good as Zezel had been setting up Kerr on the power play, Eklund was even better, putting the big guy on a pace for an NHL-record 34 goals with the man advantage. When I was quoted that season as saying our goaltending was just as good as it had been the previous year, I wasn't just saying it for the sake of Frosty's confidence. I meant it. Throughout my career, whenever I played in front of a goalie who was not good enough, I'd have to change my game to try and block more shots, even from bad angles. But I never thought to do that with Froese.

Keenan, however, never seemed to think Bob was better than a backup. When the coach named Froese to the midseason All-Star Game, it was with the backhanded compliment, "The stats justify it." I think Mike also wanted to toughen Frosty with mind games. That was Keenan—so afraid the loss of Pelle would turn into a crutch for us that he pushed and pushed.

Every day—and I mean *every* day—Keenan was with the Flyers, I drove to work wondering what shit was going to hit the fan. Anybody who says he wasn't intimidated the first year would be lying. By the second season, I think some guys started to dismiss what Mike had to say, Kerr being one of the first.

Keenan was especially hard on the young guys. Zezel became the biggest whipping boy because he never got back up in Mike's face, like almost everybody else did at some point. Keenan believed negative motivation was better than no motivation at all. He wanted emotion. Guys who didn't emote—like Eriksson, Pelle's countryman who had been a tower of strength for Kerstin and the Lindbergh family—were dismissed as weak.

In February, we were up comfortably during a third period in Buffalo when a shot hit Eriksson in the knee. He came back to the bench in obvious pain, tried one more shift, but just couldn't do it. While Sudsy was looking at Thomas's knee, Keenan was berating Eriksson, calling him chickenshit and finally pushing him with his foot so hard that Thomas fell off the bench and into the boards. He tried to play another shift regardless.

The x-rays showed Thomas had a broken kneecap that would put him out for the year. I asked him, "Why did you go back out?" He said it was less painful to be on the ice with a broken kneecap than to listen to the guy behind the bench.

I had been brought up with the belief that even when the coach is wrong, he is right. There wasn't a lot of joy playing for Keenan, but the bottom line was we would win, so the leadership of the team stood behind Mike and played good cop for him sometimes, as did the assistant coaches. Guys like Sinisalo and Propp let Keenan roll off their backs. But Zezel was so down that, at Mike's request, I took him to lunch one time for a cheer-up.

Once, when Keenan canceled a day off and skated us unbelievably hard, we sat in the locker room, spitefully making ourselves late for a luncheon sponsored by Ed Snider and the organization. But Keenan could surprise us, too. Sometimes, he would call in guys he had blistered for a makeup session the next day, and occasionally provided moments of unsolicited support. One time in Calgary, when I was putting too much pressure on myself, he gave Sudsy and assistant trainer Kurt Mundt $100 and told them to get me drunk to get my mind off my play.

Another time, I was waiting to get on the bus to the rink in L.A. when Mike pulled me back into the hotel and asked, "What's wrong with you?"

"I'm playing like shit," I replied.

"He said, 'You're one of the best players in this fucking league. Forget what's happened, go play like I know you can play.'"

It was a tiny little thing, but it helped me a lot. That particular season, however, being on my way to a plus-85, I didn't need any pep talks. McCrimmon would finish at plus-83, although our running joke was to check the summaries every day to see if the two of us combined were keeping pace with Paul Coffey in the scoring race among defensemen. But my 82 points and Beast's 56 could only tie his 138.

Keenan wouldn't play Dave Richter, whom we had gotten from Minnesota for Bergen after Todd said he didn't want to play for Mike. Win or lose, we were going with a four-man rotation of Howe-McCrimmon and Crossman-Marsh. But the elephant in the room remained the goaltending. Keenan and Clarke were worried enough to send Jensen back down and pick up Chico Resch from the Devils for a draft choice at the trading deadline, but at that stage of his career, I think Chico was brought in as much for his bubbly personality as his netminding. We had become a pretty grim team, given no room to fail. We won to shut the coach up.

Chico beat the Rangers at Madison Square Garden to start a stretch drive of 11 wins in our last 13 games. Froese was as good as he had been all season in beating the Rangers 3–2 at Madison Square Garden in the final week, and when we roared from behind to beat Washington in game 80 to put away the division title, our point total was only three fewer than the season before.

We quickly erased two early deficits in game one of our five-game series against Ted Sator's Rangers, almost as if we believed we could beat at will a team we had defeated in 18 of our last 19 meetings. But the Rangers killed off a two-man advantage, Tomas Sandstrom scored off a Froese puck-handling mistake and we skated into their discipline during the entire, shocking, 6–2 loss.

Keenan called it the worst game we had played since he had become the coach. And in the days when we would play a brutal four games in five nights to start the playoffs, he wasn't going to assume we could quickly get ourselves together.

Early the next morning, we were put on a bus from the hotel and brought to the Coliseum, where, one by one, the assistants called us in, starting with Ron Sutter. "How did you think you played?" Keenan asked him. Ronnie said, "Okay," and explained why.

Keenan whacked Holmgren on the shoulder to cue a video that showed Sutter losing about six draws—never mind that he won 12—and then Mike Ridley knocking Ronnie off the puck for a Ranger goal, probably Sutter's only bad play of the night.

McCrimmon and I were the last two called, in a tandem. We sat in silence until Keenan finally said, "I need better. Get the fuck out of my office."

And we *were* better. Beast and Sutter scored early in game two, important because the well-prepared Rangers had a tight penalty-killing box against Kerr and Eklund. It was tense to the end, but we got Froese his first playoff win, 2–1, and as we carried another 2–1 lead into the third period of game three at Madison Square Garden, thought we were back to doing business as usual. But Ronnie uncharacteristically gave the puck away and Ridley was left open for a tap-in. Derrick Smith, usually so reliable, took a needless penalty that the Rangers cashed to go ahead 3–2.

After giving up two quick third-period goals in game three a year earlier in the same building, Keenan calmed us at the bench. This time he ordered everybody to face him and angrily told us we were embarrassing ourselves on national television.

"If he points at me, I'm going to hit him," Kerr whispered to me.

Off the next face-off, Froese dove out at Bob Brooke, who scored easily, and the rout was on. We fell apart like we hadn't done late in a game in two seasons, and after the 5–2 loss were one game from elimination and suddenly reliving our worst nightmares from the McCammon years.

Keenan seemed to realize he couldn't give off any more panic and allowed beer in a meeting at the hotel. When we fell behind 1–0 the next night, we remained composed. McCrimmon intercepted a puck at the point and Zezel beat John Vanbiesbrouck between the legs to tie it. Keenan replaced Eklund with Zezel on the power play to give us more bulk against the Rangers' bumping, and Peter responded with the best game I ever saw him play in a pressure situation.

Poulin scored after knocking down a Vanbiesbrouck clearout and we were on our way to a 7–1 win, rising again in the clutch like we had been doing for two years.

But now that the Rangers had been blown out of their presumed best chance to kill us off, they came to game five at the Spectrum with nothing left to lose, all the pressure seeming to revert to us.

At 1–1 in the second period of game five at the Spectrum, I got one of my shots blocked and the Rangers scored on a four-on-two. Propp pushed Don Maloney into McCrimmon, freeing up Mark Osborne for a goal 1:11 later and, down 3–1, we were in deep trouble. McCrimmon got a bouncer past the screened Vanbiesbrouck to make it 3–2, but their goalie stopped a Beast screamer through traffic before the Rangers twice hit the empty net for a 5–2 win. It was over and nobody could really believe it. Another first-round loss, just when we thought we had gotten past them.

Mike Ridley and Kelly Miller were good young players for New York. Vanbiesbrouck, except for one game, had been excellent. Sator knew the Flyers, and some Rangers who would never again perform as well rose to the occasion. New York played a composed game five and deserved the credit far more than Froese should have taken any blame. Our goalie played fine.

Were we emotionally drained from the Lindbergh tragedy? Maybe. All season, it had seemed like there was a new crisis every day. But I think the first round is hard on the favorites each year because they really can't win, only lose. Had we gotten by, maybe we would have started to roll again, taken advantage of Edmonton's loss to Calgary and won the Stanley Cup. Who really knows? We certainly had the talent and the drive, but not the breaks against a well-coached Rangers team.

None of this was any consolation through another long summer.

CHAPTER 11

The Two-Minute-and-26-Second Lifetime

As I watched rookie goalie Ron Hextall firing pucks out of his zone during the exhibition games that preceded our 1986–87 season, I figured that this kid would eventually save me some energy and hits in the back. I didn't realize he would begin to do it as soon as opening night.

A surprise starter in goal against the Oilers at the Spectrum, Hextall was scored on two minutes into the game by Jari Kurri. But when he dragged his pad to stop a Gretzky breakaway, the Spectrum crowd roared.

"Who the hell are you?" Gretzky asked Hextall.

"Who the hell are *you?*" Hextall asked Gretzky.

We got third-period goals by Ron Sutter and Peter Zezel to win 2–1. Hextall got the next start and was in the net for 18 of our first 20. He didn't just stop pucks; he cleared them. Instead of merely defying shooters, he would punish them with whacks to the leg and bait them using a cadence he'd perform with his stick against the posts before every defensive-zone draw.

Mike Keenan's pain from our first-round loss to the Rangers in 1986 had been eased watching Hextall carry the Hershey Bears to the American Hockey League final. Basically, he had won the number-one job from Bob Froese even before going unbeaten in the exhibition season. Our sixth-round draft pick in 1982 was innovative, fundamentally sound and ultracompetitive, a gift sent from the hockey gods as compensation for our tragic loss of Pelle Lindbergh.

To our trademark penalty-killing—we had compiled 62 shorthanded goals in the previous three seasons—Hextall added an unprecedented puck-handling component. Often, on opposition power plays, there was at least one lazy guy who wouldn't hustle back after a turnover, so I would give a quick yell and either Dave Poulin or Brian Propp would drive the defenseman back by going wide, enabling me to fill the slot. Sometimes Brad McCrimmon would do it, too.

We all read each other so well. Poulin had great speed and excellent vision; Propp was an all-around good player. No one was out there merely to kill two minutes. Hextall had the same mentality and was learning to use us better. Ninety-seven per cent of the time, he was going to throw the puck up the left-wing boards, so I knew if we had Propp or Poulin confronting a guy there, I could get to a good support position 20 feet away and kick the puck out for a two-on-one.

We were so good at killing penalties, leading the league in 1984–85 and coming in second and third the following two seasons, that my advice to Kjell Samuelsson—the six-foot, six-inch defenseman we acquired in December from the Rangers for Froese—was to take a penalty or two to stand up for himself. In his first few games with us, Samuelsson must have had his nose broken three times.

"Kjell, just put your stick through somebody's face," I said. "We'll kill the penalty, and sooner or later, they'll quit running you."

Can't say the big guy wasn't open to suggestion: there must have been five games in a row where he received penalties for cross-checking. We had to tell him enough was enough. Keenan didn't warm quickly to big Kjell—a rookie who hadn't been drafted until age 25—and neither did the fans, who were incredulous that we would trade a goalie with a

92–29–12 career record to a team already looking to be our first-round playoff opponent for a fifth time in six years.

It was a merry Christmas for Froese, who was happy to be free of Keenan. But not for Propp, who had 41 points in his first 27 games before suffering a kneecap fracture, denying him the opportunity for his first 100-point season.

McCrimmon had missed the first nine games in a contract holdout and returned for just a one-year deal. "They did their thing, I did mine," he said, ready to do business as usual. We were 25–7–2 before Ted Sator, already fired by new Ranger GM Phil Esposito for coaching the boring hockey that had upset both the Flyers and Capitals the preceding spring, beat us 2–1 in his first game behind the bench at Buffalo on December 23. Two days after Christmas in Vancouver, a bad first period gave us a jump on consecutive losses when Keenan came in screaming at the break.

"I fought to get you guys two days off!" he said. Actually, those two days at the holiday were mandated by the collective bargaining agreement, but never mind. Mad Mike was rolling, going around the room, winding up at one of his favorite punching bags, rookie right wing Scott Mellanby. Because Mellanby's father, Ralph, had been executive producer of *Hockey Night in Canada,* and because Scott hadn't spent any time in the minors after leaving the University of Wisconsin, Keenan accused Mellanby of "being born with a silver spoon in his mouth" and seemed determined to fill it with vinegar.

"Look at you! I sent you home to eat some turkey, not to eat the whole thing," raged Keenan. "Your face is redder than a baboon's ass."

To this day, whenever I see Scott—he played 22 seasons, pretty good longevity for a spoiled rich kid—I call him the Red Baboon.

We continued to monkey around on that trip, losing four games. Keenan was no bundle of joy, but my mood was lifted with a sudden opportunity to become a dad again. McCrimmon and I were by the pool at the L.A. Marriott when I got a page from Ginger, who was in Houston visiting her stepmother. At a neighborhood function, Ginger had heard about a young woman who, after becoming pregnant during a failed reconciliation attempt with her boyfriend, was going to put the baby up for adoption.

Ginger's pregnancy with Azia had been too difficult for her to risk bearing another child. Only occasionally—and not in the previous year—had we talked about adoption, but Ginger said we were going to have to be quick if we wanted this kid.

My first thought was to ask Marty and Mary, who couldn't have children because of complications Mary had suffered from a tubular pregnancy, and Ginger reluctantly agreed. But my brother and his wife said they had read about cases where judges had given birth parents their children back following a change of heart even two or three years later, and Marty and Mary decided they didn't want to risk that heartbreak. They settled for becoming an aunt and uncle again—as, deep down, I had hoped they would. We put the adoption wheels in motion.

The Flyers' wheels, meanwhile, were a little squeaky as 1987 began, despite our virtually insurmountable lead in the division. My back problems flared again in late January and forced me to miss 10 games. Sutter had a stress fracture in his back, and Sinisalo needed knee surgery. There was a game in Buffalo where we had eight starters out and still won, 7–4, thanks to a hat trick by Zezel. But it was largely because of Hextall that we won about half our games through all these injuries.

I had seen some competitive people in the game, but this guy was *wired.* Although he wasn't in net when we played the Devils in New Jersey, Hextall used some end-of-game shoving between Mel Bridgman and Samuelsson as an excuse to pummel the winning goalie, Alain Chevrier.

Ron even took unkindly to goals scored in practice. One night, Propp announced his intention of breaking his own record—I think it was 25—for goals scored in warmup. We warned him it wasn't a great idea, and then watched the fun unfold.

Propp annoyed Hexy greatly by scoring behind his back while he was working on stops at the other side of his crease. After Propp had banked a couple in off Hexy's butt for our final giggle, Hextall came into the locker room, took his stick and knocked down the shelf above Propp's head. Good thing there was a second one there, or else a lot of stuff would have come down on him.

Though we won back-to-back games only three times from late January on, I never thought the sky was falling. Neither of our two defensive acquisitions—J.J. Daigneault, obtained over the summer from Vancouver for Richie Sutter, and Samuelsson—had gained Keenan's trust, but we anticipated getting all our injured guys back by the first round.

Now, if only I could get some sleep. After being away on hockey trips for the birth of Travis and Azia, I had the once-in-a-lifetime experience of having 10-month-old Nolan Gerry Howe brought to our door in February.

Raised by his grandparents to that point, Nolan had never slept in his own crib, a habit we had to break. The first night, he cried non-stop from 8 p.m until 4 a.m., and we thought we would go out of our minds. When Ginger had finally had enough and went downstairs to pour herself a rare drink, I broke the game plan by sneaking into the nursery, picking up my lovely new son and holding him until his crying stopped. I put him back into his crib, hoping that my visit would go undetected by Ginger, but as soon as I did, Nolan ratted me out by starting to wail again. It was four days before he stopped crying or would take anything but his bottle.

Nolan was a challenge, but we must have been doing something right. When the social worker came for the follow-up interview, our son was all over the place, refusing to be as perfect as we wanted him to be.

"I've seen enough," she said after 10 minutes. Our hearts fell for a couple seconds until she said, "This is one of the best-adjusted babies I ever have seen."

When we formally adopted Nolan that summer in Houston, we were told that if the birth parents wanted him back in the first year, we probably wouldn't win in court. Thank God it never happened. We could only imagine that pain.

For the Flyers, the pain was real. By March, everybody except Sutter was back, but then Tocchet, Zezel and Sinisalo were lost again, putting their postseason availability in question. Keenan ran hard practices to try to build conditioning for the playoffs, which killed our legs as the anxiety built. When we gave up nine goals to the Islanders in game 80 and blew the Jennings Trophy (fewest goals-against), Clarke, who really had not interjected much over three years, told the media there was no excuse for that kind of effort and that Keenan had to share some of the blame.

Following a 3–0 shutout by Vanbiesbrouck—the Rangers' first of the year—in game one of the first round, our GM took a different tone. With Esposito having traded Mike Ridley, Kelly Miller and Bob Brooke, and then gone behind the bench after Tommy Webster developed an inner-ear problem, this opponent was a ragtag New York team bearing no resemblance to the one that had beaten us the previous year. The only thing we had to fear was the possibility of a fifth first-round flop in six years. Clarke came to our postgame meal and tried to be reassuring. He met with the captains and said it was time for us to show some leadership.

A little emotion didn't hurt, either. Dave Brown punched out George McPhee early in game two and Tocchet broke a 2–2 tie just before the second period ended. We added two more goals before Esposito switched to Froese, just as Clarke had hoped when he made the deal with the intention of playing with our nemesis Vanbiesbrouck's head, and we went on to an 8–3 win.

Esposito, angry that the Flyers had replayed Brown's pummeling of McPhee on Arenavision, jammed a hand into Jay Snider's chest before game three in New York. "You're a no-class fuck," said Espo.

"Fuck you," said Snider.

Hexy shut out the Rangers, 3–0. We should have stayed in control, but in game four we got overanxious, missed a guy coming out of the penalty box and gave up a power-play goal, falling behind 3–0. Keenan yanked Hextall, then put him back in during a Ranger power play. In between gestures at Froese and Espo—who was taunting "Ronald . . . Ronald McDonald!"—Hextall was kicking out shots left and right.

Lindsay Carson took a run at Froese, then another swing at Frosty while he headed toward the bench on a delayed penalty. Although untouched, Froese flopped to the ice and the ref added two extra minutes. We lost 6–3 to go back to Philly with the series tied 2–2.

In game five, we found ourselves in another fine mess when Hextall, killing an early Samuelsson penalty, cleared the puck over the glass, drawing a delay-of-game call. I had to clear a shot off the line that trickled behind Hextall, but we got out of the period scoreless.

After Tocchet scored early in the second period, we started to play with the realization that there was no way we would lose to these guys. Though Hexy missed a poke check on Pierre Larouche and he tied the game, Kerr converted Eklund's centering pass and we picked up the pace to a level we hadn't played at since early in the season. The Rangers were done, not only in that 3–1 win but in game six as well. Poulin (cracked ribs) and Craven (broken foot) were lost in that contest, but Tocchet and Crossman gave us a 2–0 lead, and Hextall's breezy second shutout of the series, 5–0, avenged our shocking upset of the year before.

Meeting the Rangers so often in the playoffs—seven times in nine years—made that win personal for a lot of guys. Maybe a little for me, too, but my joy was mostly in surviving the first-round pressure cooker.

Just like in 1985, we drew the Islanders in the second round. The Isles had needed four overtimes before Pat LaFontaine put Washington away in game seven. I was tired just staying up to watch that game and can only imagine how they felt, especially coming into the Spectrum for game one without Denis Potvin, Mike Bossy, Brent Sutter or Patrick Flatley.

We weren't exactly healthy ourselves, missing Poulin, Craven and Sutter, but we had more than they did in a 4–1 win. Not so when Potvin returned for game two, which was tied 1–1 going into the final minute when Zezel jumped on the ice too soon during a change. When Mikko Makela nailed a perfect shot just inside the far post with two seconds left to win the game for the Islanders, Keenan took the heat for Peter's mistake, but then put it on Propp, who was struggling again in the playoffs.

Brian was a little undersized, which doesn't help when the space for playmaking shrinks in the postseason. He was one of a few players who could score from 20 or 30 feet out, but in the playoffs, more of the goals are scored from 20 feet or closer. He wasn't considered a superstar—not that I was, either—but because we didn't have one, the heat would mount on Proppie unfairly.

Without two regular centers and Craven—who could fill in so well at the position—we needed some goals to get through the division final. So it was a tribute to our depth when Hershey call-ups Don Nachbaur and Tim Tookey came up big in game three, Tookey setting up Propp to score a confidence-builder. We pretty much smothered the Islanders in a 4–1 win, and then Eklund fed Kerr for two power-play goals in a 6–4 victory in game four that Tocchet wrapped up into the empty net.

Whenever we had a chance to finish off a series early, our joke was, "Do we really want to give Keenan extra days to bag-skate us?" But with so many guys still out, Kerr's shoulder being held in place by a harness and the key injured Islanders back for game five, we wanted this over.

Carson tried, soloing off a blocked shot to put us up 1–0. But when Hexy tripped in one of our infamous Spectrum ice ruts, the Islanders tied the game. New York got another lucky goal and escaped, 2–1, when a dump-in went into the net off Derrick Smith's legs.

For game six, we cued a rusty Sutter, back for the first time since January, but after two periods, Kerr couldn't go anymore and Bossy and Trottier both scored in a 4–2 win that forced game seven. From the two surviving lineups, one couldn't have guessed we had finished 18 points ahead of the Islanders during the regular season.

At Clarke's suggestion, Nice Mike benched Iron Mike for a night and surprised the team by taking us to the Comedy Factory Outlet, where John DeBella did a great Keenan, our kind of stand-up. It got our minds off the pressure for a few hours, but Poulin needed more than just mind over matter to suit up for game seven with cracked ribs. He submitted to a nerve block, an unnerving process that takes

Number 9 with the 1970 Junior Red Wings, with Marty (Number 3) and coach Carl Lindstrom. (Hockey Hall of Fame.)

The Howe home in Bloomfield Hills, Michigan, 1972.

Olympic silver medalists, 1972. Clockwise from bottom left: Dick McGlynn, Robbie Ftorek, Stu Irving and me.

Caddying for Gordie at Plum Hollow golf course in Detroit.

Coach George Armstrong holds up my new Toronto Marlboros jersey in 1972 as Marty watches. (Hockey Hall of Fame)

Three Howes: Marty, Gordie and me in Houston, 1973. We proved it was no publicity stunt. (O-Pee-Chee)

It took much of my first professional year to get comfortable. (Robert Shaver)

As a Hartford Whaler in 1979–80, my first NHL season. (Robert Shaver)

Mom and her Amway products stash in our Glastonbury, Connecticut, garage, 1980.

My son Travis with Gordie in Glastonbury, Connecticut.

With my wife, Ginger, in 1982, posing outside Independence Hall following my introductory press conference as a Philadelphia Flyer. (Bernie Moser)

Gordie with my daughter, Azia, and son Travis at my Moorestown, New Jersey, home.

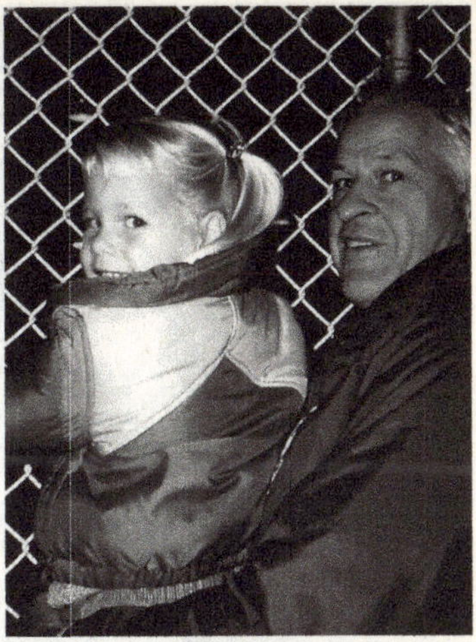

Azia and Gordie at the Flyers' practice rink, the Coliseum, in Voorhees, New Jersey.

Bobby Clarke and me wearing our snappy Cooperalls during 1982–83, my first season in Philly. (Paul Bereswill)

When Brad McCrimmon, my defense partner from 1984–88, died in a 2011 Russian plane crash, I lost the best friend I ever had in hockey. (Ed Mahan)

My children: Nolan (*left*), Travis and Azia, in Moorestown, New Jersey, in 1986.

With Dave Poulin, Captain Courageous of the Flyers, during the 1985–86 season. (Ed Mahan)

Ron Hextall (Number 27) and I battled Wayne Gretzky (Number 99) to a bitter game-seven end in the 1987 finals. (Paul Bereswill)

Skating with my Red Wing teammates Bob Probert (Number 24) and Ray Sheppard. (Mark Hicks)

Assistant captain with the Red Wings, 1995. (Mark Hicks)

With Gordie at the entrance to the Red Wings' dressing room, February 27, 1995. (Mark Hicks)

In the locker room after winning the 1997 Cup against the Flyers, with my son Nolan and Red Wings defensive pairing Nicklas Lidstrom (*far right*) and Vladimir Konstantinov (*far left*). Tragically, Vladi would become permanently impaired only days later, when a limousine taking him home from the Cup party crashed. (Mark Hicks)

With Mike Ilitch and Stanley, celebrating the 2002 Cup during a party at the Red Wings owner's home. (Focal Point)

With Gordie and Colleen at the 2002 Ilitch Cup party. (Focal Point)

30 minutes and, as I learned once in Hartford, leaves you in agony when it wears off.

With no Craven and Kerr, we needed our captain desperately. Poulin wore shoulder pads tall enough to scrape the ceiling, and that's how high we were when he assisted on Brown's tip-in, and then set up Propp to finish a two-man shorthanded breakaway. The penalty had not expired, and the roar remained unsubsided when Kelly Hrudey extended his blocker on a Marsh shot that was going a foot wide, deflecting the puck off both posts and in to give us a 3–0 lead.

Propp's playoff monkey was off his back with a dominating performance in game seven. Sinisalo put it away, 5–1, with two third-period goals. For the second time in three years, we had eliminated what might have been the best clutch team in history to reach the semifinals.

Even bigger than that win, which I thought was our best yet of the Keenan era, were the bodies of our next opponents—the defending Stanley Cup champion Canadiens. But the rookie hero of Montreal's unexpected run of the previous year, goalie Patrick Roy, had struggled most of the season, losing the starting job to Brian Hayward. So even without Kerr, and with Poulin requiring more time to recover, Hextall gave us a decent chance.

Good fortune got us though game one, when Smith put the shot of his life over Hayward's glove off an across-the-body feed by Nachbaur to tie the game late in the third period. Sinisalo's poke, with a majority of the players on the ice groping on their knees for the puck, sneaked across the line for a 4–3 win in overtime.

In game two, the Canadiens leaned hard and won 5–2. Then, in game three in Montreal, they scored two rebound goals in the first period and overwhelmed all of us except Hexy. After making 19 first-period saves, he told us in the locker room that he had done all he could without us, and he was right.

Keenan, who had been worried about little Eklund being caught in size mismatches, said screw it and put him with Tocchet and Propp in a wise attempt to back Montreal off with speed. Eklund scored twice to tie the game, and it became obvious that the way out for us against such physical domination was between Hayward's legs. Propp and Tocchet scored there, and Hextall stole game three for us, 4–3.

The Canadiens went back to Roy and his rusty glove in game four. But they were no match for Eklund, who one-handed a goal, converted a Tocchet pass-out and soloed to complete a hat trick in our 6–3 win. Although we were being territorially outplayed, we went ahead 3–1 in the series.

Hextall was killing the Canadiens' confidence. Hospodar, who dressed only for the warmups, decided to pitch in and play mind games with Claude Lemieux, who always ended his on-ice pre-game with a shot into the vacated opposition net. Before game three, Eddie had stayed on the ice a little longer, intercepted Lemieux's shot and fired it back into the Montreal goal. Prior to game four, Chico Resch joined the fun by helping Eddie turn the net around before leaving the ice. For game five, Chris Chelios swung it back around to feed Lemieux's peace of mind.

I found the whole thing amusing. We had a goalie playing so super that they were down to superstition. But early in game five, Hayward finally made some stops and the Canadiens shut off the superhighway we had been taking up the middle in a 5–2 win that sent us back to Montreal.

In game six's warmup, Hospodar and Resch waited until Lemieux went to the locker room before leaving the ice. But they were suckered. Lemieux returned, emerging from the tunnel with a puck and Shayne Corson. Eddie and Chico raced back out, but it was too late for Eddie to do anything but beat on Lemieux.

"Hospodar is out on the ice fighting!" our stick boy ran into the locker room yelling. I grabbed a stick and was out the door. Crossman had taken his skates off, so he ran out in shower slippers. Poulin, who was going to play again after missing the first five games, grabbed hold of somebody after just taking needles in his ribs. Hextall, restrained by Keenan because he feared his goalie would get sucker-punched, was the only Flyer not on the ice.

Brownie went after Chris Nilan, Nachbaur started beating on 35-year old Larry Robinson and Daryl Stanley paired off with John Kordic before the officials could get dressed and restore order. It was 15 minutes until they got us back in the locker rooms.

The officials came in and told us Corson, Brian Skrudland, Robinson and Nilan were out of the game for the Canadiens; Brown, Stanley, Hospodar and Nachbaur were gone for us. Advantage: Philadelphia, which they figured out belatedly. Ten minutes later, they came back to tell us that that only Eddie had gotten a game misconduct.

The fans booed the U.S. anthem and roared when the Canadiens scored in the first minute. Poulin—Captain Courageous—tied it with a shorthanded goal, but Robinson scored at the end of the period, just before Bobby Smith put them up 3–1 on a power play.

The Canadiens had the working margin that they used to full advantage in game five, but Hayward couldn't control a rebound, enabling Sinisalo to score. It then took only 2:40 for their two-goal lead to disappear as Mellanby, on a feed from Crossman, tied the game.

I had been in many a series where, no matter how hard you worked, the opposition had every answer. This time, we had destiny on our side, which is another way of saying we had Hextall.

Seven minutes into the third period, Propp stole the puck from Chelios and slid it across to Tocchet, who scored into the half-empty net, putting us ahead, 4–3. As the clock ran down, Crossman and I reversed a few times to beat the first forechecker, and our forwards gave us time. Hexy covered their last good chance with three minutes to go, and with Hayward pulled, Propp cleared the puck.

I waited at the blue line to bat down Montreal's last prayer and raced for Hexy, who had been amazing. We won all three games at the Forum to earn our second crack at Edmonton, and the Cup, in three seasons.

The Oilers were scarier than ever after adding Kent Nilsson and Reijo Ruotsalainen to Gretzky, Messier, Anderson, Coffey and Kurri. Surely they were hungrier, too, after losing the previous year to Calgary on the fluke of defenseman Steve Smith banking the puck into the net off his own goalie, Grant Fuhr, late in game seven.

The Flyers were not just more experienced than in 1985, but better, too, even without Kerr. Tocchet had come into his own as a scorer during the playoffs, Propp was having a great postseason and Eklund had stepped up big-time. Samuelsson, who had proved himself to Keenan as the spring went along, had arms that could unfurl as if they were on retractors. We had five good defensemen capable of logging a lot of minutes, and no other team in the league, not even Edmonton, that could say that.

You go into a series with a great goalie like Hextall, you figure that's worth one win. A second victory should be provided by your big scorer, which we didn't have without Kerr. We fulfilled the requirement of having two excellent checking centers—Sutter and Poulin—to use against Gretzky and Messier, even though Dave needed to be frozen before games. But then, we effectively lost me—or the best of me—as soon as game one began in Edmonton.

Off the opening face-off, I dumped it ahead and Messier finished a check on my leg, just below the thigh pad. By the end of the second period, I could only wave at Messier as he circled the net to feed Anderson for a 2–1 lead. At the break, I gave Mike shit for leaving me out there. He said he would rather have me on one leg than somebody else on two. I didn't necessarily agree, but stuck it out to the end of our 4–2 loss.

At least we had two days before the second contest. Our strength and conditioning guy, Pat Croce, had me crying three times a day by pushing on my leg until my heel would finally reach my butt. The process took anywhere from 30 minutes to an hour. This was a really bad charley horse. Somehow, Pat worked enough of it out to get me on the ice for game two. Beast knew my situation and assumed the majority of my usual offensive responsibilities.

We led 2–1 on goals by Propp and Smith going into the third period, but the Oilers started coming at us like a white wave. Anderson went end to end to tie it, and Coffey set up Kurri for a one-timer just inside the post to win it, 3–2, in overtime.

We had Craven back for game three, plus the next two games at home. But all the little bumps on the Spectrum's notoriously choppy ice that we had come to embrace as our advantage were dwarfed by the mountain we had to climb after Messier scored shorthanded, Coffey cranked a bullet and Anderson swooped in to put Edmonton up 3–0 in the second period.

We got one back when Craven used his stick shaft to bunt one over Fuhr on the power play. After Craven stole the puck from Kevin Lowe and Zezel's centering pass for Tocchet went in off Craig Muni, we suddenly were only down 3–2.

Early in the third period, I fed Mellanby, whose hammer went in off Fuhr's pads to tie it just 17 seconds before McCrimmon went to the net and redirected Mellanby's feed over Fuhr. Samuelsson was tremendous down the stretch—they couldn't use their speed to get wide of him—and Propp put away our 5–3 victory, the first winning rally from a three-goal deficit in a Stanley Cup final game in 41 years.

With Edmonton ahead in the series 2–1, we weren't thinking we had done ourselves proud to avoid a possible sweep. Our second time in the final, we were there to win. But the Oilers kicked themselves for letting one get away and the Great One was poised to stomp the life out of us.

In game four, after McCrimmon scored to cut Edmonton's lead to 2–1, Gretzky came out of the penalty box and fed Randy Gregg for a goal. When the lead grew to 4–1, Hexy was seething and took a full two-hander to the back of Nilsson's leg as he went by the crease.

He was okay, but we weren't. Our fans, figuring they had seen the last of us for the year after our loss, applauded respectfully to thank us for a great run. Both teams got on charters that night, one gate apart, and I remember thinking the Oilers looked pretty cocky. But what were we going to say?

As we practiced in Edmonton, the next day, the Cup was in the Northlands Coliseum for possible presentation after game five. Keenan had it brought to the locker room to remind us that it was still within our reach. The plans for Edmonton's parade appeared in their newspaper—more incentive to spoil their celebration. We didn't need the "I love you guys" speech that Mike gave us at the hotel that night—we had heard that kind of thing before in must-win situations and had become pretty cynical by now—but our coach delivered his message anyway.

It is fair to say, however, that Keenan loved Ron "Hackstall" a lot more than the booing, chanting Edmonton fans. Our goalie wasn't just determined to go down hard; he still believed we weren't going down at all, even when the Oilers scored twice in the first seven minutes of game five.

Hextall stopped Coffey on a breakaway and kept his cool when run by Marty McSorley. A third goal that should have counted, by Anderson, was waved off because referee Don Koharski lost sight of the puck, so from the bottom of the mineshaft we could still see the light when Tocchet, back playing with Eklund and Propp for the first time since the Montreal series, rapped a pass-out between Fuhr's legs.

We weren't even shaken when McSorley batted one out of the air to make it 3–1. Tocchet buried Nilsson, Crossman jumped up to beat Fuhr over his glove, and then Eklund forced a bad clear by Craig Muni and put in a rebound to tie it. After Hextall withstood the next bombardment, Propp forced Muni to give the puck away and Tocchet redirected a cross-crease feed. My God, we led, 4–3.

After hunkering down for two defensive-zone draws in the final minute, I lifted the puck off Gretzky's stick and put it in the only safe place I knew against that team—over the glass. The buzzer went off with me shaking my head in disbelief. You don't come back on that team once in a series, let alone twice. Yet we were alive and going home.

Hexy came up the tunnel like a man possessed every night, not just for game six of the final. But when the roar went up as he led us out, we didn't have to actually hear Starship's drowned-out "Nothing's Going to Stop Us Now" to believe it. We felt that way even after Gretzky got by me to feed Kevin Lowe for a tap-in and Kevin McClelland scored on a rebound to put us down 2–0. Twice in the series, we had already come back from two-goal deficits.

With only 13 shots on goal in two periods, we still had the Oilers where we wanted them. After Brad Marsh dove and stopped a Gretzky wraparound and Hextall held up the puck in his glove, we believed our fate was also in his hand. Lindsay Carson, not much of a scorer, got the puck through Lowe (an All-Star) and Brown (a fighter) tipped the puck between Fuhr's legs to get us on the board.

Propp, set up by Eklund, put one over Fuhr's glove to tie it at 2–2. The Spectrum had not lost a decibel when Daigneault, who barely played until these last two games, held off Kurri in front of our net and was waved to stay on by Keenan. Pouncing on Kurri's forced clear that died just inside the blue line, Daigneault slapped an unforgettable bouncer through everybody, including Fuhr.

On the video of that goal, the picture jumps. That's how much the Spectrum was shaking. I looked up, expecting to see chips of paint coming off the ceiling. Five minutes later, I had made it to the game I always wanted to be in: winner takes all for the Stanley Cup.

Game seven would be an NHL-record 26th playoff game in 54 days for us, but we were so high that the extra day off before game seven—there was a previous booking at Northlands Coliseum—was not our friend. We'd had the Oilers reeling, and now they had an extra day to regroup. After blowing the Calgary series the year before, there was enormous pressure on them, and they looked tight at the opening face-off.

Messier cross-checked Hextall, Coffey held Propp and Andy Van Hellemond called both penalties, giving us a two-man advantage after only 1:13. As Craven held the puck along the wing, he saw Fuhr put out his stick to cut off the passing lane. Murray shot at the goalie's skate and got the intended carom into the net. It was the first time in the entire series that we had scored the initial goal, and there still was 1:32 to go on the power play.

Crossman took an Eklund pass, swung around a diving Lowe and was about to give us a two-goal lead when Fuhr charged out to poke the puck away. Anderson blew through Carson at center, Nilsson had a speed mismatch on Brown, and so did Messier on Sutter to tap in a spectacular goal to tie the game. But even that wind tunnel didn't take our breath away. McSorley swept a puck off the line before Propp could reach it, and Sinisalo had a breakaway and a redirection that Fuhr stopped.

As the second period moved along, the Oilers got stronger. Esa Tikkanen bumped off Crossman and Gretzky threaded a pass to Kurri, who put one between Zezel's legs and just inside the far post. Edmonton, ahead 2–1, then cranked it up like I had never seen a team crank it up. We never had the puck.

As many good chances as they had, however, it wasn't implausible that we could still tie the game. Not in this series. But they were just too good. Hextall had just come across to make a stop on Messier when Anderson flew through center ice again and cranked a wicked 40-footer off the inside of Hextall's pad and into the net with 2:25 remaining.

Hexy was mad at himself for not stopping it, but how much worse than 3–1 would the final have been without him? There was no big screw-up in game seven that any of us would have to take to our graves. I knew we had lost to the best single-game performance by a team that I had ever witnessed. But my heart wasn't buying what my eyes had seen. I never felt worse after a game in my life.

We had been one goal away with 2:26 to play, and yet, basically, it was a lifetime. I was 32 years old and hoped there would be another chance, but I had the sense I might never get there again. And it did turn out to be my closest shot.

I knew what our team went through with all the injuries, 26 play-off games, three years of daily doses of Mike Keenan and even the death of an All-Star goalie. But we had kept it together with an eye on the prize, and suddenly, it was gone. In the regular season, you can vent, scream, slam something or say, "We'll get 'em tomorrow," because there is another day. This was just so final.

Before they let the media in, I looked up, and there weren't too many heads not in towels, crying. You could hear a pin drop. I went to a sink, turned on the spigot and buried my head, hoping the water would stop or at least hide my tears. It didn't work very well. We had been so close to something you play for your entire life that I couldn't even describe the pain.

"I've never been shot by a bullet," I told reporters. "But it couldn't hurt any more than this."

I don't remember whether Keenan spoke to us or not. I don't think anybody said a word on the long ride to the Edmonton airport or for the first hour of the flight, when I think I cracked a joke and it loosened things up a little. I heard later that while our coach slept on the plane, some guys had asked Clarke to fire him. I wasn't one of them.

A few days later, when Jay Snider asked for my thoughts on Mike, I said there was no way the Flyers should get rid of him. We were winning. I was willing to endure. But I told Jay to brace for a bad start to the following season since Hextall would be serving his eight-game suspension for whacking Nilsson.

Needing the time to heal my charley horse over the summer, I excused myself from Team USA for the September Canada Cup. Tocchet, Propp, Poulin, Crossman and Hextall were invited to play for Team Canada, and Keenan was asked to coach, so I knew they would all miss a portion of Flyers training camp.

But when I predicted our poor start to Snider months earlier, I had no idea that the screw Dr. John Gregg put in Kerr's shoulder would become dislodged and that the new one would become infected, keeping him out of the lineup until March.

I also would never have guessed that McCrimmon would be traded in August, but after a stubborn two-year contract battle with Clarke, Brad was dealt to Calgary for first- and third-round draft choices.

I was totally stunned and pissed that my partner was gone; I just didn't understand it at all. If the hardest thing to find in hockey is a goalie you can count on, the next is a defenseman who can play 25 minutes a game and in every situation. We were one win away from the Stanley Cup with a core of Crossman, Marsh, Samuelsson,

McCrimmon and me. Beast and Clarke were $25,000 apart, and the Flyers treated it like he was asking for the whole bank, replacing Brad with somebody who might make our team in three years.

Kerry Huffman, our number-one pick in 1986, had some ability, but they should have been breaking him in as a seventh defenseman, not our fifth. Plugging him in over his head was asking for a failure that I had seen time and again. With McCrimmon gone, we also lost an important voice in our locker room, especially when the bitching about Keenan resumed. Beast always would say, "He's a prick, but a smart hockey guy."

Brad was going to a Cup contender close to where his parents lived (in Saskatchewan), so those were positives for him, but no way did he want to get traded. The irony was that we were starting 1987–88 with too many guys who *did* want out, another condition for the perfect storm to rage.

In our fourth game of the new season, we were humiliated by the Islanders, 6–0. After Ron Sutter lost a defensive zone face-off to his brother Brent, Keenan ordered Ron to the locker room. Instead, he hung in the tunnel, which at the Spectrum was next to where the defensemen sat on the bench, and asked me what he should do.

"Spear somebody in the face; that's what he wants," I said. "You have to show him you're pissed off."

Keenan allowed Sutter to spend the rest of the game on the bench, but didn't dress him for our return match two nights later at Nassau Coliseum, which we won. With Mark LaForest in our goal, we went only 3–4–1 before Hextall returned at Madison Square Garden.

With the teams tied 2–2 during the third period, I had been going back and forth with the feisty Tomas Sandstrom, a thorn in a lot of teams' sides, but especially ours. Off a face-off, he speared me in the gut. I doubled over and glided to the bench, where I sat screaming at him, "You're dead!"

"I'll take care of it," said Dave Brown, who had retaliated for me against Sandstrom a year earlier and received a five-game suspension for a cross-check to the face shield.

"No, he's mine," I insisted. I just had to figure out how to do it without being suspended for a million games.

The next shift I was out against Sandstrom, the Rangers dumped the puck to the corner and I turned at the front of the net to look for him. There he was—at my feet, with Brownie standing over him. I had to see it on the replay. After I did, I don't know how Dave, who snapped Sandstrom's head back with a vicious cross-check between the visor and the side of the face, didn't break his neck. Brownie was suspended for 12 games, irritating the hell out of us because Sandstrom, who really was a dirty player, came off as a martyr.

Just a few months later, I got to see another side of him. When I had my son Travis with me at the All-Star Game in St. Louis, Sandstrom told me he was going up the Gateway Arch and asked if Travis wanted to come. They had a great time. Who would have thought?

Our next game against the Rangers, Sandstrom speared me again. I said, "If that's the way you want it, let's go at it," but he said, "No, I'm sorry," and didn't do it ever again. When he came to the Red Wings after I had begun scouting for them, we laughed about the old times. Tomas had scars from a lot of wars. But I doubt if anybody who ever evened a score against him was vilified to the degree of Brownie.

As our enforcer served what was then the fifth-longest suspension in NHL history, he wasn't the only Flyer holding baggage. Hextall had a new contract and an obsession with becoming the best goalie ever, an ambition he had announced when he won the Vezina Trophy a few months earlier.

For the third time, I had finished second in the Norris balloting—this time to Ray Bourque. At least I still had something to shoot for. After the playoffs, I told people I felt badly for Hextall because it would be hard to duplicate the best-goaltended season I had ever seen.

"Relax a little," I told him.

"I'm only going to play five years, but I am going to be the best goalie anybody ever saw," he said.

"Talk to you in five years and we'll see how you feel then," I said. But that's the way he was in practice every day, yelling, "Shoot the puck!" if somebody passed it behind him for tap-in, or chasing Proppie or somebody around the rink after getting scored upon during warmup.

But here I was, trying to help Ronnie when I could have really used a little aid myself. In a game against Boston, I turned to get a head start on a dump-in and got hit with the puck in the middle of my back; I had trouble breathing as games went along. After about two weeks, they finally took x-rays and discovered two of my ribs had broken off where they had connected with my vertebrae. I could still play, but not well.

Some games, like the 6–0 loss at home to the horrible Leafs, looked suspiciously like a blatant attempt to get Keenan out of our lives. But I don't think it was conscious; more a case of us not enjoying ourselves. I would never question the character of any of the guys on those teams.

I imagined Clarke and the Sniders would get crucified for firing the coach who had just gotten them to game seven of the Stanley Cup final, but there were circumstances that could have justified a change. Still, Keenan wasn't the only factor in our anxiety. Paul Coffey was holding out and refusing to return to Edmonton, and Clarke was probably interested, in which case he was necessarily offering important players off our team. When we learned that Coffey had been dealt to Pittsburgh, our apprehension lessened. But as each loss came, the thought of how many games we would have to win to make up all this ground caused panic and individualism, which never works to get a team out of its slump.

The shit hit the fan in St. Louis when Tocchet was benched from early in the second period for the duration of the game, then afterwards said it was because he had refused his coach's order to start a fight. Nobody on the bench heard such an order—or a refusal—and after the 5–2 loss, Keenan told the newspapers it was "a lie." He ripped Rick for selfishly worrying about his own stats. Meanwhile, Hexy said we were a "disgrace to the uniform." When we practiced there the next day, Mike removed a table from the center of the locker room.

"He's going to challenge me to a fight," Captain Poulin whispered to Lindsay Carson.

"Go for it," said Carson.

Instead, Mike asked each player to discuss what he was bringing to the team, then left to let us talk among ourselves.

Some guys wanted to come out and publicly announce that we had enough of Keenan as coach, but I thought that would be unprofessional and most of my teammates agreed. We said we would continue to play for each other. As we sank to 6–13–3, there were games we would play well for 50 minutes, but then just emotionally exhaust ourselves and blow the lead. Finally, even after Buffalo scored twice to create a 2–2 tie on Thanksgiving Eve, we pulled away to a 5–2 victory.

When we followed up with a win in Quebec City, Keenan did not cancel our scheduled three-day retreat in Lake Placid. We had been dreading a boot camp—practice twice a day plus team-building activities like mountain biking—but were surprised by his announcement that he would join us in afternoon scrimmages.

"All you guys who hate my guts and want to kill me, I'm all yours," he said. "But remember: after two days, you're mine again."

That was a risk some guys were happy to take. Thus, my new defensive partner was born—Mike Keenan, former ace of the blue lines at St. Lawrence University and the Roanoke Valley Rebels.

Carson, one of Mike's favorite punching bags, finally had the free shot he had wanted for more than three years. "Pass the puck in his feet," Lindsay told me. I purposely put it behind Mike so that it would carom off the boards and into his feet, forcing him to look down and leaving him vulnerable to a blindside hit. Lindsay ran over him like a freight train. Our coach got up and kept playing. Guys ran him for two days.

We had no curfew, only instructions not to drive and to do everything together. The Flyers went home regenerated and beat Hartford. When the Bruins came in, we seemed to be burying our problems until I thought we were going to have to bury Marsh, who took simultaneous body checks by Ray Bourque and Cam Neely, hit his helmetless head on the glass supports, and then slammed it on the ice.

I was the first guy over the boards to reach him. His eyes were rolled back and there was blood coming out his nose and mouth. I first thought he was dead, but he went into a seizure, forcing Sudsy to clamp Brad's jaw open to keep him from swallowing his tongue.

He woke up in the Zamboni entrance, where he jokingly asked for his chew. It was a hard thing to watch happen to a teammate we loved, and it took a full period for us to settle ourselves. The Bruins scored twice to put us behind, but our confidence was coming back and our four-goal third period proved it. Propp's insurance goal convinced a lot of fans to go to their cars. Big mistake.

Hextall went to a knee behind the net to play a Bourque dump-in, rose and wristed the puck 20 feet into the air. I had been concentrating on making the closest guy—Lyndon Byers—take a detour, then looked up to see the puck, which had been going wide, slam just inside the post.

I didn't even know who shot it. Then I saw Hexy jumping up and down and suddenly I had a good idea. He had just become the first NHL goalie in history to shoot and score a goal. Pretty neat, but I'd known he was going to do it eventually.

As cold as we had been, suddenly our team was white-hot. Craven scored when we were two men short to win a game in Winnipeg, and a 12–0–2 streak lifted us from worst to first in the division in just 31 days.

I was settling in with my new partner, Samuelsson, which had been a process. At some point during our first few games, he came to the bench, yelling at me for an error I had made. I said, "People make mistakes. That's what partners are for." He never did it again.

Defensively, I played a little higher than I had with McCrimmon, trying to steer the play to where Kjell's reach and range would get a piece of anybody coming down his side. Offensively, I increased my pursuit of the puck. Kjell could pass and communicate well, so our chemistry was fine, just not the same as what I'd had with McCrimmon.

Our winning streak ended in Edmonton with a 6–0 blasting by our nemeses, and then we lost in Calgary on a power-play goal with eight seconds remaining. We were two games removed from a

14-game winning streak that might as well have been a 14-year losing streak the way Keenan lit into us after the first period in Vancouver.

Around the room he went, one by one, until he got to Sinisalo. "You haven't done a goddamn thing in so long," Keenan said, and then looked at the stats sheet he was holding. "You have 12 goals? How the hell do you have 12 goals?"

"Power play," Ilkka said. And we all burst out laughing.

Keenan turned around and kicked a table that had to weigh a ton, and his face turned red. I'll bet he broke his toe. And now, we were laughing even more.

"You fuckers are going to pay for this," he said, and limped out.

At least that was an injury we could afford. Huffman, who had been playing okay, had to come out of the lineup with a calcium knot in his thigh. Marsh, who had been determined to be the last helmetless player in the league, came back from his severe concussion after only nine days wearing protection. It wasn't just that he looked different; he was not the same player. They didn't do the baseline testing then to measure recoveries from concussions. Brad was a step slower and Keenan was as quick as ever to lose confidence.

Although Clarke made deals to pick up a couple of veteran defensemen, Keenan had no trust in them, so they barely played. It meant that, when I hurt my back in L.A. and had to fly home, we were still short on the blue line. Before our next game in Vancouver, our GM acquired Willie Huber from the Canucks. Huber had a bad knee and a bad excuse not to dress for us that night: he said he needed time to pack.

Keenan stuck with his reliables, including Hextall in a game in which he got hit with a shot by the Rangers' Michel Petit and couldn't move his arm. Hexy gave up four goals prior to being pulled in the 5–2 loss. He also surrendered three in our 11–6 win in Detroit—a matchup that began with him vomiting in the locker room.

After 10 days, I came back on the same night that Kerr did—March 10 against Washington—and we won. But two days later, Timmy's strength in his shoulder was gone, and that win over the Caps proved to be our only one in nine games. Crossman, who had grown tired of Keenan's negativity, was begged by Poulin to play harder and didn't. Doug was convinced that the fans were booing his number, 3, because they had booed Tom Bladon and Behn Wilson—the players who wore that number previously. Crossman also read history books about the propaganda practices of despotic historical leaders and thought parallels applied to our team. He was not a happy guy.

The amazing Tim Kerr returned with a hat trick against Winnipeg, but the strength in his shoulder was quickly spent again and he had to come out of the lineup. We didn't squeak into the playoffs until the final weekend—not that Washington, our first-round opponent, finished much better.

Both Scott Stevens and Rod Langway were out of the Caps' lineup as we went to game four up 2–1. Although we were facing a team without its two best defensemen, we did nothing for 51 minutes and fell behind 4–1 before I put in Samuelsson's rebound. That woke the team up. Sammy gloved down a clearing attempt, enabling Propp to put in a feed from Tocchet, and with 51 seconds left, Kjell tied the game off a goalmouth scramble.

We were so quiet in the locker room before the overtime—it was like we couldn't believe it. Even after Craven scored at 1:18, it didn't seem real. If we had played that game 250 times, we would have won it just once. So with Hextall struggling and Kjell and me playing 35 minutes a game, it was hard to feel comfortable. Perhaps the Caps would continue to hand it to us.

But they didn't. In game five, when Washington was energized by the return of Stevens, Hexy looked even more shaky during our 5–2 loss in Landover.

Keenan asked Clarke's opinion on playing LaForest in goal for game six to give Hextall a chance to clear his head. The GM thought it was a good idea, but our coach decided to go with Hextall regardless. This time, Keenan didn't go to the "I love you guys" speech. He bag-skated us for 75 minutes, even though we were about to play our sixth playoff game in nine days.

Poulin, his groin wrapped on both sides, was smarter than I. Dave went only half-speed, defying Mike even as he screamed. "Can't hear you," Poulin would say.

With fried legs, we played well in game six for about one shift. Our team was down 2–0 when Keenan sent Brownie out against Bobby Gould, who turtled. All we got for our trouble was five extra minutes in penalties and two power-play goals against. The 7–2 loss was the only one of my career that I ever blamed on a coach.

We still had one shot left in game seven.

Kerr, with one working arm, put us up 1–0 on a two-man advantage. Trying to rehydrate myself after playing 15 first-period minutes in a hot Capital Centre, I could hear, from my seat by the locker-room door, assistant coach Paul Holmgren calling a spare defenseman we had picked up that season out into the corridor and asking if he could take a couple shifts. His answer: "If you don't need me, don't use me." I swear, I never heard anything like that in my life.

When I scored on a breakaway out of the penalty box, we went up 3–0. But we didn't have the defense or confidence to protect it. By the end of the second period, it was 3–3. After Dale Hunter put the Caps ahead, we appeared to receive an omen when a shot by the little-used Marsh got through traffic to get us to overtime. Maybe we were going to get through this after all.

The saves we would have needed from Hexy to finish the series in game five or six were suddenly coming as we took our last stand, but in overtime, it was a Washington onslaught. Larry Murphy made a quick counter off a Craven giveaway at the Capitals' line and Hunter split Marsh and Crossman to win the series on a breakaway.

Like the previous year, we had a bunch of key guys—in this case, Sutter, Poulin and Tocchet—who had come back just before the playoffs and weren't up to speed for the first round. Still, we had survived injuries in 1987 not just because Hextall had been so much better that spring, but because our defense was deeper. If we'd had McCrimmon playing 25 minutes a game in that 1988 series against Washington, there's no question in my mind we would have won.

Instead, we had a guy in the hallway saying, "If you don't need me, don't use me."

Since the Flyers hadn't fired Keenan when they had the chance in November, I really didn't know whether they would at the end of the season. But Clarke and the Sniders did in early May. I wouldn't have let Mike go, despite it all.

Keenan pushed us to two finals and three division championships. Every veteran on the team, myself included, played 20 per cent better under Mike than before he was hired.

Our two great playoff runs were foiled in the end by probably the best offensive machine in hockey history. We were as good as a lot of teams that won the Cup. McCrimmon shared the opinion of many that our window of opportunity was in 1986, when Edmonton got beat by Calgary after we had lost to the Rangers. But Montreal steamrolled the Flames in that final, so you just don't know who is going to get hot and who is going to get hurt.

We took our best shot. Moving forward, we needed a new defense more than a new coach, but actually, the Flyers would get both.

CHAPTER 12

The Little Person with the Blowtorch

After four years of mental beatdowns by Mike Keenan, we looked forward to playing for a head coach we wanted to please rather than spite. Though Paul Holmgren's only experience behind the bench was as an assistant, he received instant respect from those of us who had been his teammates. And he quickly demonstrated a different way of making his point.

Early in the 1988–89 season, I stood up on a pass to Mario Lemieux, who cleverly used his quick hands and long reach to tip the puck over my head and send himself on a breakaway. When I came to the bench, Holmgren gave me a "what are you doing?" look that was as effective as a glare or harsh words.

Actually, there wasn't much I could have done. Who else would have made that play but Lemieux? But this was Paul's gentler, yet still challenging, approach. Besides, he would flash just enough temper to scare the shit out of us. One time he broke a fiberglass stick and sent the blade winging around the locker room.

E.J. McGuire, a sweet, bright and tireless man who never had a bad day in the four years I knew him as an assistant coach, left with Keenan to go to the Chicago Blackhawks. Paul wisely chose two new assistants—Mike Eaves, an upbeat and smart guy, and Andy Murray, who handled most of the game preparation and didn't miss many details.

Doug Crossman chose not to join us on our Holmgren honeymoon, although team president Jay Snider had told me he thought a new coach could restore Doug's enthusiasm. I said, "You don't get it. He hates the fans and the organization, not just Keenan." Sure enough, Crossman asked for a trade, which he received—to Los Angeles for defenseman Jay Wells.

GM Bob Clarke also gave up on defenseman Greg Smyth, a high draft choice (22nd overall in 1984) who always came to training camp out of shape, sending him to Quebec for defenseman Terry Carkner. Smyth's Flyer legacy was limited to being a victim of one of the best practical jokes ever.

During his first camp, some of our players told him that team personnel could travel across the Walt Whitman Bridge from New Jersey into Pennsylvania without paying a toll by simply shouting the secret code word "Flyers" into the coin catcher. Smyth followed the instructions and, when the bar wouldn't go up, started arguing with the supervisor who came over to our vehicle. "I don't care who you're with," she said as guys busted a gut in the back seat.

Two more draft choices—Jeff Chychrun and Gord Murphy—made the team, giving us four new defensemen and, sadly, ending Brad Marsh's days in Philadelphia. After Clarke picked up winger Doug Sulliman, Marsh was exposed in the waiver draft and lost to Toronto.

Brad was the ultimate Flyer; I hated to see him go. He had struggled the previous season after coming back too soon from his concussion, but, if paired with a mobile, right-handed partner, he still could have helped us as a fifth defenseman, particularly since his departure left Kjell Samuelsson and me as the only holdovers. After a 4–0 start, that inexperience caught up to us, although it was not the only factor to quickly turn the fresh air of our coaching change into a tornado.

Rick Tocchet served a 10-game suspension for gouging the Islanders' Dean Chynoweth in a fight, Dave Poulin suffered a shoulder separation, and Murray Craven narrowly escaped a career-ending eye injury when cracked in the face by Mirko Frycer while scoring a winning goal in Detroit. We also lost Ron Sutter to a jaw fracture when the Rangers' James Patrick put his stick up to ward off a body check.

By December, Holmgren was so distraught by our 10–16–2 record that he offered Clarke his resignation. But the GM was more inclined to blame the underachievers who had thought they would do better with Keenan out of their lives. When we put up only 15 shots and lost to the St. Louis Blues at home for the first time in 35 games spanning 16 years, Clarke made a rare postgame locker-room appearance. "I hope there are wheels on your houses," was all he said before walking out.

Peter Zezel forgot about an appointment to meet with Holmgren and then twice misplaced checks on overtime goals that sent us to defeats against Calgary and Boston. For the second time in two seasons, Poulin and Sutter were injured and Peter was struggling at a time when we needed more from him. At the morning skate on November 29, he was told he had been traded to St. Louis for center Mike Bullard.

It ended a rough ride for Zezel in Philadelphia. Peter was the Flyers' heartthrob—you could hear the shrieks from the young ladies as soon as he hit the ice—but he had frustrated Keenan by doing things like recording his weight at 208 when he had let himself get up to 227. Mike ordered 7 a.m. and 4 p.m. workouts with Pat Croce at his place in Broomall, Pennsylvania—at least an hour away, fighting rush-hour traffic twice—in addition to the regular 10:30 am. team practices for four weeks until Peter lost the weight.

During one of our runs to the final, Keenan banished Zezel to another locker room, which was completely humiliating. The shock treatments wore him down, and one time Keenan wanted me to play good cop and take Peter out for lunch and a pep talk.

"What did you tell him?" Mike wanted to know the next day.

"I told him things could be a lot worse; he could be your son and have to hear it at home, too. I think that worked."

"That's what you said?" asked Mike.

Keenan was a good father to his daughter, Gayla—I'm not implying otherwise. But a lot of us saw more in the affable and easy-going Zezel than he delivered in stretches where he would get down on himself. I thought he had a big-time shot he didn't use enough, but he went on to play 15 NHL seasons and didn't have to apologize for a career in which he scored 608 points.

Peter, who never married, was with Vancouver in 1998–99 when he asked to be traded to the Leafs so he could be near his family—his niece was terminally ill with cancer. Instead, the Canucks dealt him to Anaheim, so he retired to run his sports camp in Toronto, only to soon be diagnosed with a rare blood disorder, hemolytic anemia. Chemotherapy achieved remission for many years, but sadly, he passed away in 2009 at age 44.

The night the Flyers traded Zezel to the Blues, I was on my way to the Spectrum for our game against Boston when a tractor-trailer jackknifed 200 yards in front of me on the Walt Whitman Bridge, closing every lane. I didn't get to the locker room until after the warmup had begun and had time only to throw my stuff on and go around the rink twice.

After Bullard scored a goal that allowed us to pull away in the third period to a 5–1 victory, he asked whether my contract stipulated that I didn't have to go out for the warmup. He was being serious, a word not often associated with Mike, a talented player who quickly was becoming a journeyman, joining his fourth team in three years. In short order, Bullard won a bunch of games for us. Meanwhile, the pinching dilemmas of our young defensemen were eased by Coach Murray's suggestion that we go to a simplifying left-wing lock. We surged over .500 by Christmas before injuries again drained us.

When Ilkka Sinisalo, who had suffered his share of health issues, went down in a Vancouver corner, guys were rolling their eyes as if to say, "What now?" When I reached him, he was holding one arm with the other. "What's wrong with it?" I asked. He let go and it flopped lifelessly—the worst broken arm I ever saw.

I ended up missing six games with groin issues and Tim Kerr was in and out of the lineup with more shoulder problems. All those years of defensemen hanging on the big guy had taken their toll.

My dad had offered long-standing advice to Timmy so he could buy himself some room: "Once a year, pick a game on national television and go crazy on some poor schmuck." But that was not his nature, any more than it was to celebrate goals by raising his stick. Kerr didn't think scoring was a big deal, just his job, and when in the lineup, he continued to do it almost as well as anybody in the NHL. His late-January hat trick in Winnipeg gave him 32 goals in the 45 games for which he had dressed.

Production from Kerr almost was as standard as Pittsburgh losses in Philadelphia. But on February 2, the Penguins finally beat us at the Spectrum, 5–3, for the first time in 43 games over 15 seasons. That Flyers streak, like ones in Los Angeles (21 games) and at home against Detroit (29) and St. Louis (35) that had ended over the previous three seasons, were points of pride for me. They all dated back to the days of the Broad Street Bullies and I didn't want them ending on my watch.

At least I wasn't on the ice or bench to see the Penguins finally congratulating each other at the Spectrum. In the second period, I had been flipped by Chris Dahlquist and landed on my knee, putting me out for another eight games. When I came back in Calgary—I hated the Saddledome because I never played well there, for whatever reason—the Flames were skating around me like I wasn't there. When the doctor had to drain 100 cubic centimeters of blood from my knee, a partial-ligament tear finally was found and I was out of the lineup again.

Kerr had started an aspirin regimen to desensitize his allergies to anti-inflammatory drugs. It worked, as did our league-best power play all season long. Hextall—backed up by Ken Wregget after he was acquired from Toronto before the trading deadline—played consistently from January on, and our addition of Keith Acton from Edmonton for Dave Brown gave us an upgrade in speed as well as another checking center.

Perhaps the most important factor was that Holmgren stayed positive throughout. Our chances at the division title were long gone, but our lead for the fourth and final playoff spot never dipped below 10 points. We liked the view from the weeds where we lay, waiting for bodies to heal.

Twice in three days during March, we received the ultimate health scare. Our Chicago-bound flight was only about 20 feet off the ground after takeoff from Philadelphia International Airport when we heard a loud crack. "This isn't good," the flight attendant said, as Scott Mellanby and I, who always sat in the back, looked at her. No kidding.

The pilot announced that we had blown a tire and were going to return. I didn't buy the explanation. When we pulled up at the gate, the presence of fire trucks and fluid dripping from the plane suggested to me that a hydraulic line had burst, which would have caused big trouble. I was happy to be back in the lineup—or *any* lineup—the next night when we rallied from a 2–0 deficit to beat Keenan's Blackhawks.

The following day, our plane was fewer than 100 feet from the runway at National Airport in Washington when Mellanby looked out the window to see a wing perpendicular to the ground. "Get it up, get it up!" Scott yelled. The pilot did, through the severe wind shear, and we barely made it over some trees. Our second landing attempt was almost as terrifying, but, thankfully, successful.

"Brutal! Brutal!" said Mellanby to the pilot as we deplaned.

A pair of air scares in three days is not what you would predict for a team named the Flyers. But perhaps our escapes were harbingers of good fortune.

Two games before the playoffs, during overtime at Montreal, Mats Naslund, tugged by Rick Tocchet, fell into my knee. I felt a sharp twinge and needed to be helped off, but the brace I had been wearing (and hating) since my return—it was uncomfortable and restrictive on turns—saved me from a long-term injury. The next day, Dr. John Gregg confirmed I probably would be able to play by halfway through the first round.

The Flyers needed only a tie against Pittsburgh in game 80 the next night to assure our 17th consecutive winning season. Instead, Holmgren pulled Hextall in overtime to go for third place, but we lost on Mario Lemieux's empty-net goal, his 199th point of the season.

A season of wild performance swings had left us at .500 and in fourth place, but our team, loaded with players who had won their share of playoff wars, still believed in itself. After years of carrying division titles on our backs like anvils, this first round had a refreshing feeling. It was Philadelphia's turn to surprise somebody, and Washington seemed like just that team. Andy Murray's scouting report advised us to put the puck into the slow feet of goalie Pete Peeters at every opportunity.

The morning of the opener at the Capital Centre, I skated to check on my knee's progress and was happily surprised to have no discomfort.

My aches and pains, and the ability to play with them, had prompted a long running joke between Kerr and me. "How you feeling tonight, Howie?" he would ask as we dressed for a game. I would reply, "Horseshit," and Timmy would roar. "Gonna win tonight, boys. Howie feels horseshit!"

Let the record show that I felt anything but horseshit when the medical staff cleared me to play game one. We ended up taking too many penalties and blew a 2–0 first-period lead, losing 3–2, but Holmgren had a positive outlook for game two as well as a smart strategy. He used Carkner and Chychrun against Mike Ridley and Kelly Miller, who usually gave me fits.

The next night, we were shorthanded too often yet again. Dino Ciccarelli got a step on me and scored on a power play just one second before the second-period buzzer. The Caps made it 2–0 early in the third off a giveaway, but we stuck to our plan. Bullard threw one in the feet of Peeters and Acton put in the rebound, then Propp scored the tying and winning goals, the last with 51 seconds remaining. It had been our turn to rally from a two-goal deficit, and the series was tied.

We couldn't hold two one-goal leads in game three before Miller, on an assist from Ridley, put one off Samuelsson's stick and under the crossbar to win it 4–3 in overtime. Foiled again by the duo of my destruction. But whoever had been sticking pins in the Dave Poulin voodoo doll at playoff time every year was defeated by our captain's resolve. His finger was broken by a Scott Stevens shot during game three, but Dave was able to play in game four thanks to DMSO—that vile, smelly stuff you rub on your skin to mask the pain but whose side effect makes you feel like you have a fungus in your mouth.

After my wraparound hit a glass support and bounced to Kerr for an easy one from the slot to put us ahead, Dave picked up a bad drop pass by Bengt Gustafsson and fired a shot that went off both the crossbar and Peeters' butt, then into the goal. We pulled away to win 5–2 to even the series.

In game five, Kerr—how great was it to finally have him in the playoffs?—created ties of 3–3 and 4–4 on setups from Pelle Eklund and me. We couldn't stop taking penalties and the Caps continued to cash them, but we kept coming back, creating a fifth deadlock at 5–5 when Tocchet's feed popped into the air, landed on Ridley's head and fell conveniently at Propp's feet for a deposit.

Eklund finished a play he had started with a brilliant move at the point, and Samuelsson put a wobbler past Peeters under the crossbar. We led 7–5, giving Hextall, still the only goalie ever to shoot and score a goal, license to risk an icing and the opportunity to repeat his feat in the playoffs. He lifted the puck in the air almost to the Caps' blue line, and it slid two feet inside the post. We won 8–5, taking a 3–2 lead in a series in which the Flyers had been shorthanded 13 more times than Washington.

We had every reason to believe this would be a seesaw to the end. After I fooled Stevens—in his earlier years, unlike his later ones, you could get to him—by circling the net to feed an unattended Propp, and Gord Murphy scored through a Tocchet screen, Washington fought back for a 2–2 tie. Rick put us ahead in the third period, but the Capitals still weren't finished. Gustafsson clearly kicked in a goal that made it 3–3. An angry Hextall hopped up in referee Denis Morel's face, but we were not rattled.

The Caps blew a chance to maintain their momentum when Ciccarelli got called for high-sticking Tocchet and we continued to find salvation in Peeters's legs. Rick threw one into the crease from the corner and the goalie's pads did the work to put us ahead 4–3 with 3:19 to go.

Five times with Peeters pulled, Ron Sutter earned a draw on defensive-zone face-offs, but the Caps' extra man won the race to the puck. Hextall had to make three good saves, and I got away with taking the net off its moorings with 19 seconds remaining to relieve the incredible pressure. Finally, Sutter cleared the puck at the buzzer.

We had avenged our previous year's painful defeat by Washington in an upset. As good as it had felt in 1985 and 1987 to survive first-round pressure cookers, it might have been even better to be victorious in a series few had picked us to win. Holmgren locked the door to his office and had a good cry. We also were a little misty-eyed about being able to repay him for being so supportive through a year of wild ups and downs. But by no means did we feel our season was made after one round of success.

Our young defensemen had played so well against the Caps, it convinced us we were deeper than Pittsburgh, which had swept the Rangers to win its first series of the Mario Lemieux era. With a huge edge in experience and a simple game plan against the multiple skills of Lemieux and Paul Coffey, Derrick Smith was assigned to bump Coffey as often as possible to negate his speed. And two of the smartest defensive centers in the NHL, Poulin and Sutter, would take shifts against the tireless Mario.

In the opener in Pittsburgh, we blew a 3–1 lead and lost 4–3 when Robbie Brown put one off my stick and over Hexy's glove midway through the third period. We bore down much harder in game two, and Kerr pumped three goals past Penguin goalie Tom Barrasso, driving him to the bench with an announced case of the flu. "Yeah, the Philly flu," mocked Kerr. Mario scored shorthanded to cut the lead to one, but Samuelsson, Poulin and Sutter were all over him the rest of the way in a series-evening 4–2 win.

Barrasso certainly didn't appear sick in game three at the Spectrum. He was the Penguins' best player as we outchanced them (26–16) and rallied from 2–0 and 3–1 deficits to tie the game 3–3 on Poulin's rebound goal. We looked like we were about to win throughout the overtime until I took a bad angle on Brown and didn't have enough leverage to keep him from getting a pass away. Phil Bourque was standing behind Hexy for a jam-in on Pittsburgh's only good opportunity of the sudden-death period.

Though down 2–1, nothing had happened to convince us we weren't the better team. In game four, Hextall stopped Lemieux on an early breakaway and Kerr scored two more on power plays before Mario hit his head on teammate Randy Cunneyworth's shoulder and couldn't finish our 4–1 victory, making number 66's availability for game five questionable.

When the Pittsburgh fans caught sight of him in the warmup, they went into a frenzy. Turned out he only had suffered from a stiff neck; then he put ours on a swivel.

Lemieux got behind Chychrun to score on a breakaway, shrugged off Sutter to feed a tap-in by Bob Errey, beat Hexy with a 30-foot screamer, then lifted the goalie's stick and scored on a wraparound to get a hat trick and an assist before the end of the first period.

Down 5–1, we reminded ourselves we still had 40 minutes to play, yet remained powerless against the best game I've ever seen an individual play. Lemieux trapped me to feed Kevin Stevens for a breakaway goal, then sent in Brown, who scored again and went into his usual windmill to celebrate—not exactly what Hexy wanted to see at that point. He started to chase the cocky little fucker but was cut off by the officials and soon flagged to the bench by Holmgren. Wregget got us through the second period down 9–3.

Holmgren kept reminding us to use the remaining time as a start toward a better game six. Either his words sunk in or Mario was exhausted from lifting his arms to celebrate. Smith and Eklund scored goals and suddenly Barrasso wasn't stopping anything, including two more by Kerr.

At 9–7, we sat on the bench saying, "We can still win this." And who knows, we might have, had Bullard not missed tipping the puck into a wide-open net in the final two minutes. That was all Pittsburgh coach Gene Ubriaco needed to see. He left Lemieux on to score his fifth goal and eighth point into the empty net, tying an NHL postseason record and putting away a wild 10–7 win.

We had just given up 10 goals and were one game from elimination, yet we still believed the true direction of the series had been re-established in that third period. When Kerr put a 35-footer over Barrasso's glove to open the scoring in game six and Hextall followed Lemieux across to stop a breakaway, Mario looked spent. Sutter ran over Zarley Zalapski to give us a two-goal lead, and the Penguins, 6–2 losers, appeared to be saving their energy.

Had they kept bearing down, the Penguins might have learned that Hextall could barely move after Bourque fell over our goalie's knee in the second period. Kerr did his postgame interviews with a towel hiding a thumb broken by a Jim Johnson slash. So now we needed to win a game seven on the road without our big scorer and with a goalie who had played in only four games in three months.

Wregget was ready, making two sharp pad saves early before Sutter pounced on a rebound and fed Propp, who scored into a wide-open net. Lemieux tied it 1–1 on a power-play wrister from the top of the circle just as Samuelsson, tangled with Brown, took Wregget's feet from under him. The surge of joy in the Civic Arena turned to anger when Propp blatantly tackled Johnson at the Flyer blue line and Poulin finished off a give-and-go with me to put us ahead.

Bullard, who had been booed out of town as a Penguin, scored the sweetest goal of his life to make it 3–1, and we didn't let Mario breathe after that. In the final minute, I chipped the puck out to

Mellanby, who soloed to the empty net and then passed the Pittsburgh bench doing a windmill to mock Brown.

It wasn't the classiest thing to do, but we enjoyed it, like all the fruits of our smart, composed, 4–1 series-clinching victory. We were in our third conference final in five years, and our high carried us through game one against a Canadiens team that had finished 35 points ahead of us. In the ultimate expression of our surging confidence, Derrick Smith stole the puck from Chris Chelios and did his only creative thing in five years as a Flyer, faking Patrick Roy almost all the way out of the net before scoring the opening goal.

We freaked on the bench, in a good way. But when a Chelios elbow drove Propp's head against the glass, we freaked in a bad way. Brian was unconscious even before his head bounced off the ice. When he came to in the locker room, Proppie still thought he was in Pittsburgh, but at least knew his phone number, just like we had memorized the number 24 on Chelios's back. Tocchet took a run at Montreal's star defenseman, but Holmgren told us no more retaliation. Indeed, Rick's insurance goal in our 4–1 win was much more useful to our cause than time in the penalty box.

The Canadiens, who had needed just nine games to get through the first two rounds, had worked off their rust by game two, a 3–0 victory that was merely a hint of how dominant they were defensively. All our efforts in game three got us only a late goal by Propp—yes, he was back that quickly—in a 5–1 loss. The puck never got to Kerr, who, playing with a frozen hand, probably wouldn't have been able to control a pass regardless. The power play that had scored 20 goals for us in the first two series couldn't be put to work against a team that didn't take penalties.

When the Canadiens beat us 3–0 in game four to take a 3–1 series lead, we had scored one goal in 186 minutes and had not really played that badly. Montreal's big defense was flawless and their forwards' play away from the puck never broke down.

Bullard, made invisible for three games like almost all of us, finally was spotted sneaking into our Montreal hotel at 4 a.m. on the morning of game five. I didn't know until six hours later at the skate, when I was tightening my laces and heard a little tremble in Holmgren's voice that made me look up.

He lifted Bullard up by the throat and put him against the locker-room wall. "You, out after curfew before a playoff game!" said Holmgren. I literally thought Paul was going to kill Mike. The way Bullard was trembling, he thought so, too.

That was plenty of inspiration for all of us before a do-or-die game. But while Paul wanted to scare a little intensity into Bullard, the message to the rest of us was to relax. Having only one goal—Smith's in game one—to put on our pre-game psych-up tape, the coach had his video guys—Leon Friedrich and Steve Romanowski—do a little editing. This time, Smith's score was followed by some quick porn of a couple screwing, followed by a shot of Derrick smiling on the bench. A fight between Chychrun and Claude Lemieux was interrupted by a battle of alien creatures. We were in hysterics.

Holmgren then said everybody was counting us out, but that we had a great organization and owner. A win in game five would bring the series home and put more money in Ed Snider's pocket.

Poulin, playing with two broken bones in his feet, had to wait until almost game time for anesthesiologist Dr. Chuck Gregg to get through customs with the novocaine. We then received a collective shot in the arm when one of us finally got body position. Smith took a Sinisalo pass-out and gave us our first lead since game one. Bullard, happy to be alive, was terrific, even though he didn't score. It was our turn to play from ahead, and we nursed that goal until Bobby Smith put one over Hextall's glove with less than five minutes remaining.

Our goalie coolly led us to overtime, when Poulin, clutch again after taking needles to be in the lineup, slammed in Gord Murphy's rebound to win game five, 2–1.

Naturally, we remembered surviving game five in Edmonton two years earlier and went home expecting more magic. Mellanby gave us the first goal again in game six, but Chychrun accidently tipped the puck into our net and the Canadiens methodically built a 4–1 lead. Propp got it back to 4–2 to give us a glimmer of hope, but the odds were long, and so were our memories about what had happened to Brian in game one. Sutter left his feet to high-stick Chelios.

Things threatened to get ugly, so with a draw coming in the Montreal end and less than two minutes to play, Homer took his time out. "We're down to our last straw with this face-off," Paul told us at the bench. "But if we don't win it, we are going down with dignity."

We lost the draw, and the puck was shot down the ice. Hextall charged Chelios at the blue line, hit him with his blocker and delivered a cross-check to the head. When Roy came to the red line to taunt Hexy, he screamed back while the fans threw trash. "So much for going down with dignity," I told Homer after a handshake line that didn't include Chelios (ordered to the locker room by coach Pat Burns). We had forgotten to let Hextall in on the plan.

For years, Propp was bitter at Chelios, whom I got to know when he came to the Red Wings. Chris told me that his elbow was retaliation for a Propp chop that had broken Chelios's hand a few years earlier. But when we were all together at a function years later, Chris walked up to Brian at my urging and they talked it out. I'm glad they did; I'm fond of them both.

Although Clarke had approached me during 1988–89 about a raise and an extension on my contract—it had two years remaining—the season had passed without him getting back to me. Entering 1989–90, he offered a three-year deal paying between $340,000 and $350,000 per year. When I asked for $385,000 to $400,000, he said the Sniders would have to sell the team to give me that much money.

The players' association had pushed through full salary disclosure that would keep us from being exploited the way Dad had been during years when the Red Wings lied that he was the highest-paid player in the league. When I learned that defenseman Doug Wilson of the Blackhawks was making $525,000, I called agent Bob Goodenow—we had grown up playing hockey together—and he agreed to represent me. Bob negotiated a contract with the Flyers starting at

$585,000 a year over three seasons. The Flyers could have had me for $385,000, but they got greedy.

Hextall—who, two years earlier, on the advice of Alan Eagleson, had accepted a long-term deal with a lot of deferred money—wanted to renegotiate, and his new agent, Rich Winter, advised him not to report to camp. Hexy was talked back by Poulin two weeks into the season and started suffering groin pulls every time he tried to play. After winning only one of our first eight games, we overcame the absences of Propp, Kerr and Hextall to get above .500. But following our December home loss to Hartford, Holmgren decided out of the blue to make a wholesale change in the club's leadership.

He replaced Poulin with Ron Sutter as captain, gave Tocchet the alternate captaincy that had been vacant since Marsh was let go a year earlier, and gave my *A* to Carkner.

Honestly, I was the most upset for Dave. He always knew the right thing to say at the right time, and just seven months earlier had proven his commitment by getting frozen for a third time in five years to play in the playoffs. What else would you want from a captain?

If a change had to be made, then Sutter, one of the best individuals I ever have met, was the right choice because of his work ethic. But he wasn't at Dave's level as a spokesman. And while giving young guys assistant captaincies to mature them makes some sense, Carkner wanted no part of any leadership role; he just wasn't cut out for it.

Apparently, the decisions had been Holmgren's, but we assumed they reflected Poulin's declining importance in the eyes of management. "I'm going to get traded," he said to me as we skated just before practice while Clarke looked down at us through the glass in his overhanging office. "The call is coming any day."

I didn't think the Flyers could deal him, but then, I didn't understand why he wasn't still captain. And I can't maintain that I wasn't also hurt by the loss of my *A*. For a while after that, I signed autographs as "Mrk Howe."

Dad was rarely captain in Detroit; like me, he led by example on the ice and wasn't one for locker-room oratory. He hadn't needed a *C* any more than I required an *A* for the sake of my ego. Nevertheless, I didn't feel I had done anything to warrant it being taken away.

Soon, I had bigger problems than bruised feelings. In late December, during an off-day in L.A., I was doing the universal military press weight machine when I felt a pop in my back. I got through our win against the Kings, but after our warmup the next night in Vancouver, I told trainer Dave Settlemyre I didn't think there was any way I could play. Holmgren, through Settlemyre, asked me to try.

By the third period, the pain put me to my knees. In previous flare-ups, my left side had been affected. This time, it was on my right, all the way down to my foot, which also had this weird sensation of having a piece of paper or something stuck on it. The nerve was really inflamed. Just handing my ticket to the agent when I boarded a plane home the next day sent me into spasm.

A CT scan couldn't identify the cause. Epidural blocks masked the pain enough for me to play two weeks later in Pittsburgh, the day Poulin was traded to Boston for Ken Linseman. I was able to get through the next game in Buffalo, and then another at home against Winnipeg—Tocchet scored four goals to give us our first win in 11 games. But two days later in Boston, I scored our only goal in a 2–1 loss and had to come out again.

Holmgren told the media that my career could be over, which he confided to me was his way of getting the team to accept the challenge of life without me.

I was not floored by the suggestion that retirement beckoned, especially since the floor was the only place where I could lie comfortably. I couldn't walk or sleep much, and riding in the car killed me. When I tried to skate, I couldn't breathe, and after about a month, when I tried pool therapy, I was unable to kick my legs. As I sat out the rest of the season, I was going crazy, while madness seemed to also descend upon my team.

Propp, traded for a second-round draft choice, joined Poulin in Boston. The Flyers finished with a losing record and missed the playoffs, both for the first time in 18 years. Jay Snider, who wanted an accelerated youth movement, fired Clarke and hired Russ Farwell, who was considered a rising star in management ranks after winning two Memorial Cup championships with Medicine Hat of the Western Hockey League.

The new general manager decided to keep Holmgren, but forced changes on the staff. Ken Hitchcock, a competitor of Farwell's in the WHL, replaced Andy Murray, who had been outspoken in his loyalty to Clarke after his firing and would join him as an assistant coach when Bob became GM of the Minnesota North Stars. Craig Hartsburg was hired as Holmgren's other assistant coach.

Sinisalo had become a free agent and left to join Clarke. Bullard and Linseman were not offered contracts, but after firing Rich Winter, Hextall got the deal he wanted and Tocchet also re-upped.

The hope was that a mediocre Patrick Division would keep the Flyers competitive through a transition. Even after Mike Ricci, taken with the fourth-overall pick, suffered a broken finger on opening night of the 1990–91 season and Hextall limped off with yet another groin pull, our morale had improved. And so, after a summer of rehab, had my back.

"Good morning," I said to one and all after stepping off the elevator at our hotel in Pittsburgh, feeling chipper about three consecutive victories. All I received were blank stares. Finally, someone said, "Guess you haven't heard. Kathy Kerr passed away."

"What?" I gasped.

After giving birth to a daughter, Kimberly, 10 days earlier, Timmy's wife had remained at Pennsylvania Hospital for treatment of a pelvic infection. When Timmy called her after we arrived in Pittsburgh, Kathy told him she expected to be going home the next day. But in the morning, she was found to have died in her bed due to what were being called "sudden cardiopulmonary complications."

I didn't see Timmy that day. After receiving a call from a doctor with the unfathomable news and crying to Holmgren for an hour, Kerr had left for the airport and the private plane Farwell and Jay Snider were bringing to take our devastated teammate home.

Penguins GM Craig Patrick ordered the doors at the Civic Arena locked so we could be alone. Keith Acton gave a prayer for Kathy before Homer and the assistants asked the captains if we wanted to go on the ice. We did, but when Hitchcock told us Timmy was going to need our support when he returned in a couple of weeks, I wondered to myself, "Will he come back at all?"

In addition to a seven-year-old stepdaughter whose father probably was going to want her back, Timmy had a 10-month-old adopted daughter and a newborn. Since my three kids were more important to me than the game, I kept thinking about what I would do in Kerr's place and concluded I probably would have seriously considered retirement. Though I really only knew Kathy from when she hosted some team gatherings and ran the annual Flyers Wives Fight for Lives charity carnival, there were reasons this death would hit me even harder than Pelle Lindbergh's.

We had only seen Kerstin Pietzsch, Pelle's fiancée, a few times after his death. When I drove her to our postseason team party that year, she quickly realized she wasn't ready for it and cried the whole way home. Kerstin soon moved to Los Angeles and then back to Sweden. Timmy's grief, however, would confront us every day. He had been through all those shoulder operations and Kathy's multiple miscarriages before she finally had a full-term pregnancy. Then, suddenly, she was gone.

As we had learned during the Lindbergh tragedy, the rink can be a sanctuary for your sorrow. After the Penguins observed a moment of silence before the game, we beat them 5–1 and, following a pregame memorial at the Spectrum two nights later, we defeated the Quebec Nordiques, too.

At Kathy's private service, the next day, we saw Timmy for the first time since her death. He joked with Sutter, his substitute on the power play, that Ron's five-on-four days were numbered, and when Pat Croce insisted on a workout together in two days, Timmy agreed to go.

Kerr's parents moved from Tecumseh, Ontario, to help take care of the babies. Croce, Jay Snider and Kerr's agent, Steve Mountain, took turns being with Timmy in the evenings. Terri Snider, Jay's wife, hosted and cleaned.

They never figured out exactly what killed Kathy, nor did I come to a full understanding of what kept her husband going. To many, his stoicism was perceived as a sign of shock, but I didn't think so because the same guy who had fought through many rehabs returned two weeks after his wife's death. As the ovation at the Spectrum swelled, and linesman Ron Asselstine respectfully waited for it to end, Kerr leaned on his stick and then looked at Asselstine, silently signaling for him to drop the puck. Timmy wanted to get on with his life.

A few weeks later, he tore cartilage in his knee and came out of the lineup, joining Hextall, who suffered a knee injury in a goalmouth collision. On November 4 in Toronto, my back forced me out again as well.

Whatever my body was trying to tell me, I wasn't listening. The day before Thanksgiving, I woke up at 5 a.m., had another epidural block at Pennsylvania Hospital, then caught a flight to Pittsburgh with Farwell to play that night.

Today, there would be not a chance on God's green earth that they would put you in the lineup on the same day you underwent an epidural. But that's how determined I was. Yet I don't remember a single word from Farwell asking how I was feeling or thanking me for trying.

Unfortunately, I didn't make it through the second period. And this time, there would be no waiting a couple of weeks for my spinal column to quiet down. Not only was I in severe pain, I was also suffering brutal headaches, chills and fevers, probably from a virus that my body was in no condition to fight off.

Ginger came home from somewhere with the kids to find me upstairs in front of a window, shivering on the floor, trying to feel some heat from the winter sun. She called Dr. Jeff Hartzell, who said he would send an ambulance. My wife was giving directions when I grabbed the phone and snapped, "Nobody is picking me up in an ambulance," and hung up.

Hartzell called back and said I probably was dehydrated and needed to be on an IV for a day or two. I agreed to go only if the ambulance would show up after dark and with the flashers off.

The IV took care of my fever and chills. I still felt there was a little person standing next to my right calf with a blowtorch, even though three MRIs and a myelogram taken over the course of two years weren't showing a problem that corresponded with my severe symptoms.

Since I was 34 years old, with a track record for playing in pain, at least the Flyers believed me. Can you imagine if I were a 22-year-old trying to make it in the game? Five different doctors who referred me to each other—and I assume consulted with one another about my case—told me maybe I should think about retiring. Wrong answer. I had to find out the reason for the pain.

Finally, one image on a CT scan showed something that might be consistent with my symptoms. So Dr. Art Bartolozzi, the Flyers' orthopedist, sent me to his associate, Dr. Richard Balderston, who looked at the picture and said he didn't think there was enough there to warrant surgery. Wrong answer again.

I took the pictures to a couple other doctors—don't remember who they were—but one said my problem was worth an operation. Right answer. Finally.

I told the Flyers I would go outside their network if necessary, which they didn't want, so Balderston agreed to do the procedure, even though he was skeptical it would help me play hockey again. Fine. This wasn't just about squeezing in a few more years on the ice, but gaining a comfort level for the rest of my life.

Dr. Balderston, who compared my herniated disk to a jelly donut in which the goo in the middle squeezed out a crack on the side and wrapped around my nerve root, said the surgery would be routine. So had childbirth seemed until Kathy Kerr developed complications. It's not that I feared dying on the table; I just was aware that things could go wrong. The night before my operation on January 19, 1991, I was nervous and sleepless.

To get my mind off it—and, I guess, onto somebody else's problems—I watched the reports of Iraqi Scud missiles hitting Israel until 2:30 a.m., an hour before Ginger and I left for Pennsylvania Hospital to make my assigned 4:45 a.m. check-in. They had an IV in me in what seemed like two minutes, and I was quickly in the operating room.

I survived. Dr. Balderston said after going in that he had been amazed by the size of the herniation—at least half my disk. I don't remember asking why a problem this big had not been obvious on multiple scans. I was just relieved that the surgeon finally was optimistic the procedure would fix my problem.

Less than four weeks later, I was skating for up to 60 minutes per session. I could bend over and, holding my legs straight, put my palms to the ground, which hadn't been possible for years. It still was only February, and the Flyers were in solid playoff position. I was excited about coming back to help.

Just four or five days away from rejoining practices, I was doing rotation work in the gym—part of the ordered therapy—and felt something pop in my back. My whole body went stiff. It was weird. There was little pain, but after being able to put my palms on the ground that morning, I suddenly could only reach my knees.

Therapy didn't help any more than it had in the past. I had been close enough to returning to be hugely disappointed. Playing, practicing and traveling little, I hadn't felt like a part of the team for more than a year, which is hard on you mentally. Holmgren understood, asking Kerr—rehabbing again from a severe muscle pull caused when he stepped on a puck during a warmup—and me to make a four-game western trip with the club during March.

Two lost hockey souls, we drove together through the Hollywood Hills in our rental car. Timmy apologized to me, saying he felt he had let everybody down.

"What could you possibly have to apologize for?" I asked him. Neither of us had wasted a second of our careers. If this was it for us, then so be it.

But then a rolfer named Robert Toporek, who had treated Jay Snider, told him that he had read about my problems and thought he could help. Snider referred Toporek to Pat Croce, who passed along the contact information. I was down to what I thought was my last option, so nobody had to talk me into going.

A rolfer stretches and separates connective tissue that has chronically thickened and shortened as a result of physical or emotional trauma. The therapy, developed by Dr. Ida Rolf, allows bodies to become straighter and more flexible.

I had already undergone treatment that concentrated mostly on my back, with limited success. But taking rolfing's holistic approach, Robert instead started on my feet and shoulders and did very little on my back until the end of my first one-hour appointment.

Reaching for the floor, I had a full foot more of flexibility than when I had walked in Toporek's door. After one session, I was a believer. And by the summer, I was feeling good again—at least about my body, if not my team.

The Flyers had blown a playoff spot by winning only two of their last 15 games. Their makeover was accelerated. Kerr, unprotected in the expansion draft, was traded by the new San Jose Sharks to the Rangers in a prearranged deal. The Flyers, looking to replace my skill on the blue line, made a three-way trade with Los Angeles and Edmonton that brought Steve Duchesne in exchange for Mellanby and Chychrun.

There was no reason to expect much from the 1991–92 Flyers, and certainly no great expectations from the Flyers about me. Having played only 59 games over the previous two seasons, I went to camp in the final year of my contact having to prove I was healthy enough to be offered a new one.

Even after stiffness forced me from the opener at the Capital Centre, I was optimistic about proving my worth. When I returned in the eighth game to be plus-5 in a 5–2 win over the North Stars, it wasn't due to a burst of adrenalin but a sigh of relief that I felt close to my old self. When I took a slash on the thumb in a game against the Devils in early

December, I was surprised but not really dismayed to learn it was broken. At least I could continue to work out and retain my core strength.

My biggest restriction, due to the cast, was that I couldn't shake hands with a parade of departing old friends. Sutter and Craven, lowballed by Farwell on contract offers, were traded—Sutter to St. Louis for center Rod Brind'Amour, who had been a high Blues draft pick, and Craven to Hartford for right wing Kevin Dineen. Tocchet was given Sutter's captaincy and struggled both with his leadership and to put the puck in the net, one thing probably having a lot to do with the other.

A week after I broke my thumb, Holmgren got booed out of the Spectrum with a 9–3 loss to Pittsburgh. Five days later, with a record of 8–14–2, he was fired by Farwell, the kind of move that happens inevitably when the talent level of a team erodes and players get slotted into levels of responsibility beyond their abilities.

With all these strangers arriving, at least Paul's replacement was somebody I knew. Bill Dineen, my first professional coach in Houston, had gone to work as a scout for the Flyers and was talked into going behind the bench to calm down a jittery team. Farwell had picked the right guy for the job.

No Flyer was going to ask Kevin Dineen for a scouting report on his dad, so my teammates questioned me. I told them I hadn't played for Foxy in 15 years, but to picture having Lieutenant Columbo for a coach.

"They fired a good man and I don't know what I can do differently than he did," said Bill as he gathered our team together the first day on the job. "But here I am and we'll try it my way.

"Three things are important to me. Number one is commitment to the team."

So he talked about that for almost five minutes.

"The second most important thing—" Dineen continued "—no, actually, I think this is more important than the first . . ."

And then he started debating with himself. By the time he got to number three, he had them ranked every which way while guys were looking at each other and at me, thinking, "What the hell is he talking about?"

But I was smiling because this was the same Dineen who had coached me to two WHA championships almost 20 years earlier. A nice guy, but no pushover. I remember that, one day, he had turned our power-play practice over to Hitchcock, but when Hitch started changing stuff around, Bill stopped him and snapped, "That's not what I want."

The Flyers finished last in the division but were an improved 24–23–9 under Dineen. For the season, they were 21–18–3 while I was in the lineup. But an offer to extend my contract never came.

If the Flyers didn't want me anymore, I was confident a contender would. As long as I recognized the danger signs and didn't push myself for one more game at the risk of missing the next three weeks, my back would remain fine. Dineen and the training staff allowed me to follow my own program. But increasingly, I needed to buy a game program to recognize my teammates.

When Tocchet and Samuelsson were traded to Pittsburgh for Mark Recchi in February, Hextall and I were the only two players left from our Stanley Cup final teams. Except for Jay Snider, who had been hugely supportive while I was able to play so little, I no longer felt any rapport with the team's management.

One day, after the players had gone out to practice—I skated on my own that morning—I saw assistant general manager John Blackwell picking discarded stick-tape rolls out of the trash and putting them back into the bins. God almighty, were we getting that cheap that we were saving 18-inch pieces of adhesive?

In two seasons, Farwell had fulfilled his mandate to make the Flyers younger and better offensively. But with the exception of Brind'Amour (as much as I loved Sutter, that was a really good trade), the character of the players who had left was unmatched by those coming in.

Recchi was the best scorer we'd had in a while, providing what Propp had done and maybe a little more. He, Ricci and Brind'Amour were a start, but we didn't have much on the back end. Gord Murphy had been traded to Boston for Garry Galley, and while the Flyers were raving about Duchesne, I could see that during those early years, he was a high-risk defenseman. I thought the Flyers were looking through rose-colored glasses at their future, and I wondered how much of one I would have with them at age 36.

Before the March trading deadline, I received a call from Mike Keenan, asking if I would come play for him in Chicago if he could make a deal. I enthusiastically told him that I would gladly sacrifice two and a half months with my family to take another run at a Stanley Cup.

On the day of the deadline, when the Flyers were on Long Island, I got a morning call in my hotel room from Rich Preston, my old Houston Aeros teammate and apartment mate, who was Keenan's assistant coach.

"We're hoping to get you and will give you a call later in the day," said Rich. I went to the morning skate excited, only to become hugely disappointed when the phone didn't ring that afternoon.

When the season ended—but before I became a free agent on July 1—I met briefly with Farwell and Jay. When I asked why I hadn't been traded, they said they wanted someone to teach the younger guys and pass on the Flyers' history and expectations. I told them if that was the case, they could have traded me to a contender for the rest of the season and then re-signed me as a free agent.

The Flyers offered a one-year deal for $500,000, plus makeable incentives that probably would get me up over $800,000. Considering that they only expected me to play about 40 games, that was pretty good money, but I wanted to see if I could get a two-year deal with a contender. So Farwell and Snider said I could shop myself around before July 1.

Bob Goodenow, who'd negotiated my last deal, had become executive director of the NHL Players' Association, so I called Ed Ferren, my lawyer buddy and former neighbor in Moorestown, New Jersey, for whom I had chaired an annual golf tournament to raise money for treatment and research on brain injures. Ed's daughter, Ann, had suffered a permanent disability when struck by a car while crossing a street.

I asked Ferren to see if the Rangers, Penguins, Red Wings, Devils or Blackhawks might be interested in me.

The most natural place to go was Detroit, my birthplace and Dad's team. But the Penguins had just won their second straight Stanley Cup and seemed loaded for more. If they had made an offer, it would have been really difficult to turn down. GM Craig Patrick later told me he didn't call back because he thought I would be too expensive. I think he would have been surprised at how affordable I would have been if offered the opportunity to join a team like his.

Rangers GM Neil Smith offered a one-year deal at $1 million. Lou Lamoriello in New Jersey said to call him back only if I got serious about going to the Rangers. Keenan asked for time to get authorization to make an offer, but he never received it from ownership.

I placed the Detroit call to owner Mike Ilitch. Bryan Murray, the Wings' coach and GM, called back in just five minutes. By late June, they offered $725,000 for a first year, $550,000 for a second, with incentives that would give me an average of $800,000 for both, plus an unspecified position in the organization for two years after my playing days were done. I told Ed to ask for that job. They aren't that easy to get in hockey, and if I was going to move my family, I wanted to be in Detroit for at least four years so that Travis, my oldest child, could get through high school and not have to be uprooted again.

The Flyers, meanwhile, were immersed in an arbitration case over Eric Lindros, arguing that Quebec owner Marcel Aubut had traded the rights to the game's presumptive next great star to them before accepting what they thought was a better deal from the Rangers. I went to the Virgin Islands for a week on a boat, having no radio, television, or reason to believe I was a high enough priority for the Flyers to match Detroit's offer.

I came back from vacation to see that Philadelphia had been awarded the rights to Lindros at the cost of sending Quebec seemingly half the organization, including defensemen Duchesne and Kerry Huffman. So the Flyers decided to match what the Red Wings offered me for two years, but there was no assurance of a job after my playing career, and their thin roster—Ricci, Hextall and top prospect Peter Forsberg had also been sent to Quebec—showed zero promise of being a Stanley Cup contender in the two years I thought I had left.

On the other hand, the Red Wings, with Steve Yzerman, Sergei Fedorov, Nick Lidstrom and Vladimir Konstantinov, appeared to be on their way. Murray indicated that he expected me to be on the second power-play unit and on the penalty kill, stuff I wanted to hear more than Farwell's assurances of a part-time job on the ice and a full-time role of mentoring young players.

Still, the Flyers suddenly really wanted me back. I felt overwhelmed; my head was pulling me toward Detroit and my heart was yanking me back to Philly.

I did what my mother had always told me to do when faced with a major decision: make two lists. There were only two items on the Philadelphia side: 1) Finishing my career on a team and in a city that I loved, and 2) Travis coming home every day saying he didn't want to leave. That was painful enough to almost balance the scales.

Here I was with an offer to a place where a part of me had always wanted to go, and another from a place that I had always loved. And I was miserable. I had a fever, flu and a migraine like the ones I had been having since childhood. I was being torn apart inside, and the stress was overwhelming.

Mr. Ilitch called that evening. "What's going on?" he asked. "I thought you wanted to come play for the Red Wings."

I told him about Travis's problem with moving and admitted my heart was in Philadelphia. Loyalty was making it difficult to leave.

"You're the type of man I want in my organization," he said.

Mr. Ilitch wanted to talk face to face, so he was sending his private jet to pick Ferren and me up the next morning.

That night, almost everybody in the Flyers organization telephoned. I was too sick to take any of the calls. On the way to the airport the next day, Ed Snider called me on my cell phone. We spoke for five or six minutes before our call got dropped because of a weak signal. I did not call back. From our brief conversation, I knew Mr. Snider was upset with me and that there wasn't much more to say.

I was at the plane. I knew if I got on, I would commit to Detroit. And that's what I did.

Within minutes of our arrival at the headquarters of Little Caesars Pizza, we were greeted by Marian and Mike Ilitch. Mr. Ilitch grabbed Ed and whisked him away to offer me a $350,000 signing bonus.

"Doesn't Mr. Ilitch know I'm here to sign his original offer?" I asked Ed.

"Do you want me to tell him we don't want it?" Ed laughed.

We turned to Mr. and Mrs. Ilitch and shook hands. The bonus beat the Philadelphia package by $250,000, but it hadn't really come down to money; rather, the clincher was the opportunity to fulfill my dream of winning a Stanley Cup.

Aside from not winning one with the Flyers, I couldn't have asked for a better hockey experience than I had in Philadelphia. As a retired player, I still think of myself first as a Flyer, because that's where I unquestionably made my reputation in the game, reaching two Cup finals and a semifinal, plus being voted three times a first team All-Star. I had gone to Philly as my father's kid and left as my own man.

CHAPTER 13

Home Groan

After 10 years in Flyer orange, it took a few pre-game warmups for my peripheral vision to no longer be jarred by the Red Wings' red on my shoulders.

Thankfully, there were no chips perched there requiring me to earn the right to don the uniform my father had made famous. By age 37, I could be my own man while wearing the winged wheel, something that would have been impossible for Gordie Howe's son to do at age 20.

Dad's Number 9 was in the Joe Louis Arena rafters. Number 2, which I wore in Philadelphia, already was taken by Brad McCrimmon, my old Flyer partner and best friend who had been a Red Wing for two seasons. But when told what was available before my July introductory press conference, I called off the search with the first option presented—the Number 4 once worn by Hall of Famer Bill Gadsby, my father's most lasting buddy in the game. It was an honor to wear the same.

I knew what my return to Detroit meant to Mom and Dad. Obviously, my father had thoroughly enjoyed playing with his sons in Houston and Hartford, but nothing he did in either place came close to the four Stanley Cups and six Hart Trophies accomplished during his 25 years as a Red Wing.

That was the only reason why, in my first home game of the 1992–93 season, I heard a little more applause than what normally would have come to a veteran player acquired for depth purposes. It did, however, feel special—being back in the city of my youth and playing for the team I had grown up idolizing. But all those emotions passed quickly because I was in Detroit on business. Still attempting to win my first Stanley Cup in my 20th professional season, I wouldn't have signed with the Red Wings had they not been a contender. Most people in the organization were more interested in how I could make a good team better than in my family's history.

The Howe name didn't even help get me on the golf course with my new teammates during training camp in Flint, Michigan. Wanting to make certain my back felt strong, I had taken a rain check on a few golf invitations early in camp. But feeling confident I could do 18 holes without compromising my health for hockey, I showed up with my clubs in the hotel lobby one afternoon, asking, "Do you have room for another?"

"We already have three foursomes," one player said.

"Well, then, maybe it would be better if I played another day," I said.

"You don't mind, do you?" they asked.

I went back up to my room, called my wife, Ginger, and said, "Wow, you're not going to believe what just happened."

It was an early introduction into the cliquish culture of my new team, but with McCrimmon there, I certainly wasn't lonely. My main defense partner was Yves Racine, but Coach Bryan Murray let Brad and me take some shifts together, just like old times in Philly. We also both played with two promising second-year defensemen—Nicklas Lidstrom and Vladimir Konstantinov—but because the Red Wings considered me an upgrade over Brad at that stage of our careers, my ice time unfortunately cut into his.

That never was going to come between us. Working side by side, we tried to try to bring that team together.

When some young players complained to Brad for a second time in two years about being frozen out by some veterans, Beast wanted to let it slide. A clear-the-air session he had called the previous season had changed nothing. But I wanted a chance to air my feelings, so we called a meeting. As it progressed, McCrimmon, his blood pressure rising, couldn't remain silent; he told a story about Wayne Gretzky loaning his Mercedes to a Los Angeles Kings rookie during camp. Meanwhile, some of our kids had been living in a hotel for two months without even being invited to lunch or dinner by veterans.

There were a lot of good people on that team, but they went their own ways. Rising young players like Sergei Fedorov, Keith Primeau and Slava Kozlov might have tended to be loners by nature, but no one was trying to bring them into the social circle.

There were no arguments in the locker room, but when the entire bench stood to cheer Steve Yzerman's goals and only half rose when Fedorov scored on an equally brilliant play, the atmosphere was not conducive to winning.

"You're not real happy, are you?" Ginger asked one day.

"Is it that obvious?" I replied.

Murray had a positive outlook and seemed to think the locker room would take care of itself. But nobody was asking why guys were hanging at the far blue line with our team ahead 4–1, or why passes were being forced toward shooters covered in the slot when teammates were open at the point. Players were not being held accountable for the team's success, which was a shame because our club was loaded with talent.

With the exception of my dad during our first season in Houston, Yzerman was the best player I ever played with. His finishing skills and creativity were brilliant. He could beat people one on one, knew when to go and when to stay, and was a cunning opportunist. The only thing Steve—who was five foot eleven and weighed 185—didn't have was size and the good fortune to be born into an era without Gretzky and Mario Lemieux, who made it impossible for Yzerman to be named to the first or second All-Star team. In my book, Yzerman was barely below those guys in terms of talent.

Fedorov was the best skater I ever saw, not just for straightaway speed, but laterally and for his change of pace. Primeau, standing six feet, five inches and with a ton of skill, was the third center behind Yzerman and Fedorov, giving us the strongest team up the middle I ever have seen.

Wingers Paul Ysebaert and Ray Sheppard could score. Goalie Tim Cheveldae played well that year. Paul Coffey, the second-greatest offensive defenseman in history after Bobby Orr, was picked up in a midseason trade with Los Angeles for Jimmy Carson. And Lidstrom and Konstantinov were on their way to becoming All- Stars.

Lidstrom already had incredible on-ice awareness. He was smooth, calm and tireless, with Go-Go Gadget arms—like the cartoon inspector—that could reach 10 feet to poke-check. Nick read plays accurately and knew how to ride guys off and put shooters at an angle. He had a hard, heavy shot that very seldom was blocked, could reach loose pucks and always was in the right spot to support his partner. Best of all, because Lidstrom rarely dumped the puck, the next person to touch it after him was on your team. Nick was everything but physical, but he didn't need that aspect of his game to eventually become one of the top three or four defensive defensemen of all time. It took the league too long to figure that out, probably because Lidstrom made it look so effortless. And, as great a player as he was, Nick was every bit as good a person.

Konstantinov was a fierce competitor with a nasty side, but he shared Nick's endurance, puck-possession skills and instincts. Plus, he was hilarious. Once, Vlady put his stick up to protect himself from a hit and cost Chicago's Jocelyn Lemieux multiple teeth and 100 stitches. A disciplinary hearing loomed near, so Mark Howe Esq. offered pro bono legal counsel to the young Russian.

"Remember," I told him, "when they call you in, just say, 'Pass puck. Follow through. Accident.'" So until his hearing—and even after as a gag—Vlady walked up to me every day reciting, "Pass puck. Follow through. Accident." It must have worked; Konstantinov escaped suspension.

One time, he was hit hard enough by huge Eric Lindros to put him out on his feet. But he never went down, and afterward told reporters, "My mother hit me harder than that."

Vlady was a rock-hard guy you could play in any situation, even offensive ones. The Red Wings had gotten him with the 221st pick in the 1989 draft, in part because it took three days to get to Murmansk, inside the Arctic Circle, to scout him. I'd say he was worth the trip.

Konstantinov wasn't the only personality on our team. I sat in the locker room between Sheldon Kennedy and Bob Probert, which was a daily experience. Kennedy's problem—the sexual abuse he suffered from convicted junior coach Graham James—was well documented. Sheldon was a hyper guy and not the easiest roommate for sleep purposes. Almost as soon as I had turned out the lights, he was walking around the room, too wound up to rest.

Probert fought a near-lifelong battle with drugs and alcohol. But I got to see that he had heart of gold. He'd counsel abusers and buy hockey tickets for underprivileged kids. In addition, Bob had a deadpan sense of humor.

Dressing on Probert's other side was Fedorov, whose huge thighs one day prompted marvel and inquiry from another player.

"I do a lot of squats in the summer," Sergei explained.

"That's what I did all summer," piped in Probert. "Squat!"

Actually, a determined Probie was a horse. One time during a tough rehabbing skate he and I were going through under assistant coach Dave Lewis, Probert looked like he was going to drop after about five minutes, but after 20 he was fresher than me. Bob started slowly in his fights, too, but would then overwhelm his combatant almost every time.

Once, when I was with the Flyers, he punched me during a final-minute puck battle. "I'll take care of this myself," I said as teammates, none of whom could have been excited about taking on the NHL's top heavyweight, reluctantly gathered to see if I needed to be avenged. "I scare him half to death."

Probert, listening, looked at me like I was nuts.

"Yeah, he's afraid he will kill me," I said.

Our guys laughed. I even got a smirk out of Probert.

While my back too often made my twilight years no barrel of laughs, I got in 60 games that first season with the Red Wings. In December, I felt a tweak, which in the past had come to mean cortisone time. But the team doctors said, "We don't do that here." Without a shot, I knew I'd spend 10 to 14 days on the shelf, and still no one gave in to my begging.

Dr. Jack Finley, who had been the primary team physician—and our family doctor, too—during my dad's tenure in Detroit, had taken a secondary role on the medical staff by 1992. He saw my panic, followed me out of the training room and quietly told me to come see him the next day for a shot of Acthar, which helps the body produce more of its own natural cortisone. The medical and coaching professionals were stunned by how quickly I had healed. As they read this, they are learning for the first time how that became possible.

A sprained neck suffered in a collision with teammate Shawn Burr—he was trying to hit Minnesota's Mike Modano—also put me out for eight games that season. Not only did I get through all those crises, but I breezed through my January return to Philly with only mild booing mixed in with some cheers. Since I had left as a free agent, I hardly expected my appearance to be a lovefest. But if people wanted to condemn a 37-year-old player who had never won a Cup for going to a place that gave him a far better chance, I wasn't going to worry about the reaction.

We beat the Flyers 7–4 to continue a January surge, and then, after a February skid, won 14 of our final 17, largely by continuing to outscore teams by wide margins. Even in 6–2 and 6–3 wins at home in games one and two of our first-round series against the Maple Leafs, we got by without doing the little things that became necessary when we arrived in Toronto. At Maple Leaf Gardens, where Coach Pat Burns could match Doug Gilmour against Yzerman, the Leafs ground out two close wins to tie the series.

We were up 4–1 in the second period of game five, then 4–2 and killing a penalty when Steve Chiasson took a shot that rimmed out of the zone, enabling Dave Ellett to cut the lead to one on the power play. Eleven minutes into the third period, my partner, Racine, had stopped at the near post to cover a Leaf and I was fighting my way through the crease to cut off a Toronto player circling the net when I was blindsided by Wendel Clark. I was in a heap beneath Cheveldae when Clark took a pass and scored to tie the game.

In overtime, Probert didn't get the puck out, Clark beat Yzerman along the boards and Gilmour backhanded one 20 feet up the slot to Mike Foligno, who beat Cheveldae through a screen to send us down 5–4, and back to Toronto trailing the series, 3–2.

Our hole became deeper in game six, as we went into the second period down 2–1, but we were bailed out when our explosive special teams scored four power-play goals and two shorthanded ones in a 7–3 victory that led us home for game seven. It was played with just one penalty, not to our advantage. Nevertheless, we came back from an early goal by Toronto's Glenn Anderson to go ahead 3–2 in the second period on a score by rookie Dallas Drake. We made that lead stand up until a bad change—Yzerman was late to come on—and brainless puck-chasing in the defensive end left both Gilmour and Bob Rouse unbelievably open in front of Cheveldae. Gilmour took a feed from Clark in the slot and tied the game, 3–3, with only 2:43 remaining.

In overtime, Clark beat Yzerman to a dump-in at the half-boards, Gilmour fed Rouse moving in from the point, and Nikolai Borschevsky redirected the crushing series winner.

It wasn't my initial experience with a first-round defeat, but it was even harder to take in Detroit than Philadelphia simply because of the difference in the number of hockey fans in the two cities. In Philly, there was loyalty, passion and a sold-out Spectrum, but not the wide base of interest around the state that Michigan's Team generates.

Having finished the season with 103 points to Toronto's 99, we were only a slight pre-series favorite, but the blown third-period leads in games five and seven were haunting. It became a god-awful, empty feeling, both for the holdovers on a team continuing to struggle to get over the playoff hump and for me—about to turn 38 and one year closer to ending my career without a Cup.

The Leafs had been grittier than us. Change had to come. McCrimmon's trade to Hartford for a draft choice caused me to lose him as a teammate for a second time, but that was a good thing because he wanted to keep playing. Ysebaert was sent to Winnipeg for defenseman Aaron Ward. Most important, however, Mr. Ilitch recognized we needed a new sheriff and brought in a legendary one—Scotty Bowman—making Murray the GM only.

Scotty's compulsions and fixations on numbers had caused Pittsburgh players and staff to call him "Rain Man," after the savant played by Dustin Hoffman in the movie of the same name. Early on, some Red Wings were rolling their eyes, but not me. I was fascinated by how quickly Bowman recognized our issues and how cleverly he tackled them.

In order to break the bad habits of our stars overstaying their shifts, one day in practice Scotty divided the team into groups according to their average ice times in recent games.

My group, the 47-to-48-second-shift group, was skated for that long in sets of five, followed by 75-second sprints for the players who averaged that length. When Scotty got to Yzerman, Coffey and about three or four more Red Wings who had been staying out for two minutes, the coach said, "I admire you trying to do your best for the team, but for two-minute shifts you need to be in a bit better shape."

The first two groups completed their work and were dismissed to ride the bike, get treatment or go home. We were showering by the time the third group came in, totally gassed and completely pissed, throwing their sticks. Scotty had not raised his voice once, but had still gotten his point across. Brilliant.

We had heard Bowman stories from his days in St. Louis, Montreal, Buffalo and Pittsburgh—making the Blues stay in the locker room after a punishment practice so they had to fight rush-hour traffic home; tipping off customs officials about purchases the Canadiens had not declared; finding matchbook covers from bars in the locker-room trash cans that allowed him to inform players he knew where they'd been the night before. I didn't see any of that in Detroit. Scotty was a coach who spoke just above a whisper, almost never after a game, and rarely ill of any player in front of his teammates.

One morning, he suddenly ordered the reassignment of every locker in the room. Most players found their new ones and got ready for practice as usual, but a few guys were screaming at the trainer, wondering why the hell everybody had been moved around. Bowman, meanwhile, was sitting in his office around the corner with his door slightly ajar, listening to all the carrying on by guys who wanted to sit by their friends.

That was Scotty's way of identifying the clique. After he had heard all he needed to hear, the players were returned to their regular lockers. I don't think it was a coincidence that a lot of the guys who had made the biggest fusses weren't Red Wings for long.

Only once do I remember Bowman letting a guy have it in front of the team. During his first week in Detroit, he scratched Shawn Burr, who had been a Red Wing for 10 seasons, in favor of young Kozlov. When Shawn complained to the media, Scotty had the teaching opportunity he wanted. He called the team together to inform Burr he was selfish and finished in Detroit. Then, in classic Bowman style, he suddenly started talking about a referee and some call that had once been made on his team in Buffalo or Pittsburgh. Five minutes later, we're still waiting for him to bring this back around to Burr, looking at each other and the assistant coaches and putting our faces behind gloves to hide our laughter.

Two or three weeks later, Scotty—who, by the way, kept Burr for two more seasons—came in between periods, yelling, "See, you guys didn't listen. I told you about that referee!" I don't remember which referee it was, but the call was exactly like the one Bowman had suffered years earlier. I often wonder if he's forgotten anything that has happened to him in his life.

Years later, when I did pre-playoff scouting for the Red Wings,

Scotty wanted me to predict how the opposing coach would react to a certain matchup, a double-shifting, or playing Yzerman and Fedorov on the same line.

Not only was Scotty two or three steps ahead on the bench, but seemingly nothing incidental got by him either. "Call security!" he once said to assistant coach Dave Lewis in the middle of a playoff game. "There's somebody in my seats. That's not my wife."

My guess is that, more than a few times along the way to nine Cups and 1,224 regular-season wins, Bowman called GMs to tell them to remove dumb players from his bench. He had little tolerance for guys without hockey sense, but apparently an appreciation for a veteran like me, who already understood too well every error I made. Scotty didn't pile on, at least not directly. One time after I screwed up to cause a goal, he called assistant coach Barry Smith over until they both stood directly behind me.

"Barry, I told you I can't tolerate that mistake," Bowman said. "If you can't teach these players, I'll get a coach who can."

It was all pointed at me, although filtered through Barry, whom Scotty had brought along from Pittsburgh and Buffalo as equal parts sounding board and whipping boy. One day, after turning a practice over to Smith, Bowman stopped it with, "Barry, this is a Junior B practice. Go stand in the corner."

The Red Wings, who felt cornered by playoff failure, were ready to buy into the success Scotty was bringing. Fedorov played his "A" game every night—the only season I saw Sergei do that—and won the Hart Trophy. And less became more for Yzerman, whose points per game started down that year as he played for Bowman and the team, not his stats, in every situation.

It was a beautiful thing to watch, and that's pretty much what I did that season, missing half of it with back problems that were wearing on my resolve.

My father, busy with his schedule of appearances and living with Mom four hours north on the beautiful bay in Traverse City, attended only some games, and when we talked, it was about his grandchildren, not very often hockey. But with my contract up at the end of the season, I gave him a call.

"How do you know when it's time to retire?" I asked.

Of course, I was asking this of someone who hadn't wanted to quit at age 52, so perhaps it was a dumb question, worthy of what I thought was the dumb answer he gave.

"You'll know," Dad said.

"Can't you give me something more than that?" I asked.

"No," he said. "You'll know."

I knew this: my problems were well down the list for the Red Wings as we entered the first round as the 100-point Western Conference champions. Our opponents were a third-year expansion team, the 33–35–16 San Jose Sharks, but Yzerman was out with a knee injury and Primeau had a bad hand, both factors that cut into our advantage up the middle.

When we lost game one, 5–4 at home, Scotty yanked goalie Bob Essensa for 21-year-old Chris Osgood, who shut out the Sharks in game two and was solid in a 3–2 win in San Jose, the first of three straight games we played there to cut down on travel.

My back was so bad for game four that the Red Wings' medical people bent their rule and gave me novocaine. We led 3–1 in the second period and appeared to have the Sharks and the series by the throat, until we gave up two goals in four minutes.

Six minutes into the third period, Ray Sheppard and I jumped into the slot for the same pass, collided, and Sergei Makarov finished off a two-on-one to put San Jose ahead. With a 4–3 loss, our control of the series was gone.

I couldn't walk for two days, let alone play in game five, when Scotty yanked Osgood after he gave up goals on the first two shots. With Yzerman back in the lineup, we kept cutting deficits to one, but couldn't get a stop from Essensa and lost 6–4, putting us suddenly one away from elimination.

In game six at the Joe, we blew out the Sharks with four first-period goals and went on to a 7–1 victory behind Osgood. But in the first minute of game seven, Igor Larionov was allowed to go up the slot and drop the puck to Johan Garpenlov for a goal, and then Makarov scored another to put us in a 2–0 hole.

Kris Draper's unassisted shorthanded goal off a steal with 13 seconds remaining in the period gave us a huge lift, and Kozlov tied it on a rebound early in the second. But Sharks goalie Arturs Irbe made some big saves and we were again going to the third period of a game seven at the mercy of a bounce.

When Doug MacLean, the GM of our farm team, the Adirondack Red Wings, stuck his head in the locker room before the third period and said, "C'mon guys, you're going to cost me my job!" it wasn't exactly a tension-breaker. How many players in that room were safe if we flopped in the first round again?

And we did. Osgood left his net for a dump-in and backhanded the puck softly up the boards. Jamie Baker controlled it with his skate and quickly shot it into the empty net with 6:35 remaining. The Sharks checked away a 3–2 game-seven road win—one of the biggest upsets ever, and one of the greater disasters of my career.

A crying Osgood told reporters he had fulfilled all the predictions of goaltending being our doom, but Irbe outplaying the kid was not the only factor in our demise. Larionov, Makarov and defenseman Sandis Ozolinsh had really good series. Still, we had lost to a team that should not have matched up against us. We were the highest-scoring team in the league during the regular season, but it got us nothing again in the playoffs.

Ilitch flirted with Mike Keenan, who had just coached the Rangers to the Stanley Cup. But Bowman, who also took the title of director of player personnel when Bryan Murray was fired as GM, ended up with more control.

That fall, at camp in Glens Falls, New York, the coaches introduced a left-wing lock that simplified the pinching options and forced players to think defense first. The trade of Steve Chiasson to Calgary brought in Mike Vernon, a veteran goalie who had won a Stanley Cup. We signed the steady Rouse to replace Chiasson and the maturing

Kris Draper and Darren McCarty improved the blue-collar quotient on our forward lines.

My contract was up, but the inner voice that Dad said would make my retirement decision for me continued to hang at the red line. I signed for one more year at $500,000 and felt good enough at camp to be happy I had done so. Then the NHL owners, as expected, locked us out before the start of the season.

I stayed in shape and received updates on the negotiations from my old agent, Bob Goodenow, who had become the executive director of the players' association. Bob kept saying it was unlikely we would play, which loomed as a death sentence for my career. I was going to be 40 by the next season, when coming back from a full year out was going to be nearly impossible. So as the stoppage dragged into December, I spent more time helping to coach my two sons' teams than I did working out.

Goodenow called in early January.

"We're going to do a deal," he said.

"Oh shit," I thought.

I did three days of crash conditioning, but, skating informally with other Red Wings while the collective bargaining agreement was being ratified, I knew I was behind the 8-ball. Whether it was because I had let things go or had simply run out of time with my 20-year-long back problems—or both—I was really stiff, requiring my rolfer, Robert Toporek, to fly out from Philly.

It took about a month to catch up, and on given days, I still had it. But physically, I was 80 per cent of the player I had been, largely because my back wouldn't let me do more than 35 minutes a day on the bike. After 40-minute workouts—a far cry from the 75 that used to be routine—I would pay the next day with stiffness. Practicing only sporadically, my confidence also began to suffer. With my diminished skill level, it was all getting to be too much to overcome.

Driving home one night that season from a convincing win and a solid plus-1 performance in my 18 minutes of ice time, it suddenly hit me: I'm done.

I should have been feeling good about that game. But all I felt was a desire to end my career.

"Now I know what you were talking about," I told Dad. And that was before our game on April 2, 1995, against St. Louis, when a hit caused my clavicle to become separated from my sternum. For two weeks, I couldn't lie down or breathe very easily, and for 13 games I couldn't play, causing the Red Wings to pick up Slava Fetisov from New Jersey for a draft choice.

It was touch and go whether I would be ready for the playoffs. But as they drew closer and I started to feel better, I was determined to take the time to smell the roses. When I did my extra work with the Black Aces (the players usually scratched from the lineup) after practice, I'd challenge the young guys to a game of two-pass. Ninety minutes later, this about-to-be-40-year-old was age eight again, putting off his mother's calls to come out of the minus-10-degree weather to eat dinner.

"I'm retiring," I told the boys. "I'm going to enjoy every second I have."

I returned to the lineup with two games remaining in the 48-game regular schedule and was minus-2 in a shutout loss to Chicago. Three nights later, in my final regular-season game, I shot a wrister from 10 feet inside the boards past St. Louis goalie Curtis Joseph and collected the puck from my 405th and final goal.

It was a third-period winner in a 3–2 victory and I was named the first star. But since I already had been on for another goal against in the game, I knew in my heart that Mike Ramsey, and not I, would be the Red Wings' sixth defenseman to start the playoffs.

The way Coffey was controlling games, and Lidstrom and Konstantinov had matured in their fourth seasons, my team had needed little from me to go 33–11–4. Our goals against had improved dramatically. We were ready to win in the playoffs.

Even coming off consecutive first-round disasters, there was no tension to our series against the Dallas Stars. We blew them out 5–1 in Texas to take a 3–0 lead and wrapped it up with a 3–1 game five win at home.

Vengeance can't be much sweeter or more complete than our second-round sweep of the Sharks by the aggregate score of 24–6.

In the conference final, Chicago goalie Eddie Belfour took us to overtime twice, but we built a 3–0 series lead. After Ramsey injured his shoulder during the Blackhawks' 5–2 stay-alive win, I saw my first action of the playoffs in game five and was on the bench and in the locker room to bear witness to our new confidence.

As we went to a third overtime of the series, somebody, I don't recall who, said, "Stay calm. We know we're going to win this; it's just a question of time." Everybody felt the same way. Kozlov's goal in the second sudden-death period put the Red Wings into their first Stanley Cup final in 29 years.

I remember Barry Smith was very concerned about the size and speed of the Devils, our opponents in the final, who were fresh off a six-game triumph over the Flyers. We thought we had our usual advantage up the middle, but Fedorov had missed a game of the Chicago series with a bad shoulder, causing Scotty to call in my dad for a suck-it-up talk with Sergei.

The Devils had a fourth line of Bobby Holik, Randy McKay and Mike Peluso that was as good as a lot of teams' second lines. Goalie Marty Brodeur was quickly establishing himself as one of the best in only his second full season, and defensemen Scott Stevens and Scott Niedermayer were two of the best in the league.

Because of Scotty's concern for the Devils' neutral-zone trap, the instructions for game one were to flip the puck into the air over their defensemen. It didn't work. Claude Lemieux's third-period goal gave New Jersey the 2–1 victory in a game where we never seemed to have the puck.

For me, that might have been a blessing. It was the only time in my career I was fearful of making a mistake, and it was not a comfortable feeling.

We played much better in game two, carrying a one-goal lead into the third period until Niedermayer—one on one against Coffey after going the length of the ice—retrieved his own rebound off the backboards and scored a spectacular goal. Jim Dowd cashed a rebound on Vernon and we lost 3–2 to go to New Jersey down 2–0.

In 1989, Calgary's Lanny McDonald had lived every hockey player's dream by scoring the Stanley Cup-winning goal in his final game. But that wasn't going to happen for me. Ramsey was ready to go for our next game. I still was eligible to get my name on the Cup, but it was going to take a big-time rally for it to happen.

I thought about how I had cried as an 11-year old in 1966—the last time the Red Wings were in the final—when the retiring 39-year-old Bill Gadsby and his team lost in six to Montreal.

When we got hammered, 5–2, in game three—Scotty said it was the worst game any of his nine Stanley Cup finalists had ever played—Gadsby's ending was about to become my own. I watched game four in a sport coat from the press box atop the Meadowlands Arena, as we lost again 5–2 and were swept away by the Devils.

It was a crappy ending to what had been a redemptive run for the franchise. At the first sign of adversity all season, we had crumbled. But as I made a quick appearance in the dressing room and then waited on the bus for it to take me away from the scene of our misery, there was no doubt in my mind that Detroit's time was coming.

Mine had expired, but I had cried more for Gadsby in '66 than I did for myself in '95. After a quiet flight that I spent hanging with the Russian guys, I went to Kozlov's house—near mine—for some beers that turned into some serious vodka drinking. I got a ride home at around 7:30 a.m. Only then, with the help of the alcohol, did tears start to flow. It hit me: my playing career was over.

Five minutes later, my eyes were dry and I was feeling good about moving on with the rest of my life—or at least better than I felt when Ginger tried to get me up hours later. I was not used to that vodka!

I wasn't in the team picture the Red Wings took a few days later. Because of the lockout and the late-running season, Ginger and I had already rebooked a scheduled vacation with friends in the Virgin Islands. So when there was some complication involving the team photographer, and the shoot had to be rescheduled, I couldn't keep three other couples waiting any longer for me on a boat in the Caribbean.

My absence seemed suspicious to people who thought I was upset about playing only three postseason games. But I wasn't angry with Scotty at all. Unlike the vast majority of players who are forced out of hockey, I was going on my terms. After 22 years, how could I feel cheated? The way my body felt at the end made the 32 seasons that Dad played—10 more years? Are you kidding me?—unfathomable.

Regrets? Not even a few. The only thing I could have done differently was to sign with Boston in 1977 instead of Hartford. But that would have denied Dad the chance to keep playing and caused me to forsake three more years of being on the ice with him. That would not have been a worthwhile sacrifice for getting to the NHL two years sooner.

Remaining in Philadelphia to finish my career might have put me in a better position with the Flyers organization for a post-retirement job. But I couldn't stay, because I really wanted to try for a Stanley Cup.

Had I wanted to leave Houston? No, but financially the Aeros were drowning, so we had little choice.

I could not control the injuries that wore me down, either. Bob Clarke blamed the severity of my back problems on overuse by Mike Keenan, but ultimately my coach wasn't as responsible for the time I missed as much as the combination of my size and the Howe streak of stubbornness. When Clarke once asked me why I chose to take hits when I could easily have skated away from them, I answered, "I would rather get injured and miss four weeks than let one person think I was afraid of being hit," a headstrong trait I'd acquired from both my mother and father.

That said, it might have helped if my parents had genetically gifted me with a slightly bigger or stronger body. The physical price I paid for playing 1,355 regular-season games and 176 playoff matches in the WHA and NHL: four broken toes, four broken ribs, four separated shoulders, a surgery on my right knee, a partially torn anterior cruciate ligament on my left knee, a skewering on the net in Hartford that could have left me paralyzed, two clavicle separations from each side of my sternum, two chipped vertebrae, 12 lost teeth, two broken noses, one punctured kidney, one broken thumb, and who knows how many stitches. The official count of concussions stopped at four, but there probably were two more—at the Olympics and during the WHA Summit Series in the Soviet Union—never diagnosed as I kept playing.

I won't leave out one totally ripped-off toenail, courtesy of a Bobby Hull slap shot, and a chronically bad back that dogged me for more than two decades, even after surgery. All of the above injuries healed, but your core strength becomes severely compromised when your back goes.

With a stronger one, perhaps I could have been a better player. But having not won a Stanley Cup, I retired with the next best thing: complete peace of mind that I got everything out of the game that my abilities and health permitted.

CHAPTER 14

Glory Days in Hockeytown

Three months after my final game in 1995, the last thing I wanted was to be reminded how much I would miss the on-ice competition and camaraderie of the locker room. When the Red Wings—who had promised me a minimum of two years' post-career employment when I signed in 1992—assigned me to pro scouting duties, I asked Jimmy Devellano, the senior vice president of hockey operations, if it was necessary for me to attend training camp.

I was relieved when he said no. But as I spent almost three months watching only the International Hockey League—teams with mostly older minor-leaguers with little development potential—this was another place my presence hardly seemed required. By December, I was hungrier than the players I was evaluating, so I went back to Jimmy D.

"Okay, I'm ready," I said. "Can you give me a real job now?"

He sent me to American Hockey League games, where there were many youthful prospects. By the next season, when he added some NHL work, the only thing I didn't like about my new job was rarely being home for dinner with my wife and kids. Of course, my contribution—and the rush I'd get from it—were nowhere near the feeling that came from blocking a shot during the final minute of a game.

But I liked being around arenas and hockey people, and I approached this job in much the same way as the one I'd had for 22 years on the ice: control what you can control and impact your team in whatever way possible.

Pre-playoff scouting quickly became what I loved most. The volume of possible opponents makes my April and May schedule change constantly, sometimes leaving me to arrange travel at 2:30 a.m., after West Coast games. You learn to go with the flow. The busier I am, the less opportunity I have to watch the Red Wings compete through the first two rounds and the easier it is on my emotions.

I remember how calm and confident our team was before the game-five overtime that put us into the 1995 final, but when you are not in the moment yourself, it's horribly nerve-racking. This was especially true while the Red Wings were knocking on the door of our first Stanley Cup since 1955.

We couldn't beat Igor Larionov in a series against the Sharks in 1994, so we had him join us in exchange for winger Ray Sheppard. Adding another versatile and creative player helped us roll to a league-record 62 wins in 1995–96. Still, goalie Nikolai Khabibulin and Winnipeg made us work through six games in the first round before the Wayne Gretzky-Mike Keenan St. Louis Blues forced double overtime in a scoreless game seven in which Steve Yzerman came to our rescue with a 58-foot shot over goalie Jon Casey's shoulder.

The Colorado Avalanche, our opponent in the Western Conference final, had acquired two-time Cup winner Patrick Roy in December to finish off a team as loaded as ours, never mind the 27-point differential between the two clubs during the regular season. Detroit's head pro scout, Dan Belisle, agreed that our series with Colorado was a virtual toss-up. We feared our tank might have been drained by the St. Louis ordeal.

Sure enough, Avalanche wins at Joe Louis Arena—in overtime and on Roy's shutout—put us behind 2–0 going to Denver. After a hit from behind by Colorado's Claude Lemieux sent Kris Draper into the boards, breaking his jaw and cheekbone, we went down bitterly in game six, and the Avalanche advanced to sweep Florida for the Cup.

The Red Wings went back to the drawing board again. We added size and subtracted nine years by trading five-foot, ten-inch, 185-pound right wing Dino Ciccarelli to Tampa Bay for a draft choice and acquiring left wing Brendan Shanahan (six foot three, 220 pounds) in a bold deal that sent center Keith Primeau and defenseman Paul Coffey to Hartford.

We missed Coffey's offense in 1996–97 and never really got on any sustained run during a 94-point regular season. In February, assistant GM Kenny Holland told me to cancel a scheduled trip and begin evaluating every potentially available defenseman in the NHL.

Scotty Bowman had coached Larry Murphy in Pittsburgh and loved him, but the fans in Toronto, with whom Murphy was spending his second season, did not. When I went to scout him, he was booed unmercifully every time he got near the puck, but he was the only Leaf defenseman making the tape-to-tape passes that were perfect for a puck-possession team like ours.

You can't recommend a player in a vacuum without understanding the needs of your team and the preferences of your coach. I told Holland and Bowman that Larry would be a great fit and we picked him up at the deadline, changing our defense for the better. Darren McCarty did the same for our psyches against the Avalanche, avenging the hit on Draper with a beating of Lemieux during a late-March game. And after we got through St. Louis and Anaheim to reach the conference final, we turned it in our favor with a 4–2 win in game two at Denver. With Sergei Fedorov outplaying Avalanche star Peter Forsberg, we badly outshot our new blood rivals in every contest but one during our hugely satisfying revenge in six games.

We had skill, experience, toughness and depth. Marty Lapointe, Kirk Maltby and McCarty had been 40- or 50-goal scorers in junior and were now on our fourth line. If you wanted to play finesse, we could play finesse. And physically, we went toe to toe with anyone. Shanahan was as good as any player at elevating his game in the final two minutes when your team needed a goal. Nick Lidstrom and Vladimir Konstantinov were rock-solid on defense, and Mike Vernon was superb in goal.

Dan Belisle and I had watched the Flyers beat a crippled Rangers team in five close games to win the East. The reports we filed said we would win the final in four games if we played well, and in five if we played just fair. Eric Lindros was a heck of a player, but Yzerman was better. And having learned defensive responsibility the hard way in so many postseason disappointments, Stevie was ready to win.

Most teams tried to counter Lindros with size and power. Bowman chose to use skill with Lidstrom and Murphy. We exploited the Flyers' thin defense in back-to-back 4–2 wins in Philadelphia, then blew them away 6–1 in game three in Detroit, making our opponent look as overwhelmed as we had been in our first trip to the final two years earlier against the Devils.

The Flyers showed up for game four, but after Lidstrom gave us the first-period lead, McCarty beat Janne Niinimaa and Ron Hextall on a spectacular second-period breakaway to make it 2–0, breathing room I needed because the scout who wrote the supremely confident report was the same guy now fearing that the next bounce would start Philadelphia on the road to one of the greatest comebacks in the history of sports. As I said, it's much harder to watch than it is to play, but Lindros's goal with only 15 seconds remaining was far too late to avoid a 2–1 Detroit victory and sweep.

The Red Wings had captured their first Stanley Cup since the last one my father won, two months before my birth. And I, finally, had an NHL championship ring.

I was happiest for the players who were winning for the first time, accomplishing what I never had done while on the ice. I was proud to be a member of the organization, but how could my contribution and satisfaction possibly be on par with the guys who put in their blood, sweat and tears? Unfortunately, I didn't need to be reminded of my place on the organizational totem pole by NHL security, which refused to let my son Nolan and me onto the ice for the celebration until John Hahn, the team's public relations director, interceded on our behalf.

Better late than never, just like for the Red Wings after 42 years. Nolan and I got our sips from the Cup, plus a picture of it with ourselves, Lidstrom and Konstantinov. There was such a crush of people in the locker room, I didn't see Dad until three hours later to share the moment with him, but it was great when he, Nolan and I had our own car in the parade down Woodward Avenue, where my father could feel the love.

The longer a franchise waits between titles, the deeper the euphoria. Ours was cruelly cut short after six days. On June 13, my daughter, Azia, ran upstairs to tell me she'd heard on the news that some Red Wings had been injured in an automobile accident.

Coming home from a team golf outing, on the way to a Cup celebration party at Chris Osgood's house, a limousine carrying Vladi Konstantinov, Slava Fetisov and Red Wings masseur Sergei Mnatsakanov had hit a tree on the median of Woodward Avenue in Birmingham, Michigan, only about four miles from my home in Bloomfield Hills. Slava would recover fully from chest and head injuries, Mnatsakanov was paralyzed from the chest down, and Konstantinov suffered permanent motor and cognitive impairment.

Vladi had wanted to take his white BMW—he drove that thing like a race-car driver—to Osgood's place just in case he decided to leave early. Not being much of a drinker, he didn't see the need to hire transportation, but he was convinced by some teammates to get in the limo, not knowing that the chauffeur's license was under suspension for a second time for drunk driving. When I visited Slava in the hospital, he told me they saw the driver fall asleep at the wheel and were pounding on the glass before they hit the tree.

We didn't see Vladi again for about a month and a half, until after he emerged from a coma. When I visited the hospital, he could answer yes-or-no questions by holding up one finger or two. You would have to put his finger down for him before the next question.

His eyes were incredibly sad. Vladi was in there somewhere and couldn't let himself out. When I told him my kids were out of school and I was going back to the Jersey Shore for the summer, his eyes became unhappier still. I felt awful walking out and even worse seeing such a good and robust guy be treated like that by fate when he had done the responsible thing. How lucky was I to play 15 more seasons after being impaled on that net in Hartford? And why was he so unfortunate?

Years later, Konstantinov's wife, Irina, and their daughter, Anastasia, relocated to West Orange, New Jersey, as Vladi stayed in Michigan. Sometimes his caregivers bring him down to the Joe Louis Arena, so I have seen him in the corridors getting around with a walker.

His short-term memory is pretty well gone. But every time I see him, I still say, "Pass puck. Follow through. Accident"—my advice when he faced the hearing for high-sticking Jocelyn Lemieux. And Vladi smiles like it was yesterday. When I think about how we were raised to hate Russians and the disrespect our players carried into international competitions during the '70s and '80s, I shake my head at our pathetic mindset. Vladi is as good a person as I ever have met.

Of course, without Konstantinov, the Red Wings weren't nearly as strong on defense as we defended our title. But the trading-deadline acquisition of Jamie Macoun from Toronto gave us another veteran hand, enough to beat the rising Dallas Stars in six games in the 1998 Western Conference final.

The difference in that series probably was our maturity. And Belisle and I, just as confident as the season before that the Red Wings had already played our toughest opponent before the final began, had an insight our veteran team could put to use against the Eastern Conference champions, Washington. The Caps had eliminated Buffalo in five games by getting leads and throwing the puck unfailingly around the sidewalls, never up the middle or across the ice. We passed the information to our coaches, and when we fell behind 4–2 in the third period of game two, Scotty or assistant coach Barry Smith gave instructions to flush the sides.

Two turnovers resulted in goals that tied the game, and we won in overtime to take a 2–0 series lead, a good example of why the Red Wings believe in live pre-scouting. Watching live, rather than on video, gives you a better feel for a team's tendencies because you can see their play away from the puck, too. From game four of the Caps' Eastern Conference final series against Buffalo, Belisle and I realized there was virtually no risk of Washington changing its strategy.

Ninety-nine percent of a team's perparation for its success comes from the coach and his assistants, and that's especially true against divisional opponents you meet repeatedly over the course of the year. But Danny and I were pretty happy that we impacted one game, leading to a second consecutive sweep of the Stanley Cup final.

The Red Wings received special dispensation from the league to put Konstantinov's name on the Cup, and even had it on his lap in his wheelchair in Washington. He hadn't played a second, but just by being there, Vladi had done what he could.

All of us want to feel we are contributing. That fall, I volunteered to be video coordinator, which meant leaving behind the press boxes to watch games from a tiny room where I prepared 35-minute tapes for assistant coaches Dave Lewis and Barry Smith to review before practice the next day.

Also principal in my duties was to have questionable penalty calls cued up when Scotty, steam coming out of his ears, came crashing through my door between periods. You can never rewind the referee's mind, but a sharp eye on the monitor can effectively alter in-game strategy. I remember a 2–0 deficit in Calgary being turned into a convincing win after Smith looked at our weak first-period forechecking—it only took one second to cue them all—and instructed our second attacker to stay higher in the zone to cut off cross-seam passes that had been burning us.

The original plan for video duties had been to split them among Belisle, Glenn Merkosky and me to keep each of us on the road for two-thirds of the season. But Dan would have needed a crash course in computers and Glenn lived in Glens Falls, New York, so for those reasons—and for the sake of continuity so the coaches could deal with just one guy—I volunteered to do it all for two seasons.

This seemed like an excellent career move when I spent the first day of my new position in Phoenix golfing with Lewis rather than scouting an AHL game in 10-degree Syracuse. But during the next season, there was a time when I had the world's worst job. With the Red Wings up 2–0 in a first-round series against Los Angeles, I was assigned the unhappy task of pointing out to our players how lucky we had been to have a sharp Chris Osgood in goal during two sloppy wins in Detroit.

The coaches, who had already watched my video, asked me to present it to the players, so I cued up all the breakdowns in our left-wing lock system, and Shanahan ended up being the first "star." I don't think Brendan spoke to me again until the next season.

By then, I had returned to scouting and passing judgment primarily on other organizations' players, but to do that effectively, you must have a feel for your own team. My evaluations really begin at our training camp, when I gain a sense of whether any player I might be asked to recommend would be an upgrade.

Jim Nill, who was the Red Wings' assistant GM—and at the time of this writing is the new GM in Dallas—would say, "I don't care if a guy can play or not, I want to know if he can help us win the Stanley Cup."

A team needs to be multi-dimensional to win four rounds. But the Red Wings' philosophy is to draft skill, because you can generally trade for the other parts. The third- or fourth-line forward or the fifth of sixth defenseman is readily available. But teams don't trade offensive stars unless they can't re-sign them—it happens less frequently since the salary cap came along—or friction grows between the organization and the player.

In any draft, the prospects who are talented, big, strong and capable of playing in the NHL within a year or two are gone in the first 10 selections. We haven't picked nearly that high since 1990, so in the pre-salary-cap era, Nill, who ran our amateur scouting, endorsed the trading of many first-rounders. His theory was that since they wouldn't play for us for four or five years, we shouldn't hesitate to use those picks to deal for somebody who would help keep our team strong during that time.

Of course, the only way that strategy won't inevitably catch up to you is if you find skill in the later rounds. And we have done that, generally in Europe—thanks largely to our scout Hakan Andersson. People knew about Henrik Zetterberg, but he was still available when we drafted 210th in 1999 because he was five foot eleven. Most teams won't use a high pick on a player who isn't going to grow to six foot two, 210 pounds, unless it's for an obvious guy like a Sidney Crosby.

A number of organizations believed for a long time that you couldn't win if you had too many Europeans. We captured Cups in 1997 and 1998 with the Russian five—Igor Larionov, Vladimir Konstantinov, Sergei Fedorov, Slava Kozlov and Slava Fetisov. Then, in 2008, we won our fourth in 12 years with nine Swedes. But the only time we used first-round picks for Europeans were for Anders Eriksson (22nd), Jiri Fischer (25th) and Niklas Kronwall (29th). Kozlov was the 45th player taken in a draft, Lidstrom and Jiri Hudler were both 53rd, Valtteri Filppula was 85th, Johan Franzen 97th, Sergei Fedorov 74th, Pavel Datsyuk 171st, Konstantinov 221st and Tomas Holmstrom 257th.

The longevity of Yzerman, Lidstrom and Holmstrom gave our draftees time to mature in Europe before we brought them to Detroit during their mid-20s. But the loss of Konstantinov forced us to pay a heavy price to remain in contention. Our permanent solution, Chris Chelios, acquired after we were dethroned by Colorado in the second round in 1999, cost us two first-rounders and Eriksson in a trade with Chicago.

That summer, we used the 25th pick in the 1998 draft on defenseman Jiri Fischer, who had grown into Konstantinov's role until suffering a heart attack on the home bench at age 25 in 2005. Prior to his next shift, he was told, "You're up, Fish," but Fischer was unconscious, falling first on Brett Lebda, then forward with his head against the inside of the boards. We had a defibrillator inside the locker room. But when Red Wings chief physician Dr. Tony Colucci—who had been seated only a few rows off the ice—quickly applied it to get Fischer back in cardiac rhythm before his brain could be damaged, his heart stopped instead. For 28 long seconds, Dr. Colucci applied chest compressions, having no idea whether they would bring Jiri back. Blessedly, they did.

A thickened heart had been detected in a training-camp physical, but a full range of tests had shown nothing to indicate it was anything but just that—a thickened heart, which a lot of athletes have, all the better to make them elite processors of oxygen. Two days after his collapse, Fischer was sent home with a monitor that tipped him off to two more episodes that put him back in the hospital over the next two weeks.

It was never completely determined what triggered the attack—might have been the perfect storm of a mineral deficiency they found in Jiri, the stress of a game, and a virus—but it was decided that professional-level physical activity, combined with the excitement of a professional athletic lifestyle, put too much risk on Fischer's heart for him to continue in the game.

Understandably, it took Jiri some time to get over the fear of another attack. But the Red Wings gave him a job—director of player development, a liaison and advisor for drafted players until they join the team—he has grown to love. There are statistics that suggest his condition is more dangerous before the age of 30 than after, and he works out religiously without ever having suffered another episode after those three. Jiri has become an advocate of defibrillators being placed in public places, not just athletic venues, and truly is living happily ever after. But even now, eight years later, the Red Wings miss a six-foot, five-inch, 225-pound defenseman who would still be in his prime, playing 25 minutes a night. So for the team, the sad chain of losing Konstantinov, and then his replacement, continues.

The 2005 collective bargaining agreement changed the draft rules. If a team hasn't signed a pick within three years, it loses his rights, so we can't be as patient with letting players mature before giving them a contract. But whatever our strategy, I don't believe any team in the NHL has done close to the job of our amateur scouts, headed by Joe McDonnell. Their task—evaluating a much larger pool of players, who are up to six years younger than the ones I scout—is much harder than mine.

Our lists of potential trade-deadline acquisitions are finished by Christmas. Then we go back for as many looks as possible. I average 145 games a year because there is no substitute for being there. If I see a guy five times and he plays three good games and two poor ones, I'm looking at a 60 per cent ratio, not enough to recommend him. If I witness 15 good ones out of 20, I have a better barometer. I might turn out to be wrong, but at least I didn't cheat myself.

Most of the players who interested us at the March trading deadline will become free agents on July 1. Until my pre-playoff scouting begins, I'm following how guys play on their new teams, as well as watching the crop of just-signed AHL players whose amateur teams have been eliminated from the playoffs.

Before free agency, we do separate lists of defensemen, forwards and goalies. We put a dollar figure on each player, based on the salaries of comparable guys around the league. If our number is $3 million and the free agent wants $5 million, we move on to the next guy on a list that could be 15 to 20 names deep. Because the cap makes it more foolish than ever to overpay, we rarely land our first or second choice.

What do I value in a player before I put in my two cents on him? Competitiveness is foremost. If a team has lost three straight, you want to see who still is banging, going to the net and blocking shots. Not as obvious is whether a player will go over the middle and risk an open-ice check, but I look for it.

I never want to see a rambunctious player going too far outside the team concept. He has to demonstrate a brain for the game. I appreciate someone trying to be a leader by example, but a player doesn't have to throw his body around to show me he is competitive.

Situations yield clues. If a team is up a goal with 45 seconds left, I don't just trust the judgment of the coach who puts a particular player out in the crucial situation; I watch to see how much he wants to be on the ice by how long he stays. Some of my Whaler teammates who averaged 1:20 on their shifts cut back to 20 seconds when we were in Philadelphia. I have no interest in guys like that.

The needs of a weak team sometimes put players into roles above their abilities, so I always try to take into account how a guy is being used. After Holland, who became GM in 1997, took a chance by signing Brett Hull in 2001 after he had shown little in the preceding playoffs, Bowman polled the people he trusted about using Brett as a penalty-killer. We all thought it was a terrible idea, but Scotty did it anyway, and that season Hull responded as a complete player in a way he never had for Ken Hitchcock in Dallas.

A lot of people thought Brian Rafalski had slipped in his final year in New Jersey before becoming a free agent, but I believed he had been overused in the first season since the retirement of Scott Stevens. My reports recommended that we sign him, and he played great for us. He was the perfect right-hand shot to play defense with Lidstrom.

My evaluations aren't made in a vacuum. If it's a Sunday and an AHL team is playing a third game in three nights after being on a bus all weekend, I take that into consideration. I'm not suggesting that stamina is not always high on my list of considerations—I don't want to see a player's energy level drop 20 seconds into a 40-second shift. But you can get a good feel for a player's intelligence when he is tired.

I also want to see how a player competes in certain arenas. Hershey probably has been the best team in the AHL the last few years, so that's a good environment to test a visitor. In 1999, after I transferred my base of operation to New Jersey to be near my summer home at the shore, I found it much more useful to watch contests in New Jersey and Philly rather than in New York, where the Rangers were struggling. I want the guy who doesn't disappear in tough games.

I feel the same about goaltenders. Their personalities are, well . . . different to begin with, but since I have never stopped a puck, fundamentals are hardest for me to judge. That said, goalies relying almost solely on technique aren't the answer anyway.

Since the best ones are big, size matters. Osgood—five-ten, 180—won two Cups for Detroit because of his intangibles, but being small can catch up to you as you age. There is a huge emphasis in today's NHL on shot-blocking, forcing goalies to make many stops through screens without seeing the pucks. So it's important for them to fill up more of the net opening. There is an art to a goalie making himself big, the way Patrick Roy did all the way to the Hall of Fame, and as J.S. Giguere did in stoning us during Anaheim's run to the 2003 final.

Big or small, the trait that good goalies have in common with superior players at any position is that they are competitive. A game after stinking it up, Osgood was as good as any netminder I ever saw at coming back and being awesome. When some of them give up a score, their shoulders slump and you see them playing deeper in the net, even yelling at their defensemen for having screened them. They begin to wilt.

When we signed Dominik Hasek in 2001, his compete level was phenomenal from the first scrimmage. Going into game six in Colorado that season, having to win to stay alive, you knew he was going to play well. He outperformed Roy in consecutive shutouts, and a round later, the Red Wings had earned another Cup.

Hasek's trademark of never giving up on any goal makes him remembered as the king of all floppers, but his quickness on his skates became an overlooked asset. From the goalie out, a player can't compete if he can't skate. I never eliminate a guy for lack of one quality, but a knock-kneed skater is hard to recommend.

You also don't just evaluate a guy at full velocity. There are decent skaters who lack the ability to change pace, and defensemen who are fine at full stride but have a hard time starting up again when defending a quick give-and-go. We all have seen countless express trains to nowhere with legs far speedier than their brains. So on my spreadsheet, the smoothness of a player's stride is never a make-or-break characteristic.

Watching Carolina's Chad LaRose in the AHL, I could understand how he'd gone undrafted. He was undersized and his skating was anything but perfect, but because his feet never stopped moving, the choppiness of his stride didn't hold him back from an NHL career. His desire was unmatched in every game I saw him play. Zach Parise is a good skater, but not an elite one. He is fast enough to get to the hard areas, where he excels. Desire and tenacity overcome average speed, and an NHL of 30 teams, combined with parity, has made the line between the major- and minor-league player so thin that 75 per cent of the talents in the AHL could come up and do a job for eight to 10 minutes a game as a depth player. If they can kill penalties in addition to contributing on a third or fourth line, those guys grow in my eyes.

But players also need a healthy understanding of their limitations. Whenever defensemen on our old AHL team in Glens Falls, New York, asked me how to reach the next level, I would say that by learning to keep the puck out of the net, they could play for anybody in the NHL. The reaction from guys scoring 65 to 70 points down there was to look at me like I had four eyes, but did they really think they were going to get to Detroit and earn power-play time over Lidstrom, Rafalski and Murphy? Most defensemen playing in the minors will reach the NHL by making simple plays, keeping the puck out of their own net and competing on a daily basis.

The distinction between the placeholders and the difference-makers is in their instincts for the game, which is why you see some guys come up and be better players in the NHL than they were in the AHL. The major-leaguers around them read situations better and provide the less-skilled guy with more options.

In today's NHL, where your average player is faster than he ever has been and the defensive mania of the coaches forces more dumping and chasing, the energy generated by your third- and fourth-line contributors probably is more important than ever. It has been the depth of our teams that has gotten us through the four-round spring minefields.

McCarty, Draper, Marty Lapointe, Kirk Maltby—and even Joe Kocur for a couple of years—were huge contributors. It didn't matter where the face-off was, what building they were in, or who they were on the ice against, they could shut down anybody and contribute goals.

Unfortunately, the salary cap has made it difficult to lock up support players and harder than ever to keep elite teams together. Fifteen years ago, Belisle and I would file pre-series reports to Bowman stating that if both teams played close to their best, the Red Wings should win in five games at most. Nowadays, we always predict that series will last six or seven.

That said, as potential opponents are narrowed down before each new round begins, I still see reasons for preferring to play one team rather than another.

In 2007, I was rooting for the less-physical Vancouver to knock out Anaheim. When the Ducks won to reach the conference final against the Red Wings, Mike Babcock, our coach, didn't like reading in my report that I thought we were underdogs in the series, but that's what I had seen from both teams. Attrition takes its toll. Most years, the Cup winner has been behind in one series—the mark of a champion—but going six or seven games through three of four rounds will cause injuries to mount.

So it helps to get a break along the way. The East was not strong in 1998, when Detroit swept Washington. In 2002, the next time we got back to the final, Carolina wasn't the best team in the Eastern Conference, just the hottest.

I thought if you took two or three players off the Hurricanes, they would have a hard time making the playoffs the following season. But when the Red Wings had to go seven to get through Colorado, and Carolina beat us in the opener at the Joe and had us in triple overtime in game three, I thought the Hurricanes were one goal away from having a really good shot at winning the Cup. Fortunately, Larionov scored and we got things back under control, shutting Carolina down in five games. Indeed, the Hurricanes missed the playoffs the following spring.

When Detroit reached the 2008 final against the Penguins—the first time we got there after Yzerman's retirement—I didn't worry about Datsyuk, Zetterberg and Kronwall stepping up. I thought our depth and experience would make the difference for us. As soon as the puck turned over, our centers smartly denied the passing lanes to Crosby, Evgeni Malkin and Jordan Staal, keeping the Pens' three scary centers from carrying the puck during our shutout wins in games one and two. They didn't adjust to a chip-and-chase style until game three, and the jump we got was a big factor in our six-game victory.

The next year, when we faced Pittsburgh again, we had finished up against Chicago on a Wednesday and started the final against the Penguins on a Saturday, a shorter-than-usual turnaround. It helped change things in a more-rested Pittsburgh's favor.

That wasn't the only factor in a matchup I rated as a toss-up. Datsyuk had missed the last three games of the series against the Blackhawks; Pittsburgh goalie Marc-Andre Fleury no longer was overplaying while going from post to post, as he had the year before, and Malkin, who took criticism for wilting against us in 2008, had been scary good in the Penguins' sweep of Carolina. He wasn't going to be denied the puck, no matter what strategies our coaches put in place.

We got Datsyuk back in game five and blew them out 5–0 to take a 3–2 series lead. But he wasn't himself, and I can't say that I was all that confident, even being only one win away. In game seven, the Penguins got the jump on two goals by Max Talbot, then showed they were a year better and more mature in holding on for a 2–1 win on our home ice.

That's how close it was to the bitter end, especially for Marian Hossa, who had left Pittsburgh to sign with us, only to be on the wrong side again. When we couldn't keep him for cap reasons and he won in Chicago the next year, I don't think I've been happier to see somebody get a ring. Marian really is a class act.

His Blackhawks' win over Philly in 2010 was during overtime in game six, another example of how little there is to choose between teams in today's NHL. Years ago, my reports used to contain things like "skate this defenseman wide" or "force him and he'll give it up." Now everybody can skate; everybody can play. You note things like

With daughter Azia and a 230-pound tuna caught in Cabo, 2005.

Dad, larger than life, is behind Marty, me, the real Gordie Howe, Marian, Mike and Chris Ilitch, plus Ken Holland (*left to right*) at the unveiling of the statue at Joe Louis Arena, April 2007. (Dave Reginek)

With my girlfriend, Sharon, at the Gordie Howe entrance to Joe Louis Arena during our visit to celebrate Dad's 80th birthday.

My kids, Azia, Nolan and Travis, at the 2006 Cup party at the Ilitches'.

Gordie, Marty, Nolan, Travis and me at Pat Verbeek's 2008 Cup party.

Fishing with Gordie at Peregrine Lodge in the Queen Charlotte Islands, near Vancouver, in 2010.

With Sharon at the Hockey Hall of Fame luncheon in November 2011.

Applauding Gordie at my Hockey Hall of Fame induction, November 2011. (David Sandford)

Most of all, I wanted to thank him for being my Dad and a role model. (Matthew Manor)

At the induction ceremony with Marty, Gordie, Cathy and Hall of Famer Bill Gadsby. (Steve Poirier)

With Gordie, Christine Burke and Nolan in 2011.

The Flyers (*left to right*: Bill Barber, Paul Holmgren and Ed Snider) joining Dad and me at my Hockey Hall of Fame induction. (AJ Messier)

Dressed in our Hall of Fame jackets, at Marty's house in Hartford.

With Azia, Ella and Gordie upon my jersey retirement in Philly. (Joe Kadlec)

The Howe Family on March 6, 2012, the night of my jersey retirement by the Flyers. *Left to right*: Nolan, Kristine (Travis's wife), Travis, me, Azia, Ella, Gordie and Azia's husband, Josh. (Joe Kadlec)

Dad giving great-granddaughter Ainsley the famous Gordie Howe elbow, June 10, 2013.

In my home office.

With family and close friends at Gordie's 85th birthday party, Detroit, 2013.

My boat, *Breakaway #2*.

With Jay Greenberg, Phoebe (Jay's golden retriever) and Gordie, March 2013.

"so-and-so will run out of position to make a hit" and "you can get under the skin of that guy," or even "you'll never see that guy go over the middle." But a fatal fundamental weakness that you can exploit over the course of a series is difficult to find.

Today's basic player is better than ever. I just wish I could say the same about the game. The elimination of the red line for offside purposes hasn't reduced the use of the neutral-zone trap; it actually has enhanced it. It's gotten so hard to carry the puck into the opposition zone that the lack of possession becomes painful to watch.

When the red line was there, I used to step up on a play to try and start a counter. Nowadays, they zing some guy down at the far end to chase the dump-in and you must honor that, leaving you 100 feet from being able to force the play at center ice. It used to be two guys in and one guy high, so just one mistake could give you a three-on-two. Now it's four or five guys back, and the way the game is obsessively coached, there are fewer breakdowns and chances.

When I played, a Kjell Samuelsson had an amazing wingspan, but now there are almost four defensemen like that on every team. You can't skate around them. When the Canadiens held my Flyers to one goal in three games in the middle of our 1989 conference final, it was remarkable to watch a defense that big, playing a step off of us and getting sticks on every puck we tried to force into scoring position. Now, you see a sealed slot on most nights.

The mistakes are fewer and the defensive fundamentals sounder than they ever have been, but I don't think the game has the entertainment value of 25 years ago. Hits are fewer and much more tentative because players deliberately turn their backs along the boards to draw boarding penalties. The fans enjoy the shootout, so I can live with it, but I don't like how teams' records are inflated by points for shootout losses. I'm waiting for the year when every team finishes above .500.

Without major rule changes, I doubt if we'll ever again see the volume of goals that there were in my era. Goaltenders are not only bigger, they are more talented because the position has become more appealing to better athletes. Their larger equipment also offers better protection and fills up more of the net. But as long as the goalies are stopping good opportunities, the quantity of goals isn't as critical to the excitement level as the amount of action around the net.

Creativity has suffered for the lack of operating room, making it more necessary to win games on power plays. To amp up the excitement, referees are instructed to call penalties and they do so excessively. When I grew up in hockey, lifting a guy's stick was considered a good defensive play, not hooking. Referees didn't control the game, they managed it, and some games needed more management than others.

Nowadays, the "Should I call it?" dilemma is gone. A little hook below the waist is a penalty, even if it doesn't impact the play.

Having the second referee has reduced some nasty goings-on behind the play, but has far from eliminated problems. It is now good strategy for a player to run a guy who can no longer defend himself by getting his stick up, then turtle to draw a retaliation penalty and become a hero when his team scores a power-play goal. It has become easier for pretenders to hide behind the referees.

I liked it better when players could police the game themselves. In 2004, Todd Bertuzzi blew a cork and did something he—and everybody in hockey—wishes he hadn't done, sucker-punching Steve Moore and ending his career. But had the Canucks, who were angry about Moore's elbow to Markus Naslund, their best player, been able to confront Moore in that game without drawing an instigator penalty, a good, old hockey fight—with perpetrators receiving five minutes apiece in penalties—would have resulted and settled the issue. Instead, things built up for the rematch five days later.

Players enforcing the code of the game can be a more effective deterrent than the presence of the referees. And the refs themselves used to be allowed to understand this.

During a preseason game in Chicago, I watched two guys drop their gloves, and then apparently think better of it. They danced around each other so embarrassingly long that fans started to boo. That's when referee Paul Stewart said, "Either you start fighting or

I'm going to start fighting you." Then he backed out and the two guys went at it.

Back in the day, Stewie was one of many refs with a personality. Unless you persisted to the point of embarrassing an official, screaming at one was as likely to draw a comment like "Yell at yourself, you're playing horseshit!" from the referee than an unsportsmanlike-conduct penalty. You can't talk to these guys anymore.

I even once got away with firing a puck—I'm not advocating this, kids—at referee Kerry Fraser during a 1986 game at Nassau Coliseum. I had been hooked around the throat as I went to shoot in a three-on-five situation, and when John Tonelli scored, I was so furious I aimed for Fraser's face. When he ducked in time, the puck almost hit Mike Bossy.

"Mark, don't be shooting the puck at my head just because we scored," said Mike.

"I'm sorry," I said. "It was intended for that fucking Fraser."

After the intermission, I had cooled off enough to apologize to Kerry for losing control. "I do it too, don't worry about it," he said. I should have been suspended for 25 games.

Kerry was not the only person to ever forgive a mistake I made. Holland didn't fire me for endorsing the signing of Uwe Krupp, a move that didn't work out. Nobody in my business has a crystal ball, only a love for the game, the wisdom that comes from experience, and hopefully a good car with a full tank of gas.

Never assume the latter. During the year I was doing video, my wife, Ginger, asked me late one afternoon to drop my son Nolan off at a hockey function across town, which left me no time to heed the illuminated warning light and stop for fuel. I barely made it on time to the coaches' meeting scheduled before the game.

Later that night, when I finished my work 90 minutes after the buzzer, there were no open gas stations near Joe Louis Arena. I was only three miles up the John Lodge Freeway when my Land Cruiser sputtered to a stop in a part of town with a lot of uninhabitable and vacant houses. Worse, in my haste, I had forgotten my cell phone.

Walking for help didn't seem like a viable option. Neither was the first good Samaritan I flagged down. The guy said he was in a hurry to get his girlfriend out of a bar before his wife got there, but promised to come back.

It was 30 minutes before another car stopped. When the driver opened the window, the minister's collar he wore was a comforting sight. The reverend said he would get me to a gas station, but first he had to make a stop at his church a few blocks away.

We walked inside, where we were greeted by 100 African American men wondering who was this white guy—in a shirt and tie, suddenly in their midst at 1:30 a.m.

"This is Gordie Howe's son," the minister announced. There being no such thing as a Detroit neighborhood where they'd never heard that name, I got the warmest of greetings. Turned out they were members of a neighborhood watch, gathering for their overnight work.

A few gentlemen and the minister took me to a gas station and then to my car, where some men helped put gasoline in the tank while others stood in the right lane of the freeway, directing the traffic around us. Before leaving, the minister asked if I wanted to take part in a prayer. Seemed like the right time for one, so we all joined hands at the side of the road. "Dear Lord, we want to thank you for keeping Mr. Howe safe this evening," he said.

We all gave a big "amen and hallelujah." Especially me. At that point, it seemed a little greedy to ask God to also throw the Red Wings another Henrik Zetterberg someday, so I passed. A scout is always looking for an edge, but in this instance, I settled for one blessing at a time.

CHAPTER 15

Colleen and Gordie

One of the first signs that something was wrong with my mother came when I listed my home in Michigan for $1.2 million and she asked about the balance on my mortgage. I told her I didn't have one.

"Then you'll never be able to sell your house," Mom said. "Nobody can afford $1.2 million." For 20 minutes, I tried to make her understand that a buyer could get his own mortgage.

When she and Dad applied for long-term health-care insurance, the interviewer asked, "If you go to the store with $10 and spend $2 for an apple and $2 for an orange, how much do you have left?" She pointed to one of the guys who worked for her and said, "I have this gentleman on my payroll. He does my shopping for me."

When I would visit their home in Traverse City, Michigan, four hours north of Detroit, the notes and records she always had organized meticulously were strewn all over the house. Computers were taking over the business world, but she couldn't comprehend how to use one.

"There is something wrong, I'm telling you," I told my youngest brother, Murray, a radiologist in Toledo. In 1996, he made an appointment for Mom with a neurologist.

In order to get her to go, Murray had to tell her it was for a routine physical—and, of course, Mom became furious when she learned otherwise. But my mother was able to charm her way through the medical evaluation. The doctor didn't think she needed testing, suggesting only that she conclude her business days earlier than the usual 2 a.m.

Mom had no intention of slowing down, but in my mind, there was little question that her brain had begun to do so. I lived in a six-street development in Bloomfield Hills, Michigan, that had just one way out onto Telegraph Road. After visiting, Mom couldn't find it, passing my house three times until my brother Marty and I stopped her. "Oh, it's so pretty in here," she said. "I just want to see it one more time."

I told Murray, "Live with her for a week and then tell me there's nothing wrong." By then, I don't think my brothers were in denial. But my mother, who had gotten the green light from the neurologist, was defensive, and her decline so gradual that four years passed before Murray, on a referral by geriatric specialist Dr. John McGreevy Jr., made her an appointment with Drs. A.J. McSweeny and Maria Kostrzewski of the neuropsychological lab at the Medical College of Ohio in Toledo.

After a five-and-a-half-hour test, the diagnosis was Pick's disease, a frontotemporal dementia that the doctors said would take her brain, and then her life, over the course of two to 10 years.

Pick's disease is not Alzheimer's, which attacks cognition and sensory perception in the parietal lobe in the back part of the brain. My mother's affliction was rarer—you will never come across it, Murray had been told at the University of Michigan Medical School—and probably more cruel. Worse than gradually robbing memory and awareness, Pick's disease causes personality changes, and its victims are conscious of the decline in their functions.

Murray and his wife—her name is Colleen, too—laid out the grim prognosis to Mom and Dad at the kitchen table. My brother said she should enjoy the good days she had left, but no longer sign anything or conduct any business.

My mother, the eternal optimist, took it well, almost as if she was relieved that she didn't have to struggle any longer with things that had gotten to be too much for her. Dad fully grasped the devastating outlook, but just didn't understand how something this horrible could happen to someone so wonderful.

Almost since the spring day in 1951 that my father finally worked up the nerve to introduce himself to the stunning 17-year-old blonde in the blue jeans he had been eyeballing for weeks at the Lucky Strike Bowling Lanes, my mother had been Dad's organizer, filter, defender and the love of his life.

"I'm Gordie," he told her. Even if he had given his last name, she wouldn't have recognized it. He offered her a ride home. Mom, who had the family car that night, had to decline and wondered if she would ever see this handsome guy again. But he got her number from the bowling alley manager and then baffled her with multiple calls without asking for a date. Good thing it didn't take that long to get his wrist shot away. But finally, they went to a movie, and then dinner at Carl's Chop House, followed by a late drink with Dad's good friend Ted and his fiancée, Pat.

Mom didn't know who Ted Lindsay was either, but noticed that the wait staff seemed particularly friendly and attentive. I don't really know how Dad's occupation never came up, but my parents had one story and stuck to it: it was only when Budd Joffa was startled to have his stepdaughter brought home by Gordie Howe that she learned this shy, sweet, unworldly guy who lived in Ma Shaw's boarding house near the bowling lanes and the Olympia was, at age 23, already a Detroit icon.

The next day, Dad left for Florida with some teammates, then home for the summer to Saskatoon, Saskatchewan, leaving the romance to bud by mail. My father was so worried about exposing his seventh-grade education, he wouldn't write a word without a dictionary by his side.

Mom was far more taken by my father's sincerity than his celebrity. He blanketed her with a sense of security my mother had not known in childhood.

Her mother, Margaret Sidney, had been married at age 17 to Howard Mulvaney, a big-band trombonist. When they divorced, she was unable to support her only child, so Mom's preschool years were spent with her great-aunt Elsie and great-uncle Hughie in a farmhouse in Sandusky, Michigan, that was heated only by a woodstove.

When her mother remarried, Mom liked her stepfather, Budd, but after that union also failed, she lost contact and never heard from him again.

Perhaps it was coming from a broken home or the strained relationship she had with her mother that helped Mom become fiercely independent. Her first job, as an usherette at Detroit's Riviera Theatre, lasted only a couple of weeks until they found out she was 13, not 16. But as soon as she reached legal working age, she successfully charmed her interviewer for a file clerk's position at Bethlehem Steel by reciting the alphabet backward.

Mom knew what she wanted and how to get it. When Dad had to break one of their early dates because of last-second orders from the Red Wings to attend a banquet, my steaming mother called a prior boyfriend. They were catching up on old times in a bar/restaurant when Dad walked in with some people who had been at his dinner.

The next day, she didn't get the usual call from my father that her ticket would be left at the box office, or much warmth from him when she brazenly telephoned to ask if they could meet after the game. "I have a date," Dad said.

Mom bought her own ticket and walked up to Ma Shaw, who was seated next to Dad's date, announcing, "Please tell Gordie I'm sorry, but I have to cancel for after the game." It wasn't until years later that Dad found out why his evening went so badly.

"How old do you a think a fella should be before he gets married?" he had asked Mom the first time they went out, At first, she suspected it was a line, but he really wanted her opinion, and ultimately she said a two-year courtship was long enough. She refused to go to Saskatoon to meet his parents without being Mrs. Gordie Howe, which she became on April 15, 1953, at Detroit's Calvary Presbyterian

Church, not far from the Lucky Strike Bowling Lanes, the Olympia and Ma Shaw's.

A man about town, this superstar athlete was not. And Mom wasn't satisfied being the smiling trophy wife. She hated the team's playoff quarantines at a motel in Toledo mandated by coach/GM Jack Adams, who often complained to reporters that wives and girlfriends were distractions to his players.

Dad's investment in an auto parts business with teammates Ted Lindsay and Marty Pavelich—my brother's namesake, by the way—drew a public rant from Adams about money taking a higher priority than winning. So Mom and Pat Lindsay created a photo opportunity by wearing borrowed mink stoles to the Olympia and lighting their cigarettes with Monopoly money.

When Billy McNeill—who had not been excused from a game in Chicago to stay with his wife, Joannie, who was ill—was traded to the Rangers soon after her shocking death, my mother was horrified by Adams's insensitivity.

Mom became the leader of the Red Wing wives, organizing social activities like ski trips. But her full-time job turned out to be functioning as the first female hockey executive, soliciting sponsors for her sons' teams, picking their coaches and eventually founding the Detroit Junior Red Wings, the initial U.S.-based development team to play in a Canadian league.

She eventually became afraid to fly after enduring two frightening plane rides, one in a private prop that ended with an emergency landing on I-75, the other when a commercial flight out of Toronto for Winnipeg—where she was joining my dad on a promotional tour for Eaton's department store—had to ditch fuel and return. Mom boarded a train, but then thought better of the three-day trip, got off in Parry Sound, Ontario, and returned to Toronto, only to check into the Royal York Hotel hours before part of the building caught fire. She wrapped herself in a wet sheet and took a back stairway to the lobby.

Having married one of the most anxious-to-please men on

earth—a multiple Hart Trophy winner who filled in a meager $1,000 raise on the blank contract that Adams put before him every year—my mother decided to protect her husband from himself, making sure he was properly compensated for the demands on his time.

When Dad was declined representation by Arnold Palmer's agent, the powerful Mark McCormack of International Management Group, my mother learned how to market him herself. After Gordie retired for the first time in 1971 and the Red Wings were too dumb to listen to him on hockey matters, Mom was by his side during aborted attempts to involve him in Red Wing owner Bruce Norris's other enterprises. The "good old boys," Norris included, sneered at the presence of a woman in a man's world. But Dad, who had dropped out of school because his undiagnosed dyslexia made him feel self-conscious, wanted and probably needed Mom at his side.

As far as I know, Dad never ran anything in his life. He was extraordinarily gifted at lighting up both the bulb behind the goal and a room filled with people. My mother took care of the rest.

When the opportunity arose for us to go to Houston in 1973, Mom recruited Gerry Patterson, an attorney and friend, to help negotiate the deal. But when it ran out in 1977, my mother had become our full-fledged agent and Whalers president Howard Baldwin suffered the goat bites to prove it. Mom and Dad were conducting cattle-breeding business at the Calderone-Curran Ranch in Michigan when Baldwin traveled there with the offer that would send our family to Hartford.

The price of feed had skyrocketed, and the Polled Hereford enterprise went sour. Mom moved on to managing a successful Amway distributorship in Connecticut and even took a run at a seat in the U.S. Congress. When I personally knew three of the five people in the alleged man-on-the-street campaign advertisement, I had to laugh. But I was proud of her for taking a shot, even though it ended in the primary. The people had spoken. It was the rare occasion Mom had to take no for an answer.

"Harry, I come to the games to see all three of my boys play," she once said to Whaler coach Harry Neale in the hallway after a game when Marty didn't get on the ice much in the third period.

As I had long held a policy of never mixing business with friends and family—I had seen too many deals and relationships go bad—I told her repeatedly, "Not interested," in getting involved in Amway.

One time when she invited Ginger, Travis and me to her house, I smelled a rat.

"No, no, just dinner," Mom insisted. But when the door opened to reveal an ongoing Amway meeting, we got back in the car and went home.

Although we sometimes disagreed on the way she handled things, I could never question Mom's loyalty to family. Cross any member and she would become a pit bull.

Following the diagnosis in 2000, it was our turn to rally for her.

Traverse City is a four-hour drive from Detroit, which left my mother inaccessible to specialized medical care and her scattered family. I had moved to Philadelphia in 1999, giving the Red Wings a full-time scout in the East; Murray was in Toledo, Marty in Hartford and Cathy in Montana, while Dad continued making personal appearances. We all agreed our parents would be better off in Detroit.

When they put their beloved home on the bay up for sale, Mom accepted a first offer that was $75,000 below the asking price and signed off on it before we could intercede.

They moved into my old house in Bloomfield Hills. One night, when I was visiting, I woke up to my mother trying to make the bed where I was lying. The incessant, hunched-over pacing around the house had begun, along with a violent aversion to water that made shower times hellacious. When mom was still well enough to travel with Dad by car to visit us at the Jersey Shore, my daughter, Azia, tried to help her grandmother and took a smack in the face for her efforts.

Another time, I introduced Mom to my good New Jersey friend, Dominic Mazzella, and she hauled off and hit him.

"What are you doing, Colleen?" asked Edna Gadsby as Mom paced around the dinner table. She responded by slugging her best friend.

"I know it's not your mother," Edna said, but she and Bill left 10 minutes later. I think she just couldn't stand seeing my mom in that state.

Neither could Dad, but he had to live it. If fate wasn't taking good care of his wife, he was determined to do so himself. It was two years before he could be talked into even three days a week with caregivers, leaving him to clean the sheets, go through the ruckus in the bathroom and endure my mother's involuntary and incessant arm squeezing.

"Ow, ow, you're hurting me," said one of the world's strongest and most patient men, as he neared the end of his rope.

I was able to arrange my scouting schedule so I could be there for a week out of every four or five. One time, I came out of the room where I had been doing some laptop work to see Dad's face a seasick shade of gray. When I checked his pulse, it went from 40 beats per minute to 180, back down to 70. So I took him to the hospital, where they paddled him to bring his heart back into rhythm, then put him on medication that would require constant adjustments. Tests showed constriction in a main artery of his heart, eventually requiring the insertion of a stent. Good thing I had been there that night.

Hoping to give Dad a break, we made arrangements for 24-hour help for Mom and flew him to Atlantic City for what was scheduled to be seven days of fishing with me in Beach Haven, New Jersey. We had a good first night, catching six to eight tuna and mahi-mahi before getting back to port in the wee hours to clean the fish and the boat.

After waking up, I asked Dad what he wanted to do the rest of the day. He said, "I need to get home to your mother. She needs me." He felt so guilty about enjoying himself that we put him back on a plane in the evening.

My mother's affliction clearly was taking the life out of two people. Over a 24-month period, Dad suffered chest pains and dizzy spells that I would estimate required 10 different hospital trips. The last thing he needed to be doing was getting Mom in and out of bed and bathing her.

"Dad, we gotta do something about getting you more help," I said. But he kept insisting, "Your mother doesn't want it."

"It's not for her, Dad, it's for you," I said. "You weren't meant to do this, and you don't have to. I know how much it is going to cost and it's not a problem. Everything is set up, just a phone call away."

I never tried to jam anything down Dad's throat, just lay it out there to help him make up his own mind. Suddenly, one day, he said, "Well, I think your mother's maybe ready for care now."

Before he could change his mind, I made the phone call to a service recommended by the Gadsbys, whose son-in-law had died of cancer. We went to care seven days a week for all of Mom's awake hours—8 a.m to 8 p.m. That still left Dad 12 hours at night to roam the house alone with his thoughts. But we hired good help that was raised one more notch when Stacey Stanley took over my mother's care. Stacey changed medications she believed were suppressing Mom's appetite and, just when I thought she wouldn't last six more months, she put on 30 pounds.

Once you got Mom through the shower ordeal, she usually was placid and sometimes even interactive. I bought her a hot chocolate maker and candy bars and she loved them. Stacey would take my parents out on the lake where she lived to see the swans and visit farms where Mom enjoyed being with the animals.

At my request, Travis, who was just starting up with Selects Hockey—a company that runs camps and arranges competitions for elite youth players—moved to Bloomfield Hills in 2006. He made sure the bills were forwarded to the accountant, picked up the prescriptions and chauffeured his grandfather, who was getting lost on his own, wherever he wanted to go. Most importantly, whenever Dad got lonely after the caregivers went home, Travis was at the house on five minutes' notice. And if he had to travel for his job, my youngest son, Nolan, would fill in.

Never far from Dad's side throughout Mom's illness was his best friend in the world, Felix Gatt. When Felix was a 16-year-old hanging at the Olympia, Terry Sawchuk refused to give him an autograph. After my father scolded the crabby goalie into doing the right thing, Felix more than ever became a worshiper of my dad's legend, showing up for his signings and assembling the world's greatest Gordie Howe collection, including a six-foot statue of my father that Felix rescued from a museum in Indiana that was going out of business.

Felix enjoyed the real Gordie Howe even more than the wax version. At least twice a week, they had lunch at T.J. Coney Island in Troy, Michigan, near Felix's print shop. It was the only place in town where Mom and Dad's teacup poodle, Rocket—my father had a sarcastic side, naming a representative of one of the world's smallest breeds after his great and grumpy rival, Maurice Richard—would be served bowls of bacon and water.

By the fourth anniversary of Mom's diagnosis, it had become more difficult than ever to carry on a phone conversation with her. You needed to be there in person. On a good day, maybe you could have a five-minute talk.

When I told her my daughter, Azia, had passed her CPA exam, my mother went, "Woooo," obviously excited. But those moments had become few. On the bad days, there was a complete void in her eyes, like a shark's. The pacing stopped when her muscles began to atrophy, putting her in a wheelchair.

"How long does this go on?" I asked Stacey.

"Until she stops eating," was the reply.

That had not happened when I went to see her during the first week of February 2009. The Red Wings' annual midwinter scouting meetings in Florida kept me from her 76th birthday celebration on February 17. But Felix, his wife, Rita, and Murray and his family thought Mom seemed to be listening to the table conversation. And there was no question she enjoyed a big piece of her birthday cake.

"Be back in a week, Mom," Murray said as he left. "I'll bring pizza."

"Pizza!" my mother said, but the next day, she stopped eating. Murray's theory was she decided that she had had a full life topped by a piece of chocolate cake, and that it was time to go.

On the night of March 5, I had just gotten home to New Jersey from a 10-day trip when Marty called to say Stacey had just told him Mom could pass at any time. "We'll talk in the morning about going out there," I said.

The next morning, the phone rang. It was Travis.

"Dad . . . ," he said, hesitantly, as I had 38 years earlier before proving incapable of informing my father that his mother had fallen down the stairs to her death. You could hear in my son's voice that something was terribly wrong.

"Travis, I know one of my parents died," I said. "Which one?"

"Grandma died," he said. Sixteen years since we had started to see the changes and nine after Mom was diagnosed, Stacey had walked into the bedroom to find my mother not breathing. The light of my father's life had gone out.

He called Felix first. "Colleen just passed away," said Dad. Felix and Rita were at the house before Mom's body was taken away.

"She is in a better place," Felix told Dad as they went for a walk, but when I arrived that night, I found Dad looking like a lost soul. Mom hadn't been conversant in two and a half years. The quality of her life was so poor that death had seemed to be a blessing. But not to Dad. No matter how ready you think you are for the inevitable, a wife's passing takes a part of you with her.

As we gathered around my mother at the Desmond Funeral Home in Troy for a private family-only viewing before cremation, Dad broke down. "Let me hold the dog," I said as he clung to Rocket. The poor thing almost got out of my arms and jumped into the casket.

The next day, we had a public viewing of Mom's ashes and photos. Wayne Gretzky, his Phoenix Coyotes in town to play the Red Wings, stopped by. So did my old Aeros teammate Rich Preston, as well as Mike Keenan and a lot of Red Wing alumni.

The following afternoon, Coach Mike Babcock and the Red Wings attended the memorial service at St. Hugo of the Hills Church in Bloomfield Hills.

In her eulogy, Mom's good friend Edna shared my mother's

brainstorm to defy team rules and join their husbands on a road trip to Montreal. They paid for their own room and had dinner and an expensive wine brought up, only to have the boys arrive with the same bottle purchased down the street for $7.95.

When one of the couples took the key for Dad and Bill's room, Edna said they all felt "naughty and nice." The Red Wings even sneaked out of the Forum with a win the next night, Gordie scoring two goals and Bill two assists. The perfect caper.

"Colleen has experienced an early Easter," Edna told the mourners. "She is an angel among the angels, probably organizing some event.

"Her motto was, 'If you want a friend, be one.'"

Murray told the congregation how our mother went about that:

"If you met Colleen Howe, you were immediately her friend. She would find out what you needed and then get it for you.

"My brothers' idea of how to deal with a bully who threw balls and rocks at me at age eight was to hit him hard with a hockey stick. Mom invited him to my birthday party, probably the first time he ever had been included in one. My enemy became a friend.

"The Osmond brothers came to Detroit years ago, and my sister, Cathy, was in love with Donny. After the concert, their limousine sped away before we could get their autograph, so Mom said, 'Gord, why not go to their hotel and meet them?' So we did, in their pajamas in their room at the Pontchartrain.

"Her middle name was 'Why Not.' Why not run for Congress to fix the country? Why not put your house up for collateral to build the first [community] hockey rink in Detroit? Why not create the first junior hockey team in the United States?

"'Hey Gordie, why not come out of retirement at the age of 45 so you can play on the same team as your sons? I'll be the first female sports agent and represent you.

"'Why not surprise our friends with a trip to Hawaii for their 25th anniversary and go with them?' *Carpe diem.* Seize the day.

"I have no doubt Mom is alive and with us right now, savoring the love we are sharing in this room. And she is waiting for us to step out of these doors and love each other with everything we have."

Dad's legs almost gave out when he rose in his pew. We had to help him to the limo that took us to the Hockeytown Cafe, the Ilitches' restaurant, for a celebration of my mother's life.

Michael Prainito, the Red Wings' vice president of corporate hospitality, had taken all the funeral preparations out of our hands. From handling the media, to recommending the funeral director and church and taking care of the food, I can't say enough about what the team did.

My father had made us promise that Mom could stay in her house until the end. Now Dad wanted to continue living there, but his support group was having health issues that were increasingly isolating him.

The Gadsbys had been coming by every Sunday for years, especially after Mom got sick, but Bill's health was declining. Genevieve and Jack Finley, the Red Wings' and Howes' physician when I was a kid, were loyal and attentive until Jack suffered a stroke, and then Felix had one, too. Both have recovered, thankfully, but Felix was unable to drive anymore. As responsive as Travis was about transportation, he no longer could take his grandfather to see Felix almost every day. We had Stacey stay on to attend to Dad five days a week for eight hours a day during the next six months, but when she left, the house was so very quiet and empty.

My father still brightened up at appearances, which we all agreed were good for him as long as he wanted to do them. At home, though, he would pick up a Red Wings team picture from the '40s and point down the rows of players, saying: "He's dead. He's dead." Then he would come to himself and say, "I should be dead."

That's it, I said to myself. I have to get him out of here.

So Dad began spending days rotating among the homes of all his children. He and Felix talk at least twice a week and I make sure my father checks in with the Gadsbys.

We have kept the house. I sometimes stay there when I am in Detroit, which gives me the opportunity to go through my mother's records and get to know her even better than I did during her life. In organized box after box in the basement were about 40 years of checks, bills, tax returns and every memo she ever received from her assistant, Dorothy Ringler. Anything with Dad's signature has monetary value to it, but the real hidden treasures were in every letter ever written to her by her kids, grandkids and Edna.

I sent them back to the family members and friends who wrote them. And I didn't throw away even one of what I presume to be every fan letter ever written to my dad, numbering in the hundreds of thousands. Perhaps one of his grandchildren will want to do a book with them one day.

I read my mother's life in those boxes, including the changes in her in the mid-'90s, when she also filed away junk mail or anything with a pretty picture. All of Dad's memorabilia was catalogued meticulously, but in a code that reflected her growing paranoia. It took some deciphering, but she had accounted for pretty much every piece.

For years, my mother desperately tried to establish a Gordie Howe museum. It isn't financially feasible, but I think we can continue the legacy in another way, by auctioning off some of the stuff and having the proceeds go to the Howe Foundation my mom started years ago.

The foundation put on a golf tournament in 2011 to benefit head-trauma patients and makes contributions to Ilitch Charities. But I think with an auction we can generate a lot of money and turn it into something everlasting—perhaps scholarships to help kids in hockey, business or whatever. Mom would have wanted that much more than her kids selling off their father's keepsakes and dividing up the money.

With the lead of Baycrest, a Canadian firm that provides aging care and does research in brain health, we have established the Gordie and Colleen Howe Fund for Alzheimer's, contributions mostly coming through Dad's appearance at an annual pro-am hockey tournament in Toronto. I'm certain that if Pick's disease had afflicted another member of the family instead of my mother, she would be as tireless for that cause as my parents were for others.

When Dad played for the Red Wings, he was the annual honorary chairperson for the Michigan March of Dimes, which he loved the most of any of his philanthropic endeavors because it was for the kids. To this day, when he walks into a room full of people, he'll go to where the children are to joke and play.

The tour Mom organized for Dad's 65th birthday in 1993 didn't get as much cooperation from NHL teams as she would have liked, and it drew some criticism as self-congratulation for profit. But those 65 stops raised $2.5 million for various charities. I would estimate that, over their lifetimes, the total generosity of my parents has come to more than $10 million—and still counting. Sure, they made some money, but they would have socked away millions more had they not been so philanthropic.

My mother insisted she never looked at bill-paying as drudgery; rather, she was thrilled to have the money to meet her obligations. I'm certain growing up in a broken home that had some financial struggles inspired a lifetime of giving. If she saw a table of handicapped persons in a restaurant, Mom always would go over and often picked up their tab. She loved to watch the faces when they found out. Her desire was for everybody to have the happy life her family enjoyed.

The deeper into those boxes I went, the more evidence of my mother's caring. And that brought me closer to her than ever.

CHAPTER 16

Nothing for Granted

In 2005, I made the hardest decision of my life. After 28 years of marriage, I left Ginger.

Mutual neglect of the relationship and poor communication left us both feeling on our own. We had been pulling in different directions for a long time.

She wanted me to either increase my earning power by getting into coaching or to relocate my scouting base to her native Houston. I wasn't interested in coaching—a lot of my fellow scouts thought it was the worst job they ever had—so money didn't motivate me to try it, and I had become adjusted to the life of a pro scout. I liked what I was doing and where I was doing it from, based close to our Jersey Shore summer place in Beach Haven.

Because my decision to leave went against everything I had always been taught and believed in, for more than three years I felt like a loser and a bad person, reluctant to be around anybody who might bring up the subject. The worst shame I ever felt after playing horribly and losing a playoff series was not in the same solar system as the failure of my marriage. But while it would have been a much easier decision to remain under the same roof, I always would have regretted staying. I was tired of the loneliness and bickering.

I am grateful Ginger brought our two natural-born children, Travis and Azia, into this world and that she was the catalyst in bringing adopted Nolan into our lives. No one will ever be prouder of three kids than I am, thanks largely to the job done by their mother.

Three months after we separated, the son of my best friend outside hockey, John Thomas, was performing in a band concert at a bar in Barnegat Light, New Jersey. I asked Sharon Battaglino, with whom Ginger and I had been Shelter Harbor Marina friends since we first started renting seasonally at Beach Haven in 1984, to accompany me for the evening.

I quickly realized how compatible we were. We allow each other to be ourselves, and that relationship has since grown to a level different from anything I ever experienced. Sharon, apart from her husband for 12 years, has interests in the same things I do, starting with going to hockey games. As soon as tax season ends—she is an accountant who works with her daughter Dee—Sharon joins me on selected trips.

Ginger was pretty upset when I first told her about my deepening bond with Sharon. Over time, she too has gotten past our troubled times and moved on with her life. I'm happy she chose to go back to Houston, where she has been in a relationship for three years. Ginger, who travels to Europe quite a bit with her boyfriend, is doing what she wants, and so am I. We now communicate better with each other than we did for a long time.

My kids, who saw all the fighting, were not surprised that we split. I believe they see both their mother and father happy and have come to understand that our separation was the best thing that could have happened. But it took Azia a couple of years to accept it, because she expected more from her father. She had been raised with the same values I was taught by my parents.

My daughter always has been adaptable. When we moved to Michigan in 1992, Azia, who was 11, came home from her first day at school with three new friends. Travis, then 14, would come in the door and lock himself in his room. That went on until Christmas before his first good Michigan friend, Ian Higgins, drew my son out of his funk. Travis then made up for lost time as his friends became more important to him than hockey. Motivated mostly by a social life and turned off by some selfishness on his Compuware Midget team, Travis quit the sport at age 16.

"You can't," Ginger advised him. "You put too much time and effort into it." But I told Travis if he wasn't having fun, I was in total support.

A year later, Bloomfield Hills High School started a team that rekindled his enthusiasm, even though the competition was a step below Compuware. No matter; my son was playing for enjoyment, no longer toward attempting a professional career. Travis was feisty and could skate, but he topped out at five foot eight and never had the instincts on a rink that I did.

After graduating high school and spending a few years at Oakland Community College, Travis got a call from Jack Lyons, his old coach with the Junior Flyers, who made my son assistant hockey director at Flyers Skate Zone in Voorhees, New Jersey. When Jack left, Travis became director, and did some coaching until 2006, when I asked him to work in Detroit for Power Play International, my mom and dad's business.

This time, he went to Michigan happily, rekindling a high school relationship with Kristine Herb and tirelessly taking care of my father while Selects Hockey, a company that conducts camps and arranges competition for elite developing players, became his full-time vocation.

Azia was disappointed I didn't ask her, rather than Travis, to move to Detroit. She wanted to be there for her grandmother, but we had caregivers for Mom and what I needed most was companionship for Dad. Plus, Azia had a budding accounting career with lots of potential and I didn't want to put her career on hold. Travis's company was in its infancy and could be run from any location. He was the obvious and perfect choice for me. Regardless, Azia would take one of her vacation weeks every year to sit with her grandmother, even after she became non-conversant.

That's the kind of person Azia is. Last Christmas, rather than buying presents for each other, she and her husband, Josh Saubers, an airline pilot, found a family with three children suffering financial hardship and brought them gifts and a holiday dinner. This past Christmas, they sent gifts to children of some friends whose lives were turned upside down by Hurricane Sandy.

Azia graduated from Stockton State College and went to work for a forensic accounting firm in Old City Philadelphia. A big raise, a lower cost of living and proximity to her mother took my daughter to Houston, where she met Josh. She passed her CPA exam and works at Core Laboratories, an oil and gas company in Houston that transports natural gas around the globe.

Nolan was an endearing yet mischievous boy who developed an attitude and a sense of entitlement as a teenager, making parenting a more challenging task than it had been with Travis and Azia. He had pent-up feelings that we couldn't reach. We tried every way to get him on the right track, and not even two years at Valley Forge Military Academy worked. Having left the ice while Nolan was growing up, I was able to spend more time with him than I had with Travis and Azia. On scouting trips and in coaching his minor hockey teams, I always saw the good side to Nolan that it just took a little longer for him to consistently unearth.

My friend John Thomas says most boys don't grow up until they are 25. He was dead on with Nolan, whose focus is no longer on himself but is directed toward the betterment of the Spinal Burst, the 12-year-old elite team he coaches in Bristol, Pennsylvania. He also works with Evolving Athletes' Vince Maltz, once a youth hockey teammate of Travis's, to give skating and hockey lessons out of Pro Skate in Monmouth Junction, New Jersey.

Nolan has become a man of his word—which, to me, is the measure of a person. He can now look at himself in the mirror and be proud.

I never doubted Nolan's pride in his father, whether I ever got into the Hockey Hall of Fame or not. Most years of the 13 I waited, calls would come from reporters before the late-June selection meeting, asking about my expectations. My story never changed—the Hall should be for the elite of the elite, which was out of my class, but there were plenty of members with credentials not better than mine. And I always said that, given the choice between being in the Hall of Fame and playing for six years with my father, the time with Dad would continue to mean more to me.

Still, the calls couldn't help but get me thinking, leaving me dejected for a day or so after the inductees were announced and my name wasn't among them. Before the 2011 vote, I heard from nobody and became totally oblivious to the time of year.

Just back from a week in Cabo San Lucas, Mexico, I spent June 27 and 28 at the shore, checking on my place and my boat, paying bills, running errands and getting ready to pack for another week-long trip for the Red Wings' pre-free-agency organizational meetings in Detroit.

On the hour-long drive home, I received three unidentified calls from the 416 area code—Toronto. No message had been left, so I figured it probably wasn't important. About 10 minutes later, I got a text from Kathi Wyatt at the Red Wings office telling me somebody from Toronto had been trying to get hold of me. "They want your Dad to do an appearance," she texted.

I called back and told her to give them Marty's number, because he handles Dad's business stuff, but Kathi said they wanted to speak to me for some reason or another. "All right, have them phone," I said. "If it's a 416 area code, I'll answer."

I was about 15 miles from home when the call came. It was Bill Hay, the CEO of the Hall of Fame, whom I had met. But when I next heard two voices I recognized—Jim Gregory's and Pat Quinn's—it hit me like a ton of bricks. Omigod, these guys are on the Hall of Fame committee! I think I'm actually getting in!

My heart pounded. After 14 years of eligibility, it happened. I was joining Oliver and Earl Seibert, Lester and Lynn Patrick, and Bobby and Brett Hull as part of only the fourth father-and-son combination to be inducted into a Hall of Fame in any North American team sport, not just hockey, as players (others had been enshrined as executives or builders). So guess who I wanted to tell first?

"When can I call Dad?' I asked. I was told to wait until after Kelly Masse, the Hall's director of media relations, hooked me up on a media conference call with Joe Nieuwendyk, Eddie Belfour and Doug Gilmour, my fellow honorees.

When that session ended, I called Marty, who was with my father attending Joe Carter's fundraiser in Toronto.

"We already know," said Marty. "Congratulations. I'll have Dad call you as soon as he gets free."

My father was pretty tired when Marty put him on the phone at 9:30 that night. He asked, "How's it going? How was your day?" and made other chitchat before finally I had to say, "I just want to let you know I got into the Hall of Fame."

"Oh yeah, I heard something about that today," Dad said.

You take his memory loss with a grain of salt. He called the next day to say how proud he was, but I didn't have to hear it from him personally to know. I already had hatched a plan to make my induction about Dad, too.

I remembered that, about a month after I retired, he had told me, "I wish you had worn my Number 9 for the Red Wings for even just one game." I said, "Oh man, that would have been great. Why didn't you ask me a month ago? I might have been able to accommodate you."

As a kid, I had never asked for Number 9. Every team just gave it to me until we went to Houston, where, obviously, it was going to be Dad's number. By the time I got to Detroit, "HOWE 9" had been hanging in the rafters for two decades, so requesting it was the last thing that would have occurred to me. The numbers in the rafters were worn by hockey heroes, and I would never have thought to ask about wearing any of them, not even Dad's. But I don't know if there have been more than three or four things during my life that my father ever asked of me, so I doubt what he said was in jest. At my November 14 induction, I would have an even larger stage to fulfill his wish.

I was a Hall of Famer. Azia was pregnant with my first grandchild. Travis was getting married in February. Nolan was becoming the person I always knew he would be. My relationship with Sharon was awesome. And I had finally pretty much forgiven myself for leaving Ginger. If I was ever in a better mental place than through the summer of 2011, I couldn't remember it. So I hardly needed to be told to savor every moment of every blessing.

On September 7, I was reminded regardless.

In mid-morning, after working a few hours on my PC, I came downstairs, where I had left my phone, to see about 12 voice messages awaiting me. Before I could even begin to listen to them, the phone rang again.

It was Dave Poulin.

"Have you heard?" he asked.

"What?" I said.

"Brad McCrimmon's team went down in a plane crash."

The jolt going through me was sickeningly familiar. As with Pelle Lindbergh and Kathy Kerr, this news was too devastating to be quickly believed.

The Internet told me that a plane carrying Lokomotiv Yaroslavl to its opening game of the Kontinental Hockey League season in Minsk, Belarus, had crashed on takeoff. But the manifest had not yet been released, so conflicting reports about players being left behind or coaches possibly flying separately gave me flickers of false hope that quickly faded.

I remembered the last time I had talked to Brad, in August, when he called from the airport as he waited to board his plane for Russia. Typecast as an assistant coach for 12 years with four NHL teams, he was excited about the opportunity to prove himself to be NHL head-coaching material by running a bench in the top Russian league. Hard as it was going to be to leave his wife, Maureen; 20-year-old daughter, Carlin; and 14-year-old son, Liam, for at least a year, he thought this was the right opportunity.

Before we hung up, I had told him that the other half of the duplex I owned in Beach Haven was going up for sale. Might he be interested in buying it? Brad said we would talk about it.

I went through the Yaroslavl roster to discover too many familiar names. Pavol Demitra had scored 304 NHL goals. I had played against Brad's assistant coach Alexander Karpovtsev when he was with the Rangers. Ruslan Salei had been a Red Wing in 2011 and we had spent two days together on a boat, fishing, during training camp in Traverse City. His wife had just given birth to their third child.

Maureen surprised me by picking up the telephone when I called. She was in shock, and I can't imagine I was of any comfort. All I could tell her was that I would be there for her, including financially if she suffered a shortfall before any insurance settlements. Maureen said money was not going to be a problem.

I took almost every call that day. Having never been one of those players who hide from the media after a loss—in fact, I urged teammates to make themselves available, if only for two minutes—I always respected that reporters had a job to do. But I also was hurting, and it always helps for me to talk rather than hold things in.

By the time they released the manifest, I pretty well had accepted the reality. Brad McCrimmon, the best friend I ever had in hockey, was gone.

In Calgary, where he won a Stanley Cup in 1989, they called him "Sarge" because he drilled the principles of team discipline into the Flames' barracks. In Philadelphia, he was the Beast for more reasons than his barrel chest and thick, hairy body.

The Flyers' self-appointed epicure and social organizer, he might as well have been the maître d' at his favorite spot, Chez Guido in Quebec City, where they put out awesome, garlic-laden feasts.

Normally, 10 or 12 guys would come out for dinner with us. At practice the next morning, you could easily pick out which ones had been at Chez Guido the night before. Brad wordlessly declared the evening a complete success by running to the waste can to let out the loudest and smelliest fart you ever could imagine. And everyone would gag and laugh with the Beast at the same time.

When we roomed together, he always took the bed closest to the window; I slept in the one nearer the door. One day, after we had arrived at our hotel in Washington at something like 4 a.m.—and Mike Keenan had decided on a bus tour of D.C. instead of a morning skate—we had three hours to sleep before leaving for the game.

Our room had to be pitch black or there would be no shut-eye for Brad. "The sun is going right into my eyes," he would complain about the slightest crack of light, and then he'd stuff towels and wedge chairs and desks against the curtain. Eventually he brought thumbtacks so he could pin the curtain edges to the wall instead of using furniture. Always entertaining to watch.

That afternoon in Washington, we finally settled into Beast Blackness—having put the "Do Not Disturb" card on the doorknob, of course. The chambermaid knocked regardless. No thanks, we said, go away, please. But she pounded again and then a third time until Brad flew over my bed and whipped the door open.

"*Ahhhhhhhhhhhhhhhh!!!*" he screamed, stark naked in front of this tiny Asian maid, who went sprinting down the hall. Our door didn't get touched the rest of the afternoon.

As soon as the Flyers would board the bus home from Madison Square Garden, the Meadowlands, Capital Centre or Nassau Coliseum, McCrimmon would run to the back, take off his jacket, shirt and tie and put on a pair of silk shorts. The Beast always felt hot.

One winter morning in Buffalo, we awoke under bedcovers at the Adam's Mark Hotel in a room so cold you could see your breath. I always liked it on the cool side myself. But before turning out the lights, the Beast had turned the heat off completely.

The thermostat was only five feet from my bed, but—probably for the only time in my life—I invoked seniority. "You wanted the room this cold. You turn the heat on," I said. It was a tough 15 feet, even by the Beast's always-stoic standards, but he made the dash to the wall and back under the covers, where we stayed until thawing.

At least that room had a thermostat, unlike the one in our Calgary hotel, which featured only master heat. It was set far too warm for Brad, of course. The front desk said there was no such thing as thermostat-controlled heat in any room in the joint, but the Beast didn't have to threaten to go naked on them to procure us a suite with a sliding patio door. We left it open for the night in the 25-degree cold and awoke the next morning to six inches of snow inside our door.

The defenseman to my right in our best Flyer years leaned in that direction politically, too, enjoying Rush Limbaugh. Brad not only was a big-time reader of political publications, but also of the Swedish magazines, translated into English, that Pelle Eklund would receive. The Beast's favorite parts, of course, were the personal ads.

"When I retire, I'm moving to Stockholm and becoming a porn star like the rest of the country," he would tell Eklund, getting a big laugh.

One day, Keenan ordered one-on-two drills, with Pelle against Beast and me. As soon as the coach saw we couldn't stop him, he sent Eklund again and again. Pelle kept dancing on us and scoring, leaving Keenan laughing and McCrimmon and me fuming.

"He's going down this time, no matter what," Brad vowed, and he got just enough of a piece of Eklund that I could two-hand his stick, sawing it off about two inches from his top hand. Eklund was stunned, but the joke really was on us. It was the only way we could stop him that day.

I needed to remember those laughs when I thought of my world without Brad McCrimmon. Only the Flyers' Stanley Cup chances, not our friendship, dissipated the day Bob Clarke traded Brad to Calgary for draft choices. Six years later, we spent much of our one season together in Detroit trying to fix a broken locker room. Because the Red Wings thought I had more left at that stage of our careers, Brad lost his job, but none of the trust he had in me.

Traded to Hartford, then pushed out in an Islanders purge from his first assistant coaching job, Brad asked me for advice on his next career move. "All good assistants have been a head coach somewhere," I said. "See if you can get a job in the American Hockey League. If not, go back to junior."

I wasn't the only person telling him that. So he went to the Saskatoon Blades, where he educated their teenagers to the franchise's first winning season in five. That got him back into the NHL with Calgary and, after the entire coaching staff was let go midway through his third season, Brad was hired by Bob Hartley in Atlanta.

When Hartley, who got the Thrashers to the only playoff berth in their history in 2006–07, was fired after an 0–6 start the next year, GM Donny Waddell went behind the bench himself to some initial success (thanks in part to a number of Beast's ideas behind the scenes). After a short while, Waddell turned over the reins to Brad, who had been the players' choice all along. He coached the team through the rest of their 82-game schedule and was offered a head-coaching position only through the next season. It might be the only one-year coaching offer I have ever heard of in the NHL.

Brad knew that if the Thrashers missed the playoffs—which they would—he was set up to fail in what might be his only chance to be an NHL head coach. He turned down that weakest of offers to go back to Detroit under Mike Babcock, staying for three years. Beast was the buffer between the players and the coaches, much like E.J McGuire had been for Mike Keenan back in our Philadelphia days. The players all respected Brad and trusted him. However, tension started to grow between Brad and Mike near the end of his second season. No longer were they on the same page.

During Brad's last year with the Red Wings, I met up with the team and flew back to Detroit on the charter. He was unhappy like I had never seen him before. Coaching is a difficult, time-consuming job that will eat you up if you don't love it. I told him he had to go someplace where he could enjoy the game again. Brad turned down more NHL assistant offers to go to Yaroslavl. He wanted to be his own boss and do it his way.

I dreaded so much calling Brad's father, Byron, that, driving to Traverse City for Red Wings training camp two days after the plane crash, I was all the way to Ohio before I'd mustered the courage. Brad's dad knew how close I was to his son, just like I knew my friend was as close to his father as I was to mine.

Byron told me that Brad had reported in a phone call from Yaroslavl that the team owners already had backed him on an issue. My friend was the happiest he had been in years.

Maureen had flown to Russia to bring back Brad's body. The entire Red Wing team came from Traverse City for the funeral, where I sat with Brian Propp, Scott Mellanby and Rick Tocchet. There were six to eight people present from every team where Brad had been.

Proppie, who played on a junior team in Brandon with McCrimmon that lost only five games in 1978–79, knew him the longest, so at the wake I urged him to do the toast.

Propp recalled that the Beast was the best he ever knew for picking up a phone and staying in touch with friends. Sharing with the guests how McCrimmon lit up any room into which he walked, Brian urged us to remember the good times, and we tried. Telling stories about Beast made us laugh. But talking about Brad, gone at age 52, was painful.

Because he had always been complimentary toward his Calgary teammate Gary Roberts, I introduced myself and told him how much Brad respected him. "He said the same thing about you," Roberts said.

A lot of defensemen—Wade Redden and Garnet Exelby among them—attended to show their appreciation for what McCrimmon had done for their careers. I'm sure he'd talked hockey over beers with a lot of these guys until 3 a.m., just like he had done so many times with me.

Brad's brother, Kelly, and his daughter, Carlin, spoke at the service. The Red Wings flew back to camp, but I stayed with Propp to spend an hour with Byron, and then went to Maureen's house in Northville with the family and close friends. I tried to leave at 1:30 a.m., but Maureen wouldn't let me go until 4:30.

Barely missing a deer on I-75, I got back to Traverse City at 9:30 and went to bed, closing the shades to the morning sunlight like Brad McCrimmon, the all-time master of that craft, had taught me.

Over the next few months, there was enough daylight cast upon the causes of the crash to make me sick about what a horrible and unnecessary waste of 43 lives—the flight engineer was the only survivor—the accident had been.

The pilot and co-pilot falsified documents that they had been trained in the use of that type of aircraft. An autopsy found phenobarbital in the co-pilot's system. The investigation concluded that the plane never got more than a few feet off the ground before hitting a tower and crashing into a riverbank because either the pilot or co-pilot hit the brake while the other was accelerating.

The heartbroken owner of the Yaroslavl team promised that all the contracts would be paid to the survivors, but Maureen quickly ran into bureaucracy that raised her suspicions. Igor Larionov, a man of power and influence in Russia, pledged to work with me to do what we could.

At my Hall induction in two months, I would have a platform from which to urge the Russians to do the right thing. I was determined to use it and also honor my dad's 16-year-old request. I wasn't sure he remembered, but I certainly did.

The previous five months had produced some of the highest highs of my life and one of the lowest lows. I think it all caught up to me on my induction weekend in Toronto.

The night before the ceremony, Sam Ciccolini, a longtime Toronto friend of Mom and Dad's with whom they had done a number of charity functions, lined up a private dinner with about 45 family members and close friends. After Sam did a long introduction about me and my family, he handed me the microphone. I hadn't even gotten past thanking everyone for taking the time to be able to share the evening with me before Bill Hay and the HOF staff started carrying the Stanley Cup into the room. My emotions all came to a head at that moment and I broke down. I looked over at Dad, whom I had seen cry only when my mother and grandmother died, and he was shedding tears, too. I couldn't get myself together until, finally, my big brother, Marty, stood and gave me a big hug to help me through it.

"I'm going to be crying so bad tomorrow," predicted Nolan.

"Better not while I'm talking about you," I warned. "If I break up giving a speech on national television, I'm not going to be very happy."

The only people who knew my plan to put on Dad's Number 9 were Sharon and Marty, whom I'd called to see if we had a Red Wings jersey. All the ones we had lying around at home were autographed, so Marty bought one that wasn't. I didn't think it would look right having a signed jersey on national television.

As it turned out, I don't think that would have been nearly as noticeable as the price tag on the sleeve that I forgot to remove before stuffing the jersey into the shoe bag that came with my tuxedo. And I still needed to solve the problem of getting it up on stage, where I had to shake the hand of Bill Hay and accept the plaque. I couldn't do both with a bag in my hand, so as soon as they announced my turn to speak, I stood up from my first row seat and flung it to the bottom of the dais, trying to be as discreet as possible.

After congratulating Gilmour, Nieuwendyk and Belfour, I made my call to the hockey world to make certain the families of the Yaroslavl crash victims received full compensation, and I acknowledged Maureen in the audience.

I credited the most instrumental persons in my development—Carl Lindstrom, Bobby Goodenow, George Armstrong, Ed Van Impe, Robbie Ftorek and the 1972 U.S. Olympic Team. I expressed my gratitude to the WHA for the early start in pro hockey and the opportunity to play alongside Marty and Dad, as well as to Aeros coach Bill Dineen for being one of the finest persons I've ever met.

I noted my appreciation to Ed Snider, Keith Allen and Bob McCammon for bringing me to Philadelphia; Mike Keenan for raising my bar; and my primary defense partners during my best years—Glen Cochrane, Kjell Samuelsson, and of course, McCrimmon.

Marian and Mike Ilitch, Jimmy Devellano and Bryan Murray drew my gratitude for the opportunity to end it in Detroit with the team of my youth and my father. I thanked Ginger for bringing our three children into the world and for the commitment she made as their mother.

I acknowledged my brothers for taking care of me—Murray, in advance, for medical care I am certain to need in my old age, and Marty for protecting his little brother when we were young. Also my sister, Cathy, who had to endure so many cold rinks and countless miles so that her brother could play hockey.

Sharon drew my praise for being such a loving and caring person and for making me feel good about myself and the person I am.

Having watched my father's induction in 1972, I told Travis, Azia and Nolan I knew how they felt and that they were the most important people in my life. When I looked at my youngest, his lip was starting to quiver. "Don't cry on me, Nolan," I said and we both held it together.

I needed only one "sorry" to get through my talk with just one catch in my throat, even as I told my mother I knew she was here on this night, just as she had been there to drive me to games, build the backyard rink, teach me the difference between right and wrong, and how to be the son of Gordie Howe.

I noted my appreciation to my father for being my linemate for six years, for elbows to the opponents who took dirty shots at me and for being the greatest hockey player ever. But more important, I said, was being the husband, father, person and role model that he is.

Then I reminded him of his after-the-fact request that I wear Number 9 just one time, and I put on his jersey—much better 16 years late then never. He came toward the stage and shook my hand.

Because I have had opportunities no one else ever has or ever will, I never take anything for granted. That included giving my Hall of Fame induction speech without becoming a blubbering mess. I made it through—one more thing to appreciate on the most grateful night of my life.

Epilogue

After you make the Hockey Hall of Fame, the culmination of your life's work, at age 56, what's next? As my blessings continued over the next several months, I didn't suffer that problem.

On January 3, 2012, my daughter, Azia, gave birth to my first grandchild, Ella Colleen. On February 4, my son Travis married Kristine Herb.

With a first-intermission boost from three Celebrex, I scored the winning goal on a penalty shot in the Legends Game that preceded the Winter Classic at Citizens Bank Park in Philadelphia. Ella got the puck and the score sheet; I received back stiffness and numbness in my right foot that didn't go away for two months.

Well worth it. I had never played in front of 45,000 people. And it was neat to once again share a locker room with some great Flyers, including many from my era.

It also was humorous to be reminded that the more things change, the more they stay the same. At the reception afterward, the Ranger invitees were grumbling about the ice time apportioned by Mike Keenan. Even in an oldtimers' game, he didn't want to lose.

My winning streak continued with inductions into the Philadelphia Sports Hall of Fame and Michigan Sports Hall of Fame. Both were huge cross-sport honors in passionate places loaded with tradition. Philly is the city where I made a name for myself and have been a longtime part of the community. I joined Dad as the only father-and-son members in Michigan, where my foundation and development were built.

There can never be a happy ending to the Brad McCrimmon story. But at least Maureen successfully fought her way through Russian bureaucracy to receive the money promised her on her husband's contract. The misspelling of his middle name on his Canadian birth certificate—recorded as Brad Bryon, instead of Brad Byron—became one more excuse not to pay off.

My theory on those complications is that, even in Russia, he probably was known only as the Beast. But I was pleased to learn that ethical obligations were met.

Ed Snider didn't owe me anything. So when he called to say I would be the fifth Flyer to have his number retired, I probably was the first of the five to apologize to him. Bob Clarke, Bill Barber, Bernie Parent and Barry Ashbee had all won the Stanley Cup.

"The Oilers had something to do with that," Ed said. The greatest honor a franchise can ever bestow on a player was deeply appreciated and granted me the last bit of closure on the best 10 seasons of my career. The July 1992 morning that I boarded Mike Ilitch's plane to sign with the Red Wings, the Flyers' owner had just made clear to me on the phone his disappointment that I was not finishing my career in Philadelphia.

About 10 years later, I happened into Portofino's restaurant at Trump Marina in Atlantic City, where Snider, Bob Clarke and the team brain trust were eating in a back room. It would have been awkward, if not downright rude, for me not to say hello, so I risked a cool reception and was rewarded with a huge hug by Snider—albeit, followed by a "Still can't believe you left."

Ed wasn't holding a grudge against the Red Wings for taking me away. He scheduled Mark Howe Night for Detroit's only visit to the Wells Fargo Center in the 2011–12 season. The two organizations represented my hockey life since 1982. So it was an extremely classy gesture for Snider and the Flyers to schedule the ceremony on that evening.

The Red Wings provided a rental van, enabling me to sport the family around for the week, plus three days on a chartered fishing boat at Cabo. The Flyers gave me an all-expenses paid trip to Cabo for eight, and when I asked to extend the party to 12 at my own cost, they generously picked up the additional tab.

Most important to me, my Number 2 went to the rafters on March 6, 2012, with Detroit and Philadelphia players on their benches watching, Ella in my arms, and Dad with me on the ice.

My father got as big an ovation as I did. Even on Mark Howe Night in Philadelphia, I was Gordie Howe's son.

Acknowledgments

Hockey has made my life a true blessing, so I want to thank all players, coaches, trainers, front-office staff and arena personnel I have had the pleasure of working with or playing against.

The sport, which has been enriching Howes since Gordie donned his first pair of skates back in the early 1930s, continues to provide enjoyment for my two boys, who pass on the family's knowledge and passion to today's youth, the way it should be.

—Mark Howe

On the December 2011 night in the Wells Fargo Center press box, when Mark Howe told me he was "too boring" to do a book, I asked him to think more about it.

What I should have said was "Let *me* think about it," which I did thoroughly for the first time on the drive home, seeking an approach that could overcome his skepticism. As a beat guy covering seven of

Mark's 10 years in Philadelphia, I found him a compulsive truth-teller who would help me produce anything but a mundane autobiography, but merely insisting to him that his story was fascinating wasn't going to get this job done. In an email the next day, I reminded him that the book would also honor the legend of Gordie Howe, as well as prolong the memory of his best friend in hockey, Brad McCrimmon.

I also knew there would be "boring" stories about winning an Olympic silver medal at age 16, playing seven seasons with his dad and brother Marty, and surviving a gruesome run-in with a net that could have left him paralyzed. Other accomplishments, like becoming a three-time First Team NHL All-Star, playing in the most compelling Stanley Cup final ever, finishing his career in the uniform of his father, earning four championship rings as a shrewd and trusted talent evaluator in the Detroit Red Wing front office, and becoming only the fourth son of a Hall of Fame player in any sport to also be enshrined for his playing exploits, made this story one that I knew had to be shared.

But the sample chapter that I proposed to him—on growing up as Gordie's kid—had to sell Mark before it could be tried out on a publisher. When I next saw him two weeks later, after he had scored the winning goal in the Legends Game that preceded by a day the Flyers-Rangers Winter Classic at Citizens Bank Park, I didn't have to ask again.

The media mob around him had thinned to two when Mark said to the other guy still standing with me: "Jay thinks we could sell a book. I think he's crazy." He then turned to me, smiled and said, "So, you want to knock off a sample chapter?"

First, he requested a month to attend his son's wedding and meet his first grandchild. I asked that, in the interim, he make a list of childhood recollections as they popped into his head. When he showed up at my house with two written notebook pages, Mark's commitment was clear.

Our vision for this work suffered practically no conflicts, even through the selection of the title. I was playing with multiple tortured lines about overcoming his father's enormous shadow when he set the record blessedly straight. "How about just calling it *Gordie Howe's Son?*" he said. "That's who I am and who I always will be."

Sold, just as he was on the effort required to do a book worthy of their relationship, Mark proved tireless during multiple all-day taping sessions and in his responses to emails. When I asked for a few more sentences on a subject, he would promptly return a few more paragraphs. While approving each chapter, he'd send me back even more expansive and insightful thoughts.

When his recollections weren't perfect, we had significant help. Brothers Marty and Murray Howe were more than just fact-checkers for me on Mark's version of events; they volunteered stories he had forgotten. Greg Innis, Jeff Jacobs, Chuck Kaiton and Dave Poulin cheerfully accessed personal and public archives, putting in efforts that went deeper than standard professional courtesy.

Almost everyone in Mark's past and present to whom I reached out got back to me, most of them as excited about the idea of a Mark Howe autobiography as its authors. That says much with respect to the esteem in which Mark is held in the hockey community, but also about the goodwill and cheer of the following: Howard Baldwin, Howard Baldwin Jr., Sharon Battaglino, Darren Blake, Fran Blinebury, Bruce Boudreau, Chris Botta, Scotty Bowman, Craig Campbell, Keith Christiansen, Bob Clarke, Dr. Tony Colucci, Skip Cunningham, Alex Delvecchio Jr., Jimmy Devellano, Kevin Devine, Bill Dineen, Jiri Fischer, Kerry Fraser, Edna Gadsby, John Garrett, Felix Gatt, Ron Hextall, Mark Hicks, Paul Holmgren, Ed Hospodar, Bill Jamieson, Joe Kadlec, Mike Keenan, Cynthia Lambert Nehr, Jim Lever, Ed Mahan, Jim Matheson, Brian McBride, Dick McGlynn, Herb Morell, Lou Nanne, Harry Neale, Denis Potvin, Samantha Poulos, Steve Pourier, Brian Propp, Dave Reginek, Chico Resch, Mike Rogers, Bill Roose, Jeff Schultz, David Settlemyre, Karen Simmons, Harry Sinden, Ed Snider, Jay Snider, Mike Sundheim, Ron Sutter, Robert Toporek, Bob Verdi, Bob Waterman, Murray Williamson, Steve Yzerman and John Ziegler.

I had the pleasure of meeting the late Colleen Howe only once. But just as Mark described knowing that his mother was in the building during his Hall of Fame acceptance speech, she also was reading as I wrote. Her books *My Three Hockey Players* and *And Howe!* bequeathed to me more of Mark's buttons, and I wanted to push them well. As you learned in these pages, Colleen was not someone you would want to disappoint.

I hope this book is as entertaining and informative as Ed Willes's delightful history of the World Hockey Association, *The Rebel League,* which provided more vignettes to run by Mark. Tom and Jerry Caraccioli's *Streaking Silver: The Untold Story of America's Forgotten Hockey Team* gave me valuable background on Mark's 1972 silver-medal experience. As I didn't begin to follow the NHL until 1967 or cover it until 1974, Roy MacSkimming's *Gordie: A Hockey Legend* brought me a deeper appreciation of Howe's salad years with the Red Wings.

As for Number 9 himself, the coolest day I spent on this project was the one when he was at my house—hey, has Mr. Hockey ever been to *yours?*—a special treat not only for me but my golden retriever, Phoebe, who kept Gordie well entertained while Mark and I worked.

Wayne Gretzky would do almost anything for his boyhood idol and the Howe family, but Number 99 also has come through for me so many times that I was not surprised by his quick and enthusiastic agreement to write the foreword. Far beyond the call of even our good friendship, Jordan Sprechman volunteered to fact-check the entire book, saving me mistakes and anxiety and contributing some excellent editing suggestions.

My agent, Doug Grad, thought this book was a good idea even before Mark believed so, and then took the proposal to the right places. Jim Gifford, the nonfiction editorial director at HarperCollins Canada, was complimentary from his first read—always what you want to hear—and had good suggestions before the manuscript went to Lloyd Davis's thorough copyedit and error-saving research. Kelly Hope took painstaking care of the proofs and pictures.

Tongue-in-cheek thanks go to Gary Bettman and Don Fehr, who collaborated to free up Mark's time with a late start to the 2012–13 season, helping us meet our deadline. When the going got tough—the last 14 chapters had to be done in less than three months—my wife, Mona, got going with the transcriptions, saving me precious hours on top of her relentless rescues from redundancy and run-on sentences. If there is a word repeated within three paragraphs anywhere in this book, it was only because I insisted to her there wasn't a better alternative. Whatever options there were for me when we married in 1977, I made the best choice.

—Jay Greenberg

Index

Note: In this index, MH *refers to Mark Howe and* GH *refers to Gordie Howe.*

I

J

K

L

M

T